101 Careers in Counseling

SHANNON HODGES, PhD, LMHC, NCC, ACS

SPRINGER PUBLISHING COMPANY
NEW YORK

Copyright © 2012 Springer Publishing Company, LLC

Springer Publishing Company, LLC
11 West 42nd Street
New York, NY 10036
www.springerpub.com

Acquisitions Editor: Nancy Hale
Composition: Newgen Imaging

ISBN: 978-0-8261-0858-6
E-ISBN: 978-0-8261-0859-3

12 13 14 / 5 4 3 2 1

The author and the publisher of this Work have made every effort to use sources believed to be reliable to provide information that is accurate and compatible with the standards generally accepted at the time of publication. The author and publisher shall not be liable for any special, consequential, or exemplary damages resulting, in whole or in part, from the readers' use of, or reliance on, the information contained in this book. The publisher has no responsibility for the persistence or accuracy of URLs for external or third-party Internet Web sites referred to in this publication and does not guarantee that any content on such Web sites is, or will remain, accurate or appropriate.

Library of Congress Cataloging-in-Publication Data
Hodges, Shannon.
  101 careers in counseling / by Shannon Hodges.
    p. cm.
  Includes bibliographical references and index.
  ISBN 978-0-8261-0858-6 — ISBN 978-0-8261-0859-3
  1. Counseling—Vocational guidance. I. Title. II. Title: One hundred one careers in counseling. III. Title: One hundred and one careers in counseling.
  BF636.6.H63 2012
  158.3023—dc23   2011050221

Printed in the United States of America by Hamilton Printing

This book is dedicated to an anonymous counselor at the University of Arkansas's Counseling Center who spent several quality sessions helping a struggling undergraduate through an intense journey of self-discovery.
Thank you for helping me see the stars.

Contents

Foreword

Counseling as a practice and body of theory has a deep cultural history going back thousands of years within the development of families, tribes, and nations from around the world. Today, we do not often consider just how ancient and how modern are the methods of helping each other through life's challenges, enabling each other to change, and providing each other with skills, insight, and relational nurturance of various kinds that allow aspects of learning, growth, and healing.

The dual nature of counseling is important to consider when you might find yourself daydreaming about a possible career in this field. When I was in my 20s, my work was based in a sense of pastoral care and community-based practice within disability care, in aged care, and in working with youth and families. When I was in my mid-20s, I was forced by educational systems and limited job prospects to choose a career; I felt like the debt involved in gaining a master's degree was huge. So, I had to be very careful. Not only did I need a career that allowed for economic stability, but also something I was passionate about and could see myself clearly doing for the rest of my life.

My first choices back then were in creative arts and music or to become a minister. It took me time to sort out, but at the core, I realized later that my intention was to help people. This is often true of many who enter the profession realizing that counseling training is based on hands-on skills development that leads immediately to career options that enable direct work with people in many settings. Across all the fields, you will begin to realize that counselors help people in many ways with an emphasis on direct, relational, and professional care.

My choice to journey toward counseling was based at the time in wanting a career that offered maximum flexibility, independence (if I needed to sustain a private practice), growth potential not only for employment but also as a person dedicated to lifelong learning, an emphasis on hands-on practice and skills development, and a field that enabled community-based work to grow in my desire to assist people from minority GLBT and Aboriginal populations.

Overall then, the two sides to the counseling field make it a very satisfying career for many people. On one hand, we have a cultural, humanitarian, and spiritual dimension to helping people, which is supported by many of the traditions of Western and non-Western cultures in North America (including First Nation, immigrant, and "dominant or mainstream" cultural worldviews that grew from European-American traditions). On the other hand, we have a modern field comprising skills, theory and professional guidelines, codes of practice and a robust literature, and a huge diversity of areas to work within across a vast array of theoretical and/or skills-based modalities or methods of helping people.

Historically and today, by exploring counseling as an indigenous form of practice and philosophy, I believe that we can discover many of the missing keys to understanding a more holistic approach to the discipline during a time in the profession's history of becoming more and more fragmented, economically and politically driven, and divided by the internal turf wars and lack of vision, practical planning, and leadership that are necessary at state and national levels across all Western countries.

Likewise, counseling in the West is enriched and paradoxically, hindered and limited, by the bodies of theory and practice that have emerged out of the European 18th and 19th centuries, which of course go further back, but in terms of defining the emergence of the profession in a formal sense must acknowledge our roots in the Christian heritage of Europe, in the Reformation, the Enlightenment, the Industrial Revolution, and the growth of Western medicine, science, and later, particularly during the 20th century, of psychology, social work, and human services.

More contemporary movements have seen the field embrace Eastern approaches, multicultural theory and practice, gender analysis, diversity theory, minority studies, and indigenous and non-Western methods. However, most of the bachelor-level textbooks that exist now are still based on the traditional Western canon—the Western "bible" of counseling—which, from most contemporary views, is extremely limited and ought to be rewritten, not as lip service to emerging postmodern and integrative perspectives, but ought to be reconsidered once completely based on these contemporary global and including non-Northern Hemisphere perspectives.

Wider views now influence the field that draw on a richer heritage of diversity in culture, language, gender, sexuality, ability, age, and spiritual values broadly defined. These essential and often overlooked fields of knowledge and practice speak to the needs we face in today's world and provide many of the answers to your quest to consider counseling as a career.

A bit of humility is in order. The majority of cultures worldwide come from a terribly rich heritage compared with the time-limited and narrowly defined Western materialistic philosophy that has dominated the profession and the academe in the West. By knowing there is more out there, I hope you will not just seek a job in this field, but you will realize that if you want to contribute to a global revolution in the ethics of care, you have that capacity as a counselor because you will be working with people to help them define their sense of meaning in life—regardless of the area you choose to work.

Also it is important to know that after many years of practice and study, I am convinced that there is no contradiction between good science and a reasonable cultural and spiritual life. Counseling, more than other disciplines, embraces this holistic perspective. This, to me, says to young people that you can come from any tradition, you can re-form and form anew your own beliefs and values during your training, and while you are growing in this field, you can nurture as a new generation a global ethic of care to support human life and environmental sustainability. These wider trends will also be a part of your life and career and include the many challenges our societies face while global climate change, economic transformation, and educational reforms continue to manifest new forms of work and career opportunities.

At this particular juncture in the history of our profession, while the field is still struggling and growing, there is no doubt that counseling is well placed to meet the needs of a changing society. If anything shows this, the following pages are a testament to the resilience, creativity, determination, and professional integrity of countless individuals who have paved the way for the up-and-coming generations to find this field of practice ready for you to make your mark on the many new career paths that now exist, reaching out to you with an invitation to consider the counseling profession as your preferred way of working.

In whatever choices you make for your career, I wish you every blessing and peace on your path in life. It is my sincere wish and prayerful intention that you and your loved ones will remain safe and are given all the provisions and opportunities for a good life that this world has to offer.

Randolph Bowers, PhD
Adjunct Senior Lecturer
School of Humanities, Faculty of Arts and Sciences
University of New England, Australia
Consultant Counseling Psychotherapist and Educator

Preface

"What exactly is a counselor?" I asked my instructor in the early spring term of 1985. Struggling with my current graduate program, I had enrolled in a graduate counseling class for teachers. During that quarter, I studied the history of counseling, significant figures, the current situation, and the outlook for the profession in addition to learning the basics of helping relationships. By the conclusion of the term, I had a pretty good idea of what a counselor was and the settings they work in. I had also performed quite well in the class, surprising myself in the process. At the end of the semester, the instructor, a doctoral student in the counselor education program at Oregon State University, suggested I apply for the master's program in counseling. Though I still was not convinced that counseling was what I wanted to do for a career, I had nothing better going for me career-wise. So, I applied and was accepted. I eventually graduated from the counseling program, found work, returned for a doctorate degree, and continued a long journey that has culminated in my writing this text on various counseling careers.

During the past 26 years since that initial counseling class, my career as a counselor has taken me all across the United States and all over the world. I have taught in a counseling program in Australia, presented workshops in Asia and Central America, and had the privilege of working alongside some amazing colleagues. I have also come to understand that there is not *one* counseling career, but *many* counseling careers (at least 101, right?).

This book will highlight the profession of counseling in its many variations. This text is specifically written for people considering a career in the counseling field. Part of my task is to explain the counseling profession, how it is similar to and different from professions such as psychology and social work, provide a sense of the job outlook, and illustrate the many variations of counseling within the profession.

What this book cannot do is tell you whether the profession is a good fit for you. I would suggest you read this text and others, talk the matter over with people you trust (family members, close friends, a career counselor, etc.), interview a professional counselor to get a sense of what they do, and do some intense self-reflection on whether a career helping others is congruent with your interests, aptitude, and values. Twenty-six years ago I took a leap of faith and enrolled in a graduate counseling program, and that decision has profoundly changed my life in numerous positive ways. Because I cannot say that my experience will be your experience, my counsel to you is to consider the matter carefully. If this book helps reveal that the profession of counseling is not in your best interests, then reading it will have been time well spent. Conversely, if this book helps you gain clarity that counseling is potentially a good field for you, then I say welcome to the profession!

Acknowledgments

I acknowledge the supportive people who have helped this book move from concept to reality. First, my heartfelt thanks to Jennifer Perillo, former editor at Springer Publishing Company, who has supported me through two books, and I hope many more. I also thank my spouse, Shoshanna Cogan, who forgives the crests and dips that writing books tends to bring out in me. I thank the professional counselors who shared their inspiring stories in the Counselor Spotlight sections of this book. Finally, I acknowledge the hard work and sacrifice of professional counselors who work in schools, colleges, clinics, and private practice. You have built the profession.

Find Your Career
With
Springer Publishing Company

201 Careers in Nursing
Joyce J. Fitzpatrick and Emerson E. Ea

101 Careers in Psychology
Tracey Ryan

101 Careers in Public Health
Beth Seltzer

101 Careers in Social Work
Jessica Ritter, Halaevalu F. Vakalahi,
and Mary Kiernan-Stern

101 Careers in Counseling
Shannon Hodges

101 Careers in Gerontology
C. Joanne Grabinski

To learn more and order, visit www.springerpub.com

Introduction

PART
I

1 The Profession of Counseling

If you are reading this book, it is likely that you are interested in the profession of counseling. Perhaps, you are a high school student who is thinking about the future, an undergraduate psychology major looking at graduate school, a teacher interested in moving into the role of school counselor, a professional in another field considering changing careers, or simply someone curious about counselors and what they do. One of the most important concepts to remember regarding the counseling profession is that the profession is made up of *many* counseling fields. Some counseling fields, such as addictions counseling and mental health counseling, are similar to one another. Others, like creative arts counseling (e.g., dance therapy, art therapy, and music therapy), are quite distinct from general counseling fields. There are traditional counseling fields like school counseling that you may be quite familiar with and others such as genetic counseling that you may never have heard of. However, regardless of which of the 101 counseling career variations highlighted in this book, all are part of the umbrella profession known as "counseling."

Because many of you reading this book may be wondering the same thing that I was back in 1985, namely, what is a counselor, I think we need to address a question in many of your minds: Who is a counselor?

Counseling has evolved since its founding in 1952. In the early days of the profession, getting a concise definition of "counselor" would have been difficult. Although the American Personnel and Guidance Association created the profession, the reality was that the term "counselor" was generic. Today, things are drastically different. Professional

3

counselors are now licensed in all 50 U.S. states, as well as Washington, DC, and Puerto Rico. Licensed counselors are required to earn a graduate degree in counseling, spend 1 to 2 years being supervised on the job by a licensed mental health professional (e.g., licensed counselor, licensed social worker, and licensed psychologist), and pass a state counseling examination to become licensed. Once a counselor has achieved licensure in his or her state, the counselor is recognized as an autonomous professional.

Counselors are also specifically trained to counsel children, adolescents, and adults struggling with depression, anxiety, stress, unemployment, addiction, sexual abuse, posttraumatic stress disorder, and so forth. Counselors may work in P-12 schools, colleges, community colleges, universities, inpatient and outpatient mental health centers, alcohol- and drug-treatment centers, the U.S. military, and many other settings (U.S. Bureau of Labor Statistics, 2010–2011). Counselors will also provide individual counseling, play therapy, couple and family counseling, group counseling, adventure-based counseling (e.g., in the wilderness, challenge courses), and so on.

In general, the term "counselor" refers to someone who has completed a master's or doctoral degree in one of the graduate counseling specialty areas (e.g., clinical mental health counseling, school counseling, rehabilitation counseling, and marriage and family counseling). Readers would have noticed other professionals with the title "admissions counselor" or with some other title. Such people are not professional counselors (unless they have completed a master's degree in counseling), and this text will not refer to them as such. It must be acknowledged, however, that some people holding baccalaureate degrees still work as addictions counselors (though this is changing). Because some of the counseling jobs in this text are new and others are actually separate from the traditional profession of counseling (e.g., adventure-based counseling), a BA or BS degree may be all that is required. But for the sake of licensure and the ability to move upward in counseling and related professions, a master's degree will be required. In the following section, I have listed the steps to becoming a professional counselor.

STEPS TO BECOMING A PROFESSIONAL COUNSELOR IN THE UNITED STATES

1. *Graduate with a baccalaureate degree.* A BA or BS degree in psychology, sociology, or education is advantageous though not required for admission to a graduate program in counseling.
2. *Apply and be accepted to a graduate program in one of the counseling specialty areas.* Specialty areas in counseling are

clinical mental health counseling, career counseling, school counseling, rehabilitation counseling, counseling and student affairs, addictions counseling, marriage and family counseling, and so on.

3. *Complete a graduate degree in one of the counseling specialty areas.* Most counseling degrees are 2 to 3 years in length, with the majority requiring a 700-hour practicum and internship.

4. *Graduate with a master's or doctoral degree in counseling.*

5. *Get hired by an agency.* Be sure the agency has a licensed counselor, social worker, or psychologist who can provide 1 to 2 years of supervision for licensure.

6. *Pass your state/territory's licensure exam.* In addition, pass the exam for national certification[1] (see National Board for Certified Counselor [NBCC]).

TYPES OF COUNSELING

You have no doubt noticed that this book is titled *101 Careers in Counseling,* so you have some sense that counseling is a broad field. Though I will address all 101 counseling careers, there are not 101 different graduate counseling programs. The Council for the Accreditation of Counseling and Related Educational Programs (CACREP, 2009) accredits the following counseling programs:

Addictions counseling
Clinical mental health counseling
School counseling
Marriage, couple, and family counseling
Career counseling
Student affairs and college counseling
Counselor education and supervision (Note that this is a doctoral degree program.)

Rehabilitation counseling is accredited by the Council on Rehabilitation Education. In addition, some of the counseling careers highlighted in this book may be accredited by other organizations (e.g., dance and movement therapy and counseling is accredited by the American Dance Therapy Association [ADTA]).

You may possibly run across additional graduate counseling programs not listed above, but that would mean they are not recognized by

---

[1] National certification is an extra, voluntary credential. Licensure is the required credential.

CACREP, which accredits graduate counseling programs. Also notice that I mentioned "graduate" counseling programs. All professional counseling programs that lead to licensure are graduate programs. Thus, you would need to earn an undergraduate degree. Most students in graduate counseling programs earn their baccalaureate degrees in psychology, though there is no requirement for the BA or BS degree. Therefore, someone with a degree in philosophy could be admitted into a graduate counseling program and potentially perform academically as well as a graduate student with a degree in psychology.

Having read the preceding, you may still have questions in your mind regarding who is/is not a counselor. You have likely noticed many different occupations that use the term "counselor." The following occupations or jobs will use the word counselor:

- Lawyers (called "counselor" in the courtroom)
- Admissions counselor
- Financial counselor
- Camp counselor
- Pastoral counselor (Note that a minister, priest, rabbi, imam, etc., may or may not be trained as a professional counselor. If you are seeking counsel from a clergy person, you may wish to ask if he or she has a graduate degree in counseling and is licensed as a counselor.)

So remember that for our purposes, when the term "counselor" is used in this book, it refers to professional counselors who hold graduate degrees in counseling and who are licensed or being supervised for licensure.

A BRIEF HISTORY OF THE COUNSELING PROFESSION

In order to gain a sense of the profession, it is important to review the origins of the counseling profession.

In 1952, four independent associations, the National Vocational Guidance Association, the National Association of Guidance and Counselor Trainers, the Student Personnel Association for Teacher Education, and the American College Personnel Association, convened in Los Angeles for the purposes of building a strong, unified coalition (Sheeley & Stickle, 2008). This meeting gave birth to the American Personnel and Guidance Association (APGA). APGA's founding is usually referenced as the birth of the counseling profession, though as evidenced by the fact "counseling" was absent from the title, it was an inauspicious start. APGA primarily focused on high school academic and vocational counseling and training college student personnel (Aubrey, 1977). The fledging profession faced numerous obstacles: Qualifications to become a "guidance" professional were ambiguous, and there was no uniform program of study, no written code of ethics, no accreditation standards, and no credentials such as licensure or national certification. Judging by contemporary standards, the early guidance movement was arguably a semiprofession (Etzoni, 1969).

Despite challenges, the counseling movement demonstrated remarkable resilience during the period from the 1950s through the 1960s. Humanistic approaches spearheaded by Carl Rogers and Fritz Perls became readily accessible to the public through the group encounter movement (Corey, 2009). The phrase "third force" in psychology was coined to differentiate existential humanistic approaches from psychoanalytic and behavioral ones (Nugent & Jones, 2009). The school counseling movement, buoyed by the Soviet's launch of *Sputnik*, arguably provided the single biggest boost to the counseling profession: It escalated the number of guidance counselors from around 7,000 to nearly 30,000 (Aubrey, 1977). All these various forces within and outside the counseling profession resulted in popularizing counseling among the public. By the mid-1970s, the counseling profession and counselor education programs (graduate programs that train counselors) had grown exponentially (Nugent & Jones, 2009).

The 1980s to 2000

In the early 1980s, counselor education leaders created the CACREP to provide standardization and accreditation (Hollis & Dodson, 2001). CACREP, which began as part of the Association of Counselor Educators and Supervisors, is now an independent agency recognized by the U.S. Council for Higher Education Accreditation to accredit master's degrees in eight counseling specialties (e.g., school counseling, community counseling, marriage and family counseling) and doctoral programs in counselor education (CACREP, 2009). Though counselor education programs are not required to be accredited, CACREP's curricular guidelines form the basis for most states' licensure laws (Remley & Herlihy, 2007). Readers considering the counseling profession should check to see if the counseling programs they are considering are CACREP accredited. Though accreditation is no guarantee of quality, it does mean that the program of interest has met the standard in the field. Furthermore, graduating from a CACREP-accredited program may provide an advantage when searching for counseling positions.

During the same time frame as CACREP's inception, the NBCC was created. NBCC established a national credential for certifying professional counselors in states lacking counselor licensure laws. Since NBCC's creation in 1982, 50 U.S. states, Washington, DC, and Puerto Rico have passed counselor licensure laws. Certification has consequently transitioned from "licensure substitution" to identifying counseling specialty areas. NBCC offers certifications in three professional-counseling specialty areas namely Certified Clinical Mental Health Counselor (CCMHC), National Certified School Counselor (NCSC), and Master Addictions Counselor (MAC). NBCC also offers the general National Certified Counselor (NCC) certification (NBCC, 2011). Remley (1995) has argued that a license should be for general practice, while national certification should identify specialty areas.

Previous to the postmodern era (say, the last 15–20 years), the counseling profession was based on Eurocentric models and was almost exclusively a U.S. profession (Corey, 2009; D'Andrea & Arredondo, 2002). Since the late-1980s, however, multicultural considerations have become mainstream, and counseling is now an international profession. Often called the "fourth force" in counseling (D'Andrea & Arredondo, 2002), multiculturalism has had a profound impact on the profession, especially regarding culturally and linguistically diverse populations (Arthur & Pedersen, 2008). Since the late 1980s, multicultural task forces have been set up and special editions of various counseling journals have addressed issues such as culture, ethnicity, and gay, lesbian, and transgender populations. *Counseling Today*, a monthly magazine published by the American Counseling Association (ACA), also features a regular column on diversity. Multicultural competencies developed by Sue, Arredondo, and McDavis (1992) were adopted by the Association for Multicultural Counseling and Development in 1995 as well as by all 19 ACA-affiliated counseling organizations. CACREP standards also identify diversity as one of the eight core counseling areas (CACREP, 2009), and coursework in multicultural counseling is a staple in counselor education curricula. Multiculturalism will continue to play a pivotal role in shaping the counseling profession, particularly given the globalization of the field (Arthur & Pedersen, 2008).

The counseling profession has also achieved numerous professional goals (e.g., name recognition, licensure in all 50 U.S. states and major territories, third-party billing privileges, and emerging international presence) in nearly 60 years of existence. Nevertheless, concerns loom large over the counseling horizon. One of the most pressing issues is the counseling profession's attempts to achieve marketplace parity with their mental health colleagues (Gladding, 2009; Remley & Herlihy, 2007). In the United States, the first significant steps on this long journey toward parity were the profession's successes in achieving state licensure. Historically, achieving rights coincides with a long-term struggle against established forces who seldom abdicate power and privilege willingly (Marx & Engels, 1985). The counseling profession's experience has been no exception to this maxim, as psychiatrists, psychologists, and social workers have vigorously opposed the counseling profession with regard to licensure, third-party billing, Medicare reimbursement, use of psychological tests, and many other areas. Undaunted, the ACA, the American Mental Health Counselors Association, and the American School Counselor Association have pressed forward in the aforementioned areas. Such efforts have yielded considerable success (e.g., licensure and third-party billing) while leaving some major rights unachieved (e.g., Medicare billing rights). Though lobbying efforts by the ACA and its affiliate have witnessed a Medicare reimbursement bill for counselors passing both houses of Congress at separate times, Medicare reimbursement remains unachieved though well within reach. TRICARE, the U.S. military's version of Medicare, does recognize licensed counselors as reimbursable providers, but counselors are the only TRICARE mental health providers requiring physician referral. The influential Institute of Medicine has recommended that the requirement for a referral physician be removed for licensed counselors, so this hurdle will be removed very soon (AMHCA, 2010). The Veterans Administration (VA) has recently approved licensed counselors to work in VA hospitals, though it will take some time before significant numbers of counselors are hired into VA medical centers.

IMPORTANT CREDENTIALS IN COUNSELING

Counselors, like professionals such as physicians, psychologists, social workers, teachers, and engineers, must be properly credentialed in order to practice. For counselors, there are two important, yet distinct, credentials.

1. *Licensure*: The most important credential a counselor must possess is a license. Professional counseling is a licensed occupation in all 50 U.S. states, Washington, DC, Puerto Rico, and Guam. In the majority of states, counselors are required to have a license in order to practice counseling, bill insurance companies, and collect private payment (Remley & Herlihy, 2007). Counselor licensure can be either a *title act* or a *scope of practice act* (Wheeler & Bertram, 2008). Title act licensure simply means that only counselors who are licensed can advertise themselves as counselors. Scope of practice act licensure means the scope of practice is limited to counselors holding a license or counselors being supervised for licensure. Most state counseling licenses are both title act and scope of practice act. For example, in the state of New Hampshire, to

call yourself a licensed counselor, you must have a current license. Furthermore, your counseling practice is limited to the range of professional activities that are outlined in the state's counselor law. Most counselor license laws permit the counselor to provide personal, career, and group counseling; diagnose and treat mental disorders; use psychological assessments; and so forth. However, as with all professions, licensure laws will vary from state to state, so it is critical for counselors to be aware of the range and limits of their state's licensure statutes.

2. *Certification*: Certification, unlike licensure, is a voluntary credential. Counselors are not required to possess a certification in order to practice professional counseling. For counselors, certification is the purview of private corporations, educational institutions, persons, and so on, and not states. The most notable certifying organization for counselors is the NBCC, located in Greensboro, North Carolina. The original certification was the National Certified Counselor credential established in 1981 (Gladding, 2009). Certification was created in an era when only a handful of states offered counselor licensure. As it was mentioned, since all 50 U.S. states, Washington, DC, and Puerto Rico have enacted counselor licensure, certification has transitioned into identifying specialty areas of counseling. NBCC offers the following certifications:

   National Certified Counselor: This is the most common certification

   Certified Clinical Mental Health Counselor: Identifies a specialty in mental health counseling

   National Certified School Counselor: Identifies a specialty in school counseling

   Master of Addictions Counselor: Identifies a specialty in chemical dependency counseling

   Approved Clinical Supervisor: Credential for counselors providing clinical supervision in the field.

To be eligible for one of these certifications, counselors must have either earned a degree in any one of the counseling fields, such as school counseling, clinical mental health counseling, career counseling, marriage and family counseling, addictions counseling, student affairs, and college counseling. (Note that students in CACREP-accredited programs may take the certification examination in the final semester/quarter of their graduate program) or have passed the certification examination conducted by NBCC. To get a sense of the NBCC, the certifications they offer, and their history, visit their Web site at www.nbcc.org.

BRIEF COMPARISONS BETWEEN COUNSELORS AND PSYCHOLOGISTS AND SOCIAL WORKERS

Counseling is a broad field practiced by counselors, social workers, psychologists, psychiatrists, marriage and family therapists (MFTs), and pastoral counselors. All these professions are distinct from one another, though some of their professional functions overlap. Because this book is written for people considering a career in counseling, I will offer brief sketches of each mental health profession below.

Psychiatrist: A psychiatrist is arguably the most different of all the mental health professionals. Psychiatrists are medical doctors who can prescribe psychoactive medication to help alleviate or lessen mental disorders. Though some psychiatrists do provide counseling, the majority of psychiatrists provide medication management. Psychiatrists must hold a valid medical license and practice in hospitals and outpatient mental health centers. The American Psychiatric Association is the professional organization representing the psychiatric profession.

Psychologists: Psychologists, like psychiatrists, are required to hold a doctoral degree (there are some exceptions to this); psychologists most commonly have a PhD, an EdD, and now the increasingly popular PsyD. Psychologists may provide counseling, use psychological tests, and diagnose and treat mental disorders. Psychologists are required to be licensed, though school psychologists may work in P-12 schools with a state certification, as opposed to a license, in many states. Psychologists practice in hospitals and outpatient centers, schools, and industries. The American Psychological Association is the chief professional organization for psychologists.

Counselors: Counselors are among the most recent of the mental health professionals. Unlike psychiatrists and psychologists, the practitioner degree for counselors is the master's. Graduate programs in counseling (or counselor education) are usually located in colleges of education at universities, though some are housed within psychology departments and a few in miscellaneous other academic units. Counselors provide counseling (individual, group, couples, and family) in inpatient and outpatient treatment centers and in schools. Some counselors do hold a doctoral degree, though this is not required for licensure or practice. The ACA is the flagship organization for the counseling profession.

Social workers: Social workers, like counselors, may practice after earning a master's degree (usually a master's in social work). Social workers work in hospitals, inpatient and outpatient mental health centers, and P-12 schools. Social workers are also licensed professionals. Social workers and counselors will often practice alongside. Social work is a very broad field, with clinical social workers providing counseling and many other social workers serving as case managers, directors of non-profit organizations, discharge planners in hospitals, and working in P-12 schools providing some counseling and resource connections outside the schools. The National Association of Social Workers is the national organization for social workers.

Marriage and family therapists: Like counselors and social workers, MFTs typically hold master's degrees and practice in the same types of agencies. MFTs receive the bulk of their graduate training in counseling couples and families, though they will also provide individual and group counseling. The American Association for Marriage and Family Therapy is the organization representing MFTs.

Dance therapy, art therapy, music therapy, and others: Readers of this text may have noticed mental health professionals advertising themselves as art therapists, dance therapists, music therapists, and so on. In many cases, for example, an art therapist may be a counselor or social worker with advanced training in art therapy. However, dance therapy, art therapy, and so on are often referred to as "creative arts counseling" and, in some cases, may have a separate licensure. Dance therapy, for example, is often a separate graduate program at the university level, often called "dance movement therapy and counseling" or something similar. Various professional associations represent the creative arts professions: the American Art Therapy Association, the ADTA, and so on. Though the numbers of creative arts therapists/counselors are relatively small due the relative recent emergence of these professions, they do appear to be growing (U.S. Bureau of Labor Statistics, 2010–2011).

Given that the scope of practice is similar among the above professions (psychiatry is an exception due to medical training), it is no wonder that the public confuses these separate professions. For our purposes (from a counselor's point of view), the biggest difference between a counselor and these allied mental health professionals is that counselors' primary training and focus is on counseling. For psychologists, psychiatrists, and social workers, counseling is an ancillary function (Remley & Herlihy, 2007). Despite each of the above profession's best efforts to educate the public about their differences, the public will likely continue to be confused among particular mental health professions.

THE JOB MARKET FOR COUNSELORS

As would be natural, persons interested in the counseling profession will be interested in the job market and salaries for counselors. Both the job market and salaries will be impacted by the area you live in (rural vs. urban), your state of residence, your experience (beginning counselor vs.

licensed counselor with around 10 years experience), and the marketplace (the strength of the national, regional, and/or local economy). The U.S. Bureau of Labor Statistics is the governmental agency that tabulates statistics and makes predictions on occupational outlook for all recognized professions based on trends and market conditions. The occupational outlook and salary information for counselors is listed below. Be aware that there may be some shifting of national figures as the figures reported are those from 2011.

OCCUPATIONAL OUTLOOK FOR MENTAL HEALTH COUNSELORS

According to the U.S. Department of Labor, "... the occupational outlook for counselors over the next decade is expected to grow faster than the average for all occupations through 2012, and job opportunities should be very good because there are usually more job openings than graduates of counseling programs" (U.S. Department of Labor, Bureau of Labor Statistics; http://www.bls.gov/oco/ocos067.htm). In addition, *Money Magazine* (2006; May) recently rated mental health counselors as one of the top 50 occupations. The Department of Labor's Bureau of Labor Statistics (2010–2011) projections are listed in Table 1.1.

Table 1.1 Employment of Counselors: Projections for Counselor Occupational Growth

	Employment (2008)	Projected (2018)	Number	Percent Change
Total counselors	665,500	782,200	116,800	+18
Breakdown by Counseling Specialty Area				
Addictions	86,100	104,200	18,100	+21
School, educational and vocational	275,800	314,400	38,600	+14
Marriage and family	27,300	31,300	3900	+14
Mental health	113,300	140,400	27,200	+24
Rehabilitation	129,500	154,100	24,500	+19
All other counselors°	33,400	37,800	4400	+13

Source: Statistics compiled by the U.S. Bureau of Labor Statistics, 2010–2011, www.bols.gov
°The Bureau of Labor Statistics does not specify or identify "all other counselors," though this category would include creative arts counselors—art therapy, music therapy, and dance therapy.

Table 1.2 Mean Salaries for Counseling Fields

Elementary and secondary school counselors	$53,750
Colleges, universities, and professional schools	$41,780
Community/junior college	$48,240
Social service agencies	$32,370
Vocational rehabilitation services	$31,340
Mental health counselors	$34,380
Rehabilitation counselors	$29,200
Addictions counselors	$34,040
Marriage and family counselors/therapists	$43,210
Other counselors	Not listed

Source: Statistics compiled by the U.S. Bureau of Labor Statistics, 2010–2011, www.bols.gov

EARNINGS FOR COUNSELORS

Median salaries for counselors vary depending on the counseling specialty, geographic region (urban, suburban, or rural setting), level of education, and so on. The Bureau of Labor Statistics reports the mean salaries for counseling fields (Table 1.2).

SUMMARY

Counseling has emerged from its origins in the early 1950s and become one of the fastest growing mental health professions (U.S. Bureau of Labor Statistics, 2010–2011). Counselors are now licensed in all 50 U.S. states, Washington, DC, and Puerto Rico. The field has broadened, offering jobs in schools, community colleges, colleges, universities, and inpatient and outpatient treatment centers, and in virtually all vocational settings where other mental health professionals would work. Though the counseling profession has achieved significant milestones in its efforts to gain parity with psychology and social work, Medicare reimbursement remains an unachieved goal though it is well within reach and it is likely that the counseling profession will achieve Medicare reimbursement privileges in the not-too-distant future.

2   Counseling as a Career

As was discussed in Chapter 1, the profession of counseling has consistently gotten stronger, especially since the mid-1970s when Virginia became the first state to license counselors. As professions get established, licensure is likely the most salient means of demonstrating professional strength. In November 2009, when California became the 50th state to grant licensure to counselors, the counseling profession achieved a significant milestone. Licensure means counselors can bill insurance companies, work in inpatient and outpatient treatment centers, hospitals, and many areas where they were previously excluded from practice. The U.S. Bureau of Labor Statistics (BOLS) (2010–2011) has projected counseling to have sustained healthy growth for the foreseeable future, and graduate counseling programs are now very common in colleges and universities. Therefore, it is no stretch to make a statement that the counseling profession has arrived as a viable and successful member of the mental health professions.

Because counselors are among the newest of the mental health professions, they still have some growing to do before achieving parity with their colleagues in social work and psychology. As was mentioned in the previous chapter, Medicare reimbursement remains the counseling profession's most significant unmet goal. Because counselors have already achieved licensure success in all the states and major territories, won the right to bill insurance, and experienced significant growth in the marketplace, counselors are certain to achieve Medicare reimbursement in the future. Readers considering counseling as a career should feel encouraged by the occupational forecast by the U.S. BOLS. However, readers should also be aware that a healthy occupational outlook and a growing field do not mean counseling is the field for you. The next section of this chapter will outline considerations to assist you in determining whether counseling is a good occupational "fit" for you.

IS THE COUNSELING PROFESSION A GOOD FIT FOR YOU?

Counselors have a very challenging and fulfilling career, helping people who are struggling with career indecision, grief recovery, martial strife, addiction, abuse (sexual, physical, or verbal), and many other maladies. Counselors work in many settings previously mentioned, and the occupational outlook is very good. These are all positive indicators for anyone considering a career in the counseling profession. However, to borrow from famed psychologist-counselor Carl Rogers, these indicators are *necessary*, though not *sufficient*, reasons for an interested person to enter the counseling profession.

There are many reasons why a person chooses to become a counselor (Kottler, 2003). For many, the reasons may include the following: a willingness to be helpful, good job outlook, someone they admire is in the field, or, as in a good number of cases, the person benefited from counseling. This latter category seems to be a significant method of entry into the profession (Corey & Corey, 2003; Kottler, 2003). It probably makes sense that a positive experience as a client would stimulate an individual to consider taking up the counseling profession, particularly if that client is young or one who is considering a career change. As someone who has been around graduate counseling programs for over 25 years, my own experience is that at least half of the students in programs I have been affiliated with as a graduate student and faculty member have entered a counseling graduate program as a result of having been in therapy.

Personal and career counseling can be a good method of assessing whether the profession is congruent with your interests. The benefit of being a client in counseling provides an individual direct experience in what is involved in counseling. Naturally, a good counseling experience is likely to tip the scales of interest in the direction of pursuing a degree in counseling (or the related fields in social work, psychology, etc.). As a veteran counselor and professor of counselor education, I definitely feel that having been a client in counseling gives a person a sense of what the profession is all about. However, and this is the "but" part, being a client in counseling is significantly different from being a counselor in a therapeutic encounter. Being a client entails a willingness to enter counseling and face whatever issues need to be faced. Being a counselor, on the other hand, means being expected to be psychologically healthy enough to help other people with their personal struggles (a *huge* consideration), able to create therapeutic attachment (through empathy, assessment, etc.), skilled to move the counseling relationship from intake through 8 to 12 sessions of counseling, patient when therapy stagnates, and able to maintain just enough clinical detachment to ensure that the client's issues do not become the counselor's issues. The experience of being a client in counseling, though very important, is not enough of a litmus test to determine whether counseling is the right field for them.

So then, what are the factors that indicate whether counseling is a good profession for a given person? Numerous research studies have indicated that many characteristics go into the making of a counselor (Kottler, 2003). Some significant characteristics of a good counselor are being empathetic, openness to new experiences, a nonjudgmental attitude, good emotional health, detachment, healthy lifestyle, and a belief that people can change (Kottler, 2003). I would assert that all these characteristics, and more, are required in order to become a good counselor. For example, good counselors are ethical, have good work ethics, seek regular consultation, continue as lifelong learners by attending workshops and conferences, and remain active in their professional associations, such as the American Counseling Association (ACA), the American School Counselor Association (ASCA), and the American Mental Health Counselors Association (AMHCA).

As a longtime counselor, counselor educator, and counseling supervisor, I have noticed that skilled counselors possess certain characteristics that assist them in their work with individuals, couples, families, and groups. I have prepared an interactive question series in this next section, and I encourage you to answer the questions in a serious and forthright manner. The questions are not an absolute test to determine whether you should or should not enter the counseling profession, but they may assist you in your decision process.

Answer the following questions by circling the number that best fits you:

1. I believe that people are capable of changing old destructive behaviors (e.g., addictions, violence against others, and bigoted attitudes).

   1   2   3   4   5   6   7   (8)   9   10

   Can't change   Can change

2. I am able to be emotionally present and reserve personal judgment when speaking with someone whose behavior and values do not match

my own (e.g., I could listen without judgment to someone who is gay or lesbian, is considering an abortion or a sex change, or is a convicted sex offender).

1   2   3   4   5   6   (7)   8   9   10

Couldn't be present   Could be present

3. I have at least one close friendship outside my family where I can get support in times of need.

1   2   3   4   5   6   7   8   9   (10)

No   Somewhat   Yes

4. I am able to actively listen and refrain from offering advice to others when they come to me with a problem.

1   2   3   4   5   (6)   7   8   9   10

Readily offer advice   Seldom offer advice

5. I believe that most issues are not simply matters of "right" and "wrong," but generally are shades of gray.

1   2   3   4   5   6   (7)   8   9   10

Always clear   Often shades of gray

6. I accept that one culture is not superior to another and affirm people of a different ethnicity, culture, religion/spirituality, sexual orientation, gender, and social class.

1   2   3   4   5   6   7   8   9   (10)

There is one "best" way   Many cultural pathways

7. Regarding Question 6, if a client were to come to me with the goal of accepting that he or she was gay or lesbian, I would be able to assist the client without reservations or judgment.

1   2   3   4   5   6   7   8   9   (10)

Absolutely not   Yes

8. Through my diet, fitness routine, friendships, or spiritual life/life meaning, I have the ability to manage stress and anxiety.

1   2   3   4   (5)   6   7   8   9   10

Poor diet and inactive   Active and healthy diet

9. When conflict arises in the workplace, home, and friendships, I am able to work to resolve these conflicts in a nondestructive manner.

 1   2   3   4   5   (6)   7   8   9   10

No or very difficult   Confident and skilled

10. I am in touch with my emotions and am able to express the full range of emotions appropriate to the situation. I also am not governed by my emotions.

 1   2   3   4   5   (6)   7   8   9   10

Out of touch/difficulty regulating   In touch/good at emotional
emotions   regulation

Consider also the following reflection questions (write the answers out on a separate sheet of paper).

1. What are the reason(s) I want to become a counselor?
2. What fears do you have about becoming a counselor?
3. What drew you to the profession of counseling?
4. Take a sheet of paper and draw a line down the middle. Label the right hand side, *My natural strengths that will help me assist future clients.* Label the left hand side, *Personal experiences and characteristics that will challenge my ability to assist future clients.* List your strengths and challenges in the appropriate column. Then compare the balance between the two. Which side seems dominant? (Be very honest with yourself.)
5. Interview a counselor. Ask the counselor what he/she likes about being a counselor; what he/she dislikes about being a counselor; what is a typical day (if there is such a thing); and if the counselor had it to do over again, would he/she still choose to be a counselor and why or why not?
6. What excites you about the profession of counseling? (List as many reasons as possible.)
7. Part of counselor education in a graduate program (and well beyond) is the ability to receive critical feedback of your counseling work. How well are you able to give and receive feedback? Also, how prone are you to becoming defensive and angry?
8. Promoting good mental health in others requires developing a sense of resilience in ourselves. So,
   (a) How resilient are you in the face of disappointment? (Score yourself on the 1–10 scale below.)

 1   2   3   4   5   6   (7)   8   9   10
Not resilient   Somewhat resilient   Very resilient

(b) Cite important times in your life when you demonstrated resilience in the face of disappointment or even despair (death of a loved one, divorce, loss of job, etc.).

9. Regarding the counseling profession, what would be your dream job (e.g., counseling in a high school, community college/university, or community agency)? What draws you to this particular setting? (Name as many specific reasons as you can.)

10. Managing conflict is a critical skill to cultivate for a person in any occupation. Because counselors are often expected to serve as mediators or to assist couples, classmates, siblings, coworkers, and so forth to resolve their conflicts, how comfortable do you feel mediating conflicts? (Note that you can perhaps use a 1–10 scaling question such as the above.) If you do not feel confident in mediating conflicts, how could you develop such confidence?

EDUCATION AND TRAINING REQUIRED TO BECOME A COUNSELOR

Just as with any skilled profession, becoming a counselor takes time. Eligibility for licensure (and licensure is a must!) includes completion of a baccalaureate degree and a 2- or 3-year master's degree in counseling. Then, after graduating with a master's degree in clinical mental health counseling, school counseling, rehabilitation counseling, and so on, the counselor is eligible to be hired in a professional setting. Counselors must be supervised for 1 to 2 years (depending on state of residence) in order to complete the "supervised-hour" requirement for state licensure. Upon completion of the required number of hours (generally 1000 to 2000 hours, though there are exceptions), the candidates may take the licensure examination. (Check with your state of residence as the required supervised hours, exam required, and when you can take the exam vary depending on state or territory.) After completing the supervised-hour requirement and passing the exam, the counselor can successfully apply for licensure. One of the best resources for readers of this book is the ACA's published book *Licensure Requirements for Professional Counselors, 2010 edition*. This handy and inexpensive book provides details about basic licensure requirements for all 50 U.S. states, Washington, DC, and Puerto Rico.

Basically, to become a counselor and to be eligible to be hired in a professional setting, it takes 6 to 7 years of full-time college and graduate school study. Then, after obtaining a master's degree in counseling (school counseling, clinical mental health counseling, rehabilitation counseling, etc.), 1 to 2 years of full-time supervised work in a professional setting plus passing your state's licensure examination are required. So, as you can see, becoming a counselor is a winding road. However, given that counselors grapple with weighty issues such as substance abuse, sexual abuse, eating disorders, career issues, and so forth, it should not be too easy to become a counselor. (The same statement could be applied for the professions of social work and psychology.)

VARIATIONS TO BECOMING A COUNSELOR

As you examine the counseling profession, you may notice that some professionals providing counseling may have the backgrounds described above (master's degree in counseling plus a license). Because counseling is one of the newest mental health professions (Gladding, 2009), there are exceptions to the described requirements. The addictions field, for example, remains heavily populated with addictions "counselors" lacking a master's degree in counseling. Because the field of addictions was traditionally staffed by people who were formerly ex-addicts (alcohol and other drugs), there was a time when very few addictions professionals held a graduate degree. Many addictions counseling jobs required a BA/BS degree (or less) and documented sobriety for a specified period of years.

The field of addictions counseling, however, is beginning to change. Master's degrees in counseling are becoming more common for addictions counselors and the ACA has a growing affiliate division known as the International Association of Addictions and Offender Counselors. While many states continue to allow agencies to hire bachelor's-level addiction counselors and credential them with certifications such as "certified addiction counselor" or "licensed addictions and drug counselor," the preferred credential is a master's degree and a license as a mental health counselor, with the latter credential requiring a master's degree. A master's degree in counseling and a license (licensed mental health counselor, licensed professional counselor, or whatever your state's counselor licensure is titled) also provides far more room for growth and advancement in your career than a bachelor's degree. So, should you be contemplating a career as an addiction counselor, I would strongly suggest you earn a master's degree in clinical mental health counseling or addictions counseling.

Another statement regarding addictions counseling should be made at this point in the text. During the addictions counseling community's formative years, a bias for hiring former addicts existed. Though it may remain an advantage for an addictions counselor to have been in successful recovery, having been an ex-addict is no longer a "requirement" for those considering a career in the addictions field. It should also be pointed out that while many addicts in treatment will prefer former addicts as counselors, a counselor's ability to maintain a therapeutic presence in the face of client defiance is likely a better predictor of success than having been a former addict. One likely would not expect an oncologist to have suffered from cancer in order to successfully treat the disease.

Another statement regarding the term "counselor" should be explained at this point. For our purposes, counseling will refer to professionals holding a graduate degree in one of the previously mentioned counseling fields and professionals holding a license as a counselor or being supervised for a license. A recent agreed-upon definition of counseling authored by an association of counseling organizations (Known as *20/20: A Vision for the Future of Counseling*) has also emerged: "Counseling is a professional relationship that empowers diverse individuals, families, and groups to accomplish mental health, wellness, education and career goals" (Linde, 2010, p. 5).

Some professionals with related degrees have been able to become credentialed as counselors due to the laws in some states. One of the most common examples of this exception is professionals holding a master's degree in counseling or clinical psychology. Because licensed psychologists are required to hold the doctorate degree (PhD, PsyD, EdD) in all but a few states, some professionals holding master's degrees in psychology have been able to become licensed counselors in some states. While this situation is likely to continue for some period of time, the counseling profession is in the process of lobbying state legislatures to license only professionals holding a graduate degree in counseling (e.g., clinical mental health counseling, addictions counseling, school counseling). When considering enrolling in a master's degree program in, say, clinical psychology, or counseling psychology, remember that you will be licensed eligible in a small number of states. Therefore, my recommendation is that you consider only master's degree programs in aforementioned counseling programs. I do not argue that professionals with a master's degree, in say, counseling psychology, are not mental health professionals, because I believe they are. However, if they are professionals (e.g., psychologists), it would behoove you to ask why their own profession and professional association (e.g., American Psychological Association) has lobbied against master's-level psychologists and considers psychologists to be only professionals holding doctoral degrees (American Psychological Association, 2011).

BENEFITS OF A CAREER IN COUNSELING

When you enroll in a graduate counseling program, you are not simply entering a given master's degree program in counselor education/counseling at a typical state university. You are on the path to joining the counseling profession, along with some 655,000 professional counselors (BOLS, 2010–2011), with the ACA as its flagship, 19 affiliate counseling divisions, and licensure in 50 U.S. states, Washington, DC, Puerto Rico, and Guam. In addition to learning counseling techniques and interventions, you will be educated on the counseling profession, its history, and what makes the profession distinctive, and you will study the professional ethics of ACA and your respective counseling division (e.g., clinical mental health counseling, school counseling, and rehabilitation counseling). So remember, you are entering a profession, not merely seeking a "job" as a counselor.

A significant benefit of the counseling profession is that counseling is a dynamic profession with job growth faster than that in most occupations (BOLS, 2010–2011). The BOLS figures for professional counselors in the field and projected job growth were noted in Chapter 1, and you can see that the occupational outlook of the counseling profession is very bright. So first, you can feel very confident that counseling will continue to be a vibrant profession for the foreseeable future. Just remember that you must prepare yourself as well as you can for a future career. At the conclusion of this chapter, several helpful books will be listed that can assist you in preparing for your job search when the time arrives. Though listing job search texts might be viewed as "putting the cart before the horse" (pardon the cliché, but it gets the point across), it is never too early to prepare for a job search.

In joining the profession of counseling, you have also entered a world where you will likely discover few absolutes. Though this is not a philosophy text and I am a counselor, not a philosopher or theologian, at some point in our counseling career, we run head first into challenging life constructs such as suicide and euthanasia, abortion, sexual orientation, and religious conflicts. Though you may have fixed ideas regarding the "rightness" or "wrongness" of, say, abortion, your beliefs and values will be put to the test. Consider the following scenario.

THE CASE OF CARL

Carl is a 70-year-old male who came to the clinic for counseling. He informed his counselor Consuelo that he had recently received a terminal diagnosis of less than 6 months. His physician had also informed him that his disease would be very painful. Carl decided that he would like to die with dignity and on his own terms and will commit suicide before he reaches the point of excruciating pain. His reasons for coming to counseling are that it helps him prepare his family and himself for death. He further stated that he had not told his family of his decision to commit suicide.

Consuelo is sympathetic to Carl, but knows suicide is against state law and that she is required to report Carl to the authorities, as, technically speaking, he is a "danger to himself." However, checking the *American Counseling Association Code of Ethics*, the ethics seem to imply you can report or not report, depending on what is in the best interests of the client. Consuelo is unsure what is in Carl's best interest. Furthermore, she is a very religious Catholic and knows that her church opposes suicide. She feels torn between her personal religious and moral principles and her professional obligation to serve what is in her client's best interest.

What Should Consuelo Do?

Now, fortunately, Consuelo will not have to make the decision by herself. She should inform Carl that while she is sympathetic to his wishes, there are legal and ethical issues she must address with her supervisor. Consuelo must walk the delicate line of the ethical construct of working in the best interest of her client while obeying state law. This issue will likely go above the supervisor (perhaps, to the agency attorney).

Why is this scenario under the benefits section of this chapter? Well, readers should understand the serious issues they will encounter and the decisions they may be called upon to make. Because you will be a member of a profession, you have an ethical code to guide you (and your supervisor) in making a decision. In addition to the *American Counseling Association Code of Ethics* (2005), there are numerous books, DVDs, and other helpful resources. Wheeler and Bertram (2008) recommend the following risk management strategy:

1. Risk management tool kit, including
   (a) Ethical codes (e.g., ACA, ASCA, and AMHCA)
   (b) Laws/state statutes of your state of practice
   (c) Articles/checklist for what to do when subpoenaed
   (d) Know your attorney (agencies, schools, colleges, etc., will have one).
2. Colleague/supervisor consultation.
3. Informed consent: Make sure the client, such as Carl, knows the exceptions to confidentiality and when the counselor must breach confidentiality.
4. Know the policies of your employer: school, clinic, university counseling center, and so on.
5. Termination and abandonment: Avoid terminating a client in crisis. Carl is definitely in a crisis, though not one where he seems likely to attempt suicide immediately.
6. Document whatever clinical decision you and your supervisor/colleague make. The rule in a court of law is "if it isn't written down, it does not exist."

7. Manage co-occurring relationships: Dual roles with clients must be minimized. School counselors, for example, will naturally have other relationships with students, but should work to maintain appropriate distance from students.

8. Practice within your scope of competence: Recognize the limitations of your training and experience. If you have no training in, say, dream interpretation, do not attempt to practice it.

9. Supervision: You will be required to have supervision for licensure. However, even after you are licensed, you will need seasoned professionals with which to discuss clinical issues. In an agency, school, college, or residential treatment center, you will have many options for supervision. Counselors in private practice may need to pay for supervision.

10. Professional liability insurance: Purchase and maintain professional liability insurance.

Adapted from Wheeler and Bertram (2008, pp. 209–210)

As a professional counselor, you will also receive professional journals with your membership in the ACA, AMHCA, ASCA, and so on (note that a complete list of the professional counseling associations is provided in the Appendix). Your membership in ACA also provides subscriptions to the *Journal of Counseling & Development* and *Counseling Today*, an award winning monthly magazine filled with personal stories and interviews of professional counselors along with helpful information for counselors to know.

THE NECESSITY OF PROFESSIONAL MEMBERSHIP

Furthermore, all readers who do matriculate into a graduate counseling program should join the ACA and appropriate divisional affiliate. For example, graduate students in a school counseling program should also join the ASCA, those in a mental health counseling program should join the AMHCA, and those in a rehabilitation counseling program should join the American Rehabilitation Counseling Association, and so forth. I would also strongly recommend maintaining a lifetime membership in these professional organizations as they provide professional identity and important publications, and lobby in the interests of the profession and its individual counselors. As a former director of counseling programs, I would be very hesitant to hire an applicant for a counseling position if she or he lacked memberships in the appropriate counseling organizations. A lack of professional membership indicates less investment in the profession and that sends the wrong signal to the hiring committee or interviewer.

LICENSURE AND CERTIFICATION

The counseling profession has made significant professional strides by achieving licensure in all 50 U.S. states in November 2009. Professions generally define themselves in part by having state licensure as the crowning achievement for professional practice. Licensed occupations include physicians, lawyers, psychologists, social workers, teachers, and, of course, counselors. Licensure is a concrete way for professionals to say, "I've arrived" as an autonomous practitioner. Until licensed, most states require that individuals seeking licensure be supervised by a licensed professional until they meet required standards.

Like all licensed occupations in the United States, licensure is the purview of each individual state or territory. Because individual state requirements can vary considerably, a counselor licensed in Nebraska who relocates to New York may not be immediately licensed. Naturally, this is a real concern for counselors (and professionals in *any* occupation) practicing in the United States. Arguments for a national licensure have yet to make significant inroads, so variability in counselor licensure is likely to continue for the foreseeable future. As previously mentioned, the ACA has published a helpful manual listing basic licensure requirements of the 50 U.S. states, Washington, DC, and Puerto Rico, as well as Web site addresses for the licensure boards in the respective states and territories (ACA, 2009).

Basic Licensure Information

While noting the variability in state licensure, readers should be aware of general licensure requirements. Regarding licensure, counseling boards:

- Require a minimum of a master's degree in counseling for licensure
- Require a 2- to 3-year master's degree in counseling or a related field
- Require a graduate of a master's degree counseling program to work under the supervision of a licensed mental health professional (preferable licensed counselor, or licensed social worker, psychologist, etc.). State licensure boards usually require between 1000 and 3000 post-master's degree hours working under the supervision of a licensed mental health professional
- All states and territories require counselors seeking licensure to pass an examination in order to be licensed. Unfortunately, there are several different tests used for counselor licensure. The most common examinations are:
  - *National Counselor Examination (NCE):* administered by the National Board for Certified Counselors (NBCC)

- *National Clinical Mental Health Counselor Examination (NCMHCE)*: also administered by NBCC
- *Certified Rehabilitation Counselor Examination*: administered by the Commission on Rehabilitation Counselor Certification (CRCC)
- *Examination of Clinical Counselor Practice*: also administered by NBCC

For general information about these examinations, contact NBCC at (336) 547–0607 or visit them online at www.nbcc.org. CRCC can be reached at (847) 394–2104 or online at www.crccertification.com. For state-specific or territory-specific information on examination requirements, contact the appropriate state counseling board.

Certification

In addition to state licensure, which is a *required* credential for professional practice, certification is a *voluntary* credential that many counselors choose to obtain. Though licensure is the more important credential, certification arguably holds a functional place in the counseling profession.

NBCC is the primary national organization that certifies counselors. Counseling certifications offered by NBCC are in the fields of school counseling, mental health counseling, addiction counseling, and supervision. Here are the certifications offered by NBCC:

National certified counselor (NCC): NCC was the original certification established in 1981 when few states offered counselor license (Gladding, 2009). Counselors who wish to become a NCC must have a minimum of 48-semester or 72-quarter hours of graduate study in counseling or a related field. The NCC credential also requires passing the NCE.

Master addictions counselor (MAC): MAC is a certification that counseling professional working in the addictions field typically earn. The MAC requires the same type of master's degree as the NCC credential, though in a counseling program with a curriculum that addresses addictions. MAC applicants must pass the examination for master addictions counselor.

National certified school counselor (NCSC): NCSC requires a 48-semester or 72-quarter hour master's degree in school counseling. Applicants must also pass the national certified school counselor examination.

Certified clinical mental health counselor (CCMHC): CCMHC credential requires a 72-semester hour or a 90-quarter hour degree in mental health counseling and passing NCMHCE.

For complete information on certification, visit the NBCC Web page on requirements for certifications at www.nbcc.org/certifications/Default.aspx.

Now, as a reader contemplating a career in counseling, you may be confused by all the different certifications and licensure requirements. When I entered the counseling field in the 1980s, I was also confused by the difference between licensure and certification and the variations of licensure and certification. Just remember that licensure is a *required* credential and is granted by each individual state or territory. Certification is a *voluntary* credential offered by independent credentialing agencies, most notably by the NBCC.

Some professionals will question the need for continuing with a credential such as certification in an era when licensure is the required credential. Arguments for the continuation of certification persist in this age of counselor licensure. The medical profession likely is the best example to cite. In medicine, physicians are licensed, but board certified in their respective specialty area (e.g., pediatrics, orthopedics, and psychiatry). Likewise, counselors are licensed by their respective state, but certified in their specialty area (school counseling, mental health counseling, addictions counseling, etc.). Thus, certification will be strengthened by licensure than weakened by it.

STRENGTH OF THE PROFESSION

The counseling profession has overcome many growing pains to become a respected member of the mental health community. As has been mentioned thus far in the text, licensure has been achieved in 50 U.S. states, Washington, DC, and Puerto Rico. Professional counselors can bill most health insurance companies and work in military and veterans administration hospitals, schools, inpatient and outpatient treatment centers, jails, prisons, and many other settings. The BOLS (2010–2011) lists 655,000 professional counselors employed in the United States, and projects it to be 782,000 by 2018, meaning an 18% growth increase. This is a large number of professionals, and the BOLS projects counselors to grow faster than those in most occupations in the foreseeable future (BOLS, 2010–2011). ACA and its 19 professional affiliate organizations are collaborating to ensure more unification within the counseling profession, and this portends very well for counselors in all fields of counseling (e.g., school counseling, mental health counseling, and rehabilitation counseling).

The above information provides very healthy indicators for the long-term future of the counseling profession. Readers considering the counseling profession should feel reassured that the marketplace will be strong when they are seeking work in the mental health field. However, it must be admitted that the counseling profession still has ground to cover before achieving parity with its mental health colleagues in psychology. The most significant goal remaining for the counseling profession is Medicare reimbursement. The counseling profession is inching closer to achieving this goal by consistently getting a bill to the floor of the U.S. Senate and House of Representatives in Washington, DC. However, though a Medicare reimbursement bill for counselors has been passed in each separate chamber of Congress, it has yet to be cleared in both houses of Congress and sent to the President to sign into law. Medicare reimbursement remains the top priority for the counseling profession (Gladding, 2009). Given that the counseling profession has achieved licensure in all states and major territories, has privileges to bill health insurance, and has Medicaid billing vendorship, it is very likely that the Medicare privileges are not far off.

Though Medicare remains the "big prize" for the counseling profession, there are other worthy goals. For example, like psychology and social work, counseling is a broad field encompassing many different types of counseling professionals, from school counselors, mental health counselors, addiction counselors, college/university/community college counselors, and many others. (At least 101 different counseling occupations, right?) An issue with such breadth is that while the ACA is the flagship organization for counselors, 19 other affiliate organizations represent particular specialty areas in counseling. This variation can result in *splitting* the profession and weakening the overall profession. Fortunately, the various counseling organizations are working to resolve various conflicts, as evidenced by the *20/20 Initiative*, mentioned previously.

Possibly, the next major frontier for the counseling profession is the international counseling movement. As one of the more recent mental health professions, counseling has been slower to move across international boundaries. However, professional counselors now work on every continent (excluding Antarctica, I guess) and in numerous countries across the globe. The International Association for Counselling is a professional organization devoted to promoting the counseling profession abroad. Counseling has a notable presence in countries such as Canada, Singapore, Taiwan, Egypt, Australia, and New Zealand. Many readers of this text may get the opportunity to work abroad after completing their master's degree and achieving licensure. I would even venture to speculate that 10 years after the publication of this text, the counseling profession would have a strong international presence. This should surprise no one given the global marketplace connections outlined in watershed books like *The World is Flat* (Freedman, 2004). (I recommend everyone read Freedman's book as it provides a good sense of future trends.)

International counseling will also change counselor education in a significant manner. For example, in a few years, a graduate student in a small college in upstate New York may have the opportunity to do an internship in Singapore. A graduate student in Botswana could do an internship in Kansas. The profession might even witness graduate programs in the United States forming partnerships with counseling programs in other countries. Alternatively, as many U.S. universities have established campuses overseas, counselor education programs might soon become one of the common programs offered at overseas campuses. In fact, I expect the international counseling profession to grow exponentially in the next decade, particularly as counseling becomes more accepted in countries around the globe.

SUMMARY

It is an exciting time to consider a career in counseling. The profession is growing and achieving numerous professional goals. The job outlook for graduates of counseling programs looks very strong for the foreseeable future, and the international counseling movement, though in its infancy, is likely to mature in the next decade. I hope that by reading this text, you will feel informed as to the nature of the counseling profession and that you will also be excited by the opportunities offered in a challenging profession.

ADDITIONAL TEXTS FOR CAREER ASSISTANCE

American Counseling Association. (2008). *Licensure requirements for professional counselors: A state-by-state report*. Alexandria, VA: Author.

Bolles, R. N. (2011). *What color is your parachute*. Berkeley, CA: Ten Speed Press.

Cappachione, L. (2000). *Visioning: Ten steps to designing the life of your dreams*. New York: Tarcher/Putnam.

Hodges, S., & Connelly, A. R. (2009). *A job search manual for counselors and counselor educators: How to navigate and promote your counseling career*. Alexandria, VA: American Counseling Association.

Janda, L. (1999). *Career tests: 25 revealing self-tests to help you find and succeed at the perfect career*. Avon, MA: Adams Media.

Sinetar, M. (1989). *Do what you love, the money will follow*. Mahwah, NJ: Paulist Press.

Walsh, R. J., & Dasenbrook, N. D. (2009). *The complete guide to private practice for licensed mental health professionals* (4th ed.). Rockford, IL: Crysand Press.

Careers in Counseling

3 Counseling Children and Families

This section of the text commences outlining the specific counseling careers. As the title implies, 101 different careers in the counseling profession will be highlighted. In many cases, it could be argued that some of the careers mentioned have few degrees of separation from one another. For example, counseling children in intact versus single-parent families may not show a marked distinction. However, because there are counselors who only counsel children from single-parent families, it is probably acceptable to list them separately (in cases such as this example, we might say they are different counseling "jobs" and not actually separate "careers"). Nevertheless, the 101 different careers or jobs will give readers a good idea about the range of potential counseling occupations.

Counseling children and adolescents will be very different from counseling adult populations because of the simple fact that children and adolescents are minors. Minors have limited discretion in their own counseling treatment. Usually, their parents or guardians are the catalyst for accessing treatment services and not the minor. There are exceptions to this, with perhaps school counseling being the most notable. Even in school settings, the parents or guardians are in a position to influence the onset, continuance, and termination of counseling services. Thus, readers should be aware that counseling minor populations would often involve communicating with their families. In many cases, the counselor may bring in the extended family for counseling, or refer them to another counselor or other therapist.

1. COUNSELOR FOR CHILDREN IN INTACT FAMILIES

Counseling children in traditional nuclear families has become significantly less common since the 1970s (Maples & Abney, 2006). As divorce has become increasingly more common in American society, single-parent families have become as common as traditional "nuclear" or two-parent families. However, there are many two-parent families in the society, and counselors will need to become facile in communicating the results of counseling with their children. My experience in training counselors is that many beginning counselors are nervous about conferences with parents, and frequently getting the parents to take an active role in counseling is the more difficult task.

If you examine the Bureau of Labor Statistics (BOLS, 2010–2011) cited in Chapter 1, the largest percentage of counselors are school counselors who number over 275,000. If you examine the other counseling professions cited in the BOLS statistics, many of these counselors, especially mental health counselors, will spend much of their time counseling children and adolescents. Marriage and family counselors will counsel families, which also involves working with children. Counselors must also realize that families come in different assortments. You will counsel children with gay and lesbian parents, children being raised by their grandparents, blended families (remarriages), and families of diverse racial, cultural, and religious backgrounds, some of whom may be recent immigrants to the United States.

Counselors working with children of intact families often are seeing the child or adolescent who has been referred by a parent, a school counselor, an athletic coach, or a religious leader. With younger children, beginning counselors should be aware that the child might not have a good understanding of what counseling is about. Some may think that they are in trouble or that counseling is playtime. Counselors must do their best to provide the child a sense of what counseling involves. With children under the age of, say, 8 years, simple language should be used, such as counseling is to "help you feel better," or "help you adjust to a new school," or whatever the issue might be. Counselors also will need to help the younger children understand what "feeling" means. Charts with smiling and sad faces, for example, are a concrete way to teach children about feelings and accompanying emotions. In fact, the counselor's primary work with a young child will likely involve helping the child to understand his or her emotions and to understand what emotions are appropriate to the given setting. For example, laughter is a joyful emotion, though it will not be an appropriate emotion in the first-grade classroom, unless initiated by the teacher.

While counseling children, you will do a lot of hands-on teaching. Because younger children will not have a highly developed vocabulary, the use of therapeutic toys is essential. Many companies catering to the therapeutic community will offer inexpensive toys such as dolls, sandboxes, foam tools, plastic and stuffed animals, and interactive games. It is imperative that counselors working with children have extensive training in play therapy and art therapy, because play and art are natural media for a child's expression of emotions and behavior (Landreth, 2002). Counseling children seldom involves sitting in chairs and having a therapeutic conversation; it is an active process that involves counselors sitting on the floor and playing with the child, sitting at a small table as the child draws his or her family, or whatever drama has brought the child to therapy. Counselors will need to use brief sentences, one or two syllable simple words, and a soft tone of voice. Remember, the child may have been abused and a counselor, particularly a large male counselor, may initially frighten the child.

Boundaries and "Who Is My Client?"

While counseling children, the counselor must always remember that the child is in counseling to work on a personal issue. Counselors may naturally feel a sense of protection toward the child and must guard against a sense of over-alliance against the parents. For minor children, parents probably have a right to know how counseling is proceeding and how therapy is being conducted (Remley & Herlihy, 2007). Therefore, while the child is the primary client, the parents could arguably be called the secondary client as they monitor and determine the parameters of the child's world. For all counselors working with any client, it is wise to ask themselves "Who is my client?" as secondary clients may play a pivotal role. The list of secondary clients for children could potentially include parents, school officials, caseworkers, foster caregivers, a residential treatment agency, and grandparents. Therefore, counseling children may involve networking with parents and other pertinent professionals in the child's world. The most important factor is to ask, "What is in the best interests of this child?" In some cases, the best interests of the child may not be served by the child's parents due to abuse or neglect. In cases of suspected abuse or neglect, counselors are required by law to notify appropriate child protection authorities. Sadly, reporting suspected abuse is no guarantee to satisfactory resolution as a lack of viable foster care placements hampers the process, and the child often returns to the abusive or dysfunctional environment he or she was removed from. When the child returns to the abusive or neglectful environment, the maltreatment may actually increase. Furthermore, my own experience is that some factions in society blame child protection workers for "breaking up families" when they remove children from their homes. Couple this with the reality that child protection services often are faulted for not removing the children from their home soon enough and you get a sense of the challenges and contradictions involved in child maltreatment cases. Thus, addressing abuse and neglect in children can be a very painful and frustrating experience for everyone involved.

Core Competencies and Skills

- Patience
- A desire to provide counseling in creative ways
- The confidence to address issues with parents
- Strong problem-solving skills
- High degree of cultural sensitivity
- Good self-care as this job can be stressful

Educational and Credential Requirements

Counselors working with children in intact families, and in fact, virtually all counselors, must obtain a master's degree in counseling to be hired to counsel children. After earning a master's degree, counselors can be hired into an agency. The counselor then is supervised by a licensed mental health professional (e.g., counselor, social worker, and psychologist) until the required number of hours under supervision is met (anywhere from 1000 to 3500 or 1 to 3 years, depending on the state or territory (American Counseling Association, 2010). Then, the counselor must pass the state licensure examination.

Best Aspects of the Job

- Working with children from preschool to adolescents
- Learning about all the dynamics related to child abuse and neglect such as the family, school and peer relationships, substance abuse, and poverty
- The challenge of creating a safe therapeutic space for a child to explore healthy options and grow emotionally
- Assisting parents or guardians in creating a healthier environment for a child
- The variety of techniques for counseling children: art therapy, play therapy, music, dance, and so on

Challenging Aspects of the Job

- Witnessing the painful and debilitating effects of abuse and neglect on children
- The frustration of witnessing children return to abusive and neglectful environments
- The difficulty in getting parents involved in their child's treatment, or the challenge of dealing with over-involved or controlling parents
- Working in a system that defines everyone as "disordered" and requires a diagnosis that may remain with a child well into adulthood

Occupational Outlook and Salary

Because counselors working with children typically are employed in public and private agencies or treatment centers, salaries can vary widely. Naturally, licensed counselors with 5 or more years of experience or those reaching management levels will earn more money. The breakdowns for counselor earnings are general; readers must interpret the median salary earnings for counselors working with children given in Table 3.1 as national figures, with variations regarding urban versus rural settings, and the state of residence.

The occupational outlook for counselors working with children is as follows:

- Mental health counselors: 24% growth rate over next 7 to 10 years
- School counselors: 14% growth rate over next 7 to 10 years
- Marriage and family counselors: 14% growth rate over next 7 to 10 years

These three broad occupations are likely the primary general occupations for counselors working with children (BOLS, 2010–2011).

2. COUNSELOR FOR CHILDREN IN FOSTER CARE

Because the differentiation between the different counseling jobs is slight, much of the information contained in the section Counselor

Table 3.1 Median Salaries for Counselors

Elementary school counselors	$57,800
Counselors working in health practices	$40,880
Counselors working in outpatient centers	$37,590
Counselors working in residential treatment centers	$29,950

for Children in Intact Families would be roughly equal to this section Counselor for Children in Foster Care. The differences, though slight, do exist and thus the need for different sections in the respective chapters. Counseling children in foster care will be considerably different from counseling children in intact families. The biggest single difference between these respective counseling jobs is counselors working with children in foster care are counseling children removed from their homes due to some type of abuse or neglect. Such counselors must prepare themselves for demanding and often stressful work.

It is important to realize the "Catch-22" situation that the child protection caseworkers face when removing children from their homes. On the one hand, caseworkers may be criticized for leaving children under the care of abusive or neglectful parents; on the other hand, caseworkers are vulnerable to criticism for removing children from their homes as they are "breaking up families." Numerous infamous cases have sprung up in the national media over the years regarding children removed from their parents' home, or in some cases, children who were not removed from their homes.

The counselor becomes involved when the child has been removed from their home. The counselor may work for a state agency called Child Protection Services, Department of Children and Families, or something similar. In most cases, the counselor is likely to be assigned a child or young adolescent who may be angry at being taken from his or her family, siblings, home environment, friends, and local school. It would be natural for a child placed in foster care to initially show mistrust when counseling begins. After all, the child has been violated by an adult or adults and will naturally be hesitant before trusting the counselor. A critical task for counselors working with foster care children is the ability to establish trust. Establishing a trusting therapeutic relationship is likely to be far more important than theoretical approaches or the use of specific techniques. In fact, some research indicates that technique and approach may be far less important than a counselor's ability to create trust (Hubble, Duncan, & Miller, 1999; Wampole, 2001).

Issues to Understand

There are several issues counselors should be aware of when counseling foster care children. Some of them are as follows:

- Children may "act out" their anger behaviorally
- Foster care children and adolescents may be less likely to trust a counselor due to past abuse and neglect

- Sadness and depression are common due to the child "losing their family"
- Understand that, because of a shortage in foster care placements, the child may be living in an environment that is neither nurturing nor healthy
- You will need to be able to set limits with a noncompliant child and at the same time create therapeutic attachment. These two different demands may be challenging to achieve
- It is natural, even expected, that beginning counselors might have a difficult time setting aside their own personal feelings about child abuse and neglect. But, to be therapeutic, counselors must focus more on healthy therapeutic attachment and less on sympathy

Best Aspects of the Job

- The ability to provide a sense of safety to abused or neglected children
- A sense that you are providing the child with long-term skills to enable him or her to deal with future difficulties
- Giving foster care children an opportunity to understand that some adults can be trusted
- Helping to reduce a child's anxiety and depression

Challenging Aspects of the Job

- Working with abused and neglected children can be emotionally painful and physically draining
- Many of the children in foster care will return to the abusive and neglectful home environments from where they were removed
- At times, counselors working with foster care children will have to fight against their own self-doubts. (e.g., "Am I really making a difference?")
- If you are a counselor with a history of abuse in your own family, you may overidentify with the child in a manner that is psychologically challenging for you
- Regarding the previous statement, it is imperative that you maintain good self-care

Occupational Outlook and Salary

Mental health counselors are most likely a general occupation type who work with children in foster care. The median salary for mental health counselors is reported in Table 3.2.

Table 3.2 Median Salary for Mental Health Counselors

Government settings (such as Department of Children and Families)	$40,000
Outpatient settings	$37,590
Residential treatment	$29,950

Remember, some private agencies pay more than others, and counselors with more years of experience and counseling supervisors will earn more in residential treatment settings.

Occupational outlook: Mental health counselors: 24% growth rate over next 7 to 10 years.

3. COUNSELOR FOR CHILDREN IN OUTPATIENT SETTINGS

Counselors working with children in outpatient settings make up a large percentage of professional counselors. Counseling in an outpatient clinic will be distinctly different from that in an inpatient clinic, and very different from counseling in schools.

Issues to Understand

Counseling children in outpatient clinics will differ from that in inpatient clinics in that the children are likely healthier, live with their parents or guardians, and are not at the residential center; counseling will involve more standard individual and group therapy. Children in outpatient clinics may have a stronger support system given that they are living with their families (or in foster care), though this is not always the case. For young children, counselors will need to be trained in alternative therapeutic methods such as play therapy, art therapy, drama therapy, and the like. Readers interested in pursuing this part of the field need to understand that they will see many abused and neglected children and that it can be emotionally draining (Landreth, 2002). Alternative modes of therapy (e.g., play therapy, art therapy, and drama therapy) are not recreation times for the child, but involve serious and methodical work and assessment on the part of the counselor.

Counselors working with children in outpatient settings also will need to become facile in addressing issues with parents and guardians. Healthy, involved parents can be a real asset to therapeutic treatment. Likewise, neglectful or abusive parents will complicate treatment and make it challenging to achieve optimal therapeutic results. All counselors counseling children and adolescents must be aware that they are mandated reporters of child maltreatment and neglect. They will occasionally need to follow up with child protection services in their area in order to protect the child from suspected maltreatment. As it has been previously noted, reporting child abuse and neglect seldom solves the problem.

Best Aspects of the Job

A former student of mine who became a counselor working in an outpatient clinic serving children told me that the best part of her job was seeing a child transition from depression and isolation to being joyful and connected to peers. It is likely that any counselor who chooses to continue working with children in outpatient settings enjoys this same reward. Many counselors who work with children in clinic settings also enjoy the fact that counseling children is very different from counseling adults. Counseling children will require a lot of patience and creativity that goes well beyond standard talk therapy.

Challenging Aspects of the Job

If readers were to poll a sample of counselors working with children in any setting, it is likely that the biggest challenge cited would be abusive or neglectful parents. Counseling with children will necessitate dialoguing with angry, disgruntled, overwhelmed, overcontrolling, and neglectful parents or guardians. To maintain a therapeutic mindset, counselors must find a way to engage such parents in meaningful dialogues (though in many cases, this may not be possible). As a counselor who has worked with children and adolescents, it is very disheartening to watch abused children return to the abusive environment that damaged them in the first place.

Occupational Outlook and Salary

The occupational outlook for counselors working with children is very good. Mental health counselors are the segment of the field providing most of the counseling to children in outpatient settings.

The growth rate is projected at 24%, and the median salary is $37,590. Achieving licensure and becoming a clinical supervisor or clinic director would likely involve a significant increase in salary.

4. COUNSELOR FOR CHILDREN IN INPATIENT SETTINGS

Counseling children in inpatient settings is both a rewarding and challenging career. Many counselors, especially those who have recently graduated with their master's degree, often begin their career in inpatient settings. One of the reasons for this is that, in my experience, residential psychiatric programs are often willing to take a large number of graduate interns. An internship provides a natural "practice" situation to see if the student is a good candidate to work at the treatment center. If a graduate intern does a good job, she or he may be able to parley an internship into a job (provided there is a vacancy).

Issues to Understand

It is likely that all careers and jobs within the counseling profession are challenging, as they all involve assisting people who are struggling with some part of their lives. It may be, however, that inpatient setting is the most demanding due to the nature of the clients who reside there. Children are placed in inpatient settings because they have been removed from the family home due to neglect or abuse or due to extreme behavior. In both instances, the children in the residential psychiatric center will be emotionally and behaviorally difficult to counsel. However, being "difficult" should not imply that said children would not make progress and graduate from the setting; most children in residential settings will indeed make enough progress to be released to their families or to foster care. However, some children will exhibit symptoms of early-onset severe mental illness (e.g., schizophrenia, bipolar disorder, and depression). Most, if not all, of the children on an inpatient psychiatric center will be on psychoactive medication. Because the counseling profession often prides itself on having a "healthy" approach to treatment (Gladding, 2009), beginning counselors may have difficulty accepting the reality of children being treated with psychoactive medication. Inpatient psychiatric treatment setting (whether as part of a hospital or as a stand-alone campus or building) will likely involve the counselor occasionally being required to help with physical restraints. I can recall as a recent graduate of a counseling program feeling very upset at having to restrain a violent child my first week on the job!

Best Aspects of the Job

The best part of counseling children residing in inpatient psychiatric units may be the opportunity to make a difference with one of the most vulnerable segments of our society. Many counselors will decide to remain in residential programs long after they have graduated from their program and will make a career of this work.

Having worked in a residential psychiatric setting and having supervised scores of graduate students who have interned and gone on to work in residential psychiatric treatment, I feel that a strong desire to help children in serious need is a definite requirement. Counselors interested in working on inpatient units will also need a strong sense of resilience as they will work daily with severely abused, neglected, and emotionally and behaviorally disturbed children. Inpatient work can be very draining, and a good support system along with an active routine (jogging, aerobics, skiing, swimming, etc.) is a must.

Challenging Aspects of the Job

The challenging aspects of counseling children in residential psychiatric settings have been discussed in the above passages. Children will display a lot of acting-out behavior, will require medication, may be oppositional and defiant, abused and very angry, self-injurious, and in general initially resistant to treatment. Having made these statements, the flip side of this equation is that such children present a real opportunity for counselors who enjoy working with difficult-to-treat children.

Occupational Outlook and Salary

The occupational outlook for counselors working in residential setting is very good. One reason for this is that such jobs likely turn over regularly due to the demanding and occasionally stressful nature of the work involved. Mental health counselors are the most likely to work in residential settings, and the BOLS (2010–2011) estimates their job growth at 24% over the next several years. Unfortunately, starting salaries for counselors working in residential treatment are significantly lower than for counselors in outpatient settings. The median salary for counselors in residential settings is $29,950. Now, once again, counselors who remain in residential settings after achieving licensure and who move into supervisory and management roles will earn considerable higher salaries.

5. COUNSELOR FOR FAMILIES

According to the Bureau of Labor Statistics (BOLS, 2010–2011), there are some 25,000 marriage and family therapists or counselors in the United States. Now, this figure is somewhat deceptive as the International Association for Marriage and Family Counselors and the American Association for Marriage and Family Therapists credential "marriage and family counselors" and "marriage and family therapists," respectively. The terms "therapist" and "counselor" are used interchangeably and can be confusing to anyone outside the counseling profession. In this section, I will be consistent and continue to use the term "counselor" to refer to professionals providing family and couples therapy, while realizing at the same time that marriage and family therapy is a field vibrant and distinct from family counseling.

Issues to Understand

Family counseling is distinctly different from individual or group counseling in that you have a group of people related to one another in a therapeutic setting. Instead of considering the needs of a single client, family counselors must address the needs of the family system and how systems outside the family impact the quality of family functioning (Bowen, 1960). There is no question that family counseling with children and parents in the same treatment room complicates the role of the counselor. Family counselors must consider whose issues to address and in what order they are to be addressed, and gauge whether family counseling is a "safe" place should domestic violence arise as an issue.

There are many additional issues to consider in family counseling. First, what defines a family? Today, more than half the couples who marry will end up divorcing (Maples & Abney, 2006). This means a family may be a mother and dependent children, two unmarried partners and children, two gay or lesbian partners and children, grandparents and grandchildren, or foster parents and children. The traditional nuclear family you might see in counseling is likely to be the minority in the counseling setting and beyond.

A key issue that will often emerge in family counseling is who has custody of the children. What if the noncustodial parent wants information on the session with his ex-wife and children? What if you are caught between a nasty custody battle involving the former spouses? Will you be able to accept two gay or lesbian parents and their children in a counseling session? What if you discover that a child is being abused and the legal requirement to report the abuse clashes with your desire to keep the family intact? Family counselors walk these and other "tightropes" on a regular basis.

Another issue that makes counseling more complicated for family counselors lies in the fact that there are several people in the session of different genders, ages, and developmental needs. Counseling will be more complicated for all these reasons, and counselors must be able to balance numerous demands and keep track of the multiple individual and family issues. Because of the number of people and the additional issues involved, family sessions are usually 90 minutes instead of the traditional 1-hour sessions in individual counseling. Family counselors also will use many intervention techniques to educate the family, such as genograms, which are therapeutic family trees, role plays, having the family do homework each week (such as caring days where they do something helpful for another family member), simple dialogue from siblings and the partners, and much more.

Best Aspects of the Job

A family counselor once said, at a conference, "The best aspect of being a family counselor lies in helping family members to have closer and more rewarding relationship with each other." Another aspect is helping parents address the needs of behaviorally challenging children, facilitating dialogue between feuding siblings, and sometimes assisting divorcing partners in how to break up without tearing themselves and their children apart. Another rewarding part of family counseling is that the counselor has the opportunity to treat the entire family, or at least a significant part, instead of just one member. Because families serve as the foundation for growth and development, or perhaps the opposite of that, treating the family instead of a single individual carries distinct advantages over individual counseling (Whitaker, 1977).

Challenging Aspects of the Job

First, family counseling is more complex than individual counseling and likely more difficult. Family counselors will also have many families that break up before or after the family counseling has been completed. In family counseling, as in couples counseling, the motivation of the individuals in the session may vary considerably. Finally, verbal, physical, and sexual abuse will sometimes be disclosed, forcing the counselor to remove the offending party, often at the protest of the remaining family members.

Occupational Outlook and Salary

BOLS (2010–2011) projects the profession of family counseling to grow by a rate of 12% over the next 7 to 10 years. Median earnings for marriage and family counselors are roughly $45,000, though there may be considerable variation depending on the work setting.

6. COUNSELOR FOR COUPLES

Marriage and family counselors will counsel couples as well as couples and their children. As a counselor who has counseled couples and families, I find that counseling couples is likely to be less complicated than counseling couples and their dependents, as the number of people in the session has been reduced to two. Naturally, counseling couples will also involve addressing parenting issues (if they have children), issues each partner brings from their own family of origin, and the current situation of their relationship.

Issues to Understand

Couples counseling will be more akin to family counseling than group counseling or individual counseling. However, couples counseling will differ from family counseling in that children will not be present in the session. Most counselors will find couples counseling simpler than family counseling due to addressing the needs of two versus three to five people. Just as in family counseling, counselors must be attuned to issues of abuse. Some research estimates that more than 40% of couples who attend counseling have experienced domestic abuse (Gladding, 2009). Couples counselors must also be aware of potential child abuse, addiction, unemployment or underemployment, family-of-origin issues, and many more.

Perhaps one of the more interesting issues that couples counselors face is that the quality of couples counseling may not involve whether or not the couples remain together. In my experience of many years counseling couples, I found that more than 50% of couples chose to break up. Yet, virtually all couples I counseled seemed to feel that counseling was helpful. Some partners come to counseling to improve their relationship and others see counseling as a safe, orderly place to break up. Couples counselors should remember that it is not their job to keep couples together, but rather to provide them the tools to have a healthier relationship either together or separately.

Best Aspects of the Job

Many couples counselors are likely to express that assisting a couple to have a healthier, more fulfilling relationship is one of the more rewarding parts of the job. Couples counselors will also be able to witness relationship changes on a weekly basis, as they will see the couple regularly. Through homework in session role play, writing, drawing, and drama therapy, the couples counselor has a front row seat to promoting healthy change in the relationship.

Challenging Aspects of the Job

Perhaps the most difficult part of the couples counselor's job is that many couples will utilize couples counseling as a place to dissolve their relationship. Beginning couples counselors may have a lot of difficulty with this reality. Also, physical, sexual, and verbal abuse will be present in the relationships of many couples who come to counseling. Couples in counseling will often exhibit outright anger and hostility and will occasionally transfer that animus onto the counselor. When issues of domestic abuse arise, the battered partner will often defend the abuser much to the chagrin of the counselor. Basically, counseling couples can be emotionally challenging work.

Occupational Outlook and Salary

The occupational outlook and salary for couples counselors will generally mirror that of family counseling reported previously.

7. COUNSELOR FOR COUPLES WISHING TO ADOPT

Many couples in the United States are unable to have children (or more children) and attempt to adopt nonbiological children. My brother adopted a child, and my niece and her husband adopted a child. Therefore, my knowledge of adoption is more personal than that of most academic counselors. While social workers have traditionally been the professionals who facilitate adoption, many counselors will counsel with couples wishing to explore adoption.

Issues to Understand

There are a multitude of issues to explore with couples wishing to adopt. First, adoption can take a frustratingly long period of time before couples welcome a child into their homes. Though there is no set timetable, adoption can take a year or more depending on the availability of a child, in-country or out-of-country adoption, the expense involved, legal issues, child-welfare investigation, and so on. In many states, biological parents giving their baby up for adoption may agree to the adoption, but still have a set period of time in which they can change their minds. Counselors counseling couples wishing to adopt must prepare clients for the emotional "roller coaster" adoptive efforts often bring.

One of the critical issues for couples wishing to adopt is the investigation into the couple's background. Stable employment, length of marriage, education, salary earnings, and household debt are just some of the issues an adoption investigation will examine. The most frustrating part of the adoptive process is likely to be the excruciatingly long period of time it takes to complete the process of adoption. Some couples literally wait several years! One of the reasons for this delay is that child protection workers are caught in a double bind: If they place a child with an abusive family, they are criticized for not being careful enough and if they do not place a child soon enough, they are criticized for keeping a child from a happy home.

Counselors must prepare and support potential adoptive parents for the challenges and difficulties through this long period of time. Another factor is that adoption can be expensive, given attorney costs, court costs, occasional travel (should the adoption be out of state), and so forth. Because of the difficulty in adopting children in the United States, many couples choose to go overseas as adoption may be much quicker. This being said, families adopting children from other countries will likely pay a high adoption price. In addition, travel to some countries (Asian countries are a common destination) is very expensive because of the distance and lodging.

Best Aspects of the Job

Best aspects of the job include supporting couples through the adoption process, especially when the couple's persistence pays off in an adoption.

Challenging Aspects of the Job

Adoption is a lengthy, costly, and drawn-out process that can be stressful on the couple who wish to adopt. Couples pursuing adoption are likely to transition through a cycle that may parallel Kübler-Ross's stages of grief (1969). While many couples will finally see a payoff in a successful adoption, many others will not, and some will discontinue their efforts because of stress and emotional exhaustion. Some couples will break up over the stress of the adoptive process.

Another difficulty for many counselors is that many otherwise suitable parents will not be allowed to adopt, including many single parents and gay and lesbian parents. Though single people can and do adopt children, they are a distinct minority. Gay and lesbian couples also adopt children, though many states and regions of the country will prohibit them from doing so either by law or by simply discriminatory practices.

Occupational Outlook and Salary

Because counseling adoptive parents is typically a part of the broader range of a counselor's job and not often a separate career, occupational outlook is probably somewhat similar to that of mental health counselors and marriage and family counselors. Thus, hard figures are difficult to "tease" out of the BOLS-reported statistics. Perusing the previously listed median earnings for both mental health counselors and marriage and family counselors will provide a rough idea of salary and occupational outlook.

8. COUNSELOR AND PLAY THERAPY

Counseling children and play therapy naturally go together as play is a child's natural language (Landreth, 2002). Many counselors choose to work with young children as opposed to older adolescents or adults because they enjoy helping children learn to live healthier, more joyful lives. Another factor in play therapy is that it is very creative and engaging in ways that counseling with adults may not be. Play therapy will be explored below.

Issues to Understand

Counselors providing play therapy to children will usually be working with children under the age of 12, presenting with a plethora of issues such as sexual, physical, or emotional abuse; attachment disorder; acting-out behavior; depression; hyperactivity; school problems; break up of the child's family; and victims of bullying behavior, to cite some reasons (Knell & Ruma, 1996). Young children placed in play therapy may not initially understand what therapy is about or their reasons for being there (Landreth, 2002), and the counselor must be careful to explain play therapy in terms the child can understand. Counselors must also illustrate that play therapy is not "play time." Though the child and counselor will use a number of toys, the toys are intended for therapeutic use.

Therapeutic toys are available through many companies marketing their products to the counseling profession. Common "toys" are dolls, sandtrays, crayons and drawing papers, nontoxic clay, watercolors, and dinosaurs. The counselor providing play therapy will attempt to elicit through interactive play the issues the child has been dealing with. In drawing, the counselor may look on from a close distance and state things such as, "I see you have drawn a house with several people together and one person off to the side. I wonder what is going on with the person off to the side?" or "I wonder how the person off to the side is feeling at being alone?" Counselors must be careful not to lead children in play therapy, but rather to ask the child for clarification (Landreth, 2002).

Best Aspects of the Job

Play therapy is very creative and provides a natural mechanism for counselors to engage children in the therapeutic milieu. Play therapy also offers the opportunity to meet the child where he or she is developmentally, in a language (play) the child can relate to. Play therapy is also likely to be less intimidating to children than a couch, chair, and question-and-answer "talk" therapy.

Challenging Aspects of the Job

Many children in play therapy have suffered serious neglect or abuse, and working full-time with such children can be emotionally challenging. Counselors providing play therapy may also struggle to get parents (or the parent or guardian) interested in the child's treatment. Some parents, school officials, and community members may not understand that play therapy is serious work, and may see only colorful toys, paintings, and sandboxes. This occasional devaluation of the play therapists' work by outsiders can be frustrating. Like anyone counseling children, play therapists must work to keep themselves healthy due to the emotional demands placed on them.

Occupational Outlook and Salary

Most counselors providing play therapy will work in outpatient settings, though some will work in inpatient psychiatric settings, and some play therapy counselors will work in schools, particularly elementary and middle schools and alternative schools. Salaries will vary considerably, with elementary and middle-school counselors earning the highest pay with a median salary of $57,800. Play therapy counselors in residential treatment earn a median salary of $29,950, which is considerably less. Mental health counselors working in more traditional outpatient clinics earn a median salary of $36,810. It must be mentioned that play therapy will likely be only one service the school counselor provides (e.g., academic counseling, group counseling, serving as consultant to teachers).

The occupational outlook for school counselors is 14% job growth, while job growth for mental health counselors is considerably better at 24%. (Mental health counselors are likely the largest counseling occupation working in residential psychiatric treatment centers.)

9. COUNSELOR AS PARENT EFFECTIVENESS TRAINER

From the information presented in this chapter, it is clear that counselors perform many jobs and roles. Counselors will work with the children, their families, and the agencies that address child welfare. One of the growing roles (jobs, functions, duties, etc.) for counselors is parent training. Parent training is scarcely a new concept for counselors. From the profession's inception in the early 1950s, counselors have worked to assist parents, grandparents, and guardians in becoming more functional parents. In many cases, counselors taught psychoeducational classes in which single parents (many of them teenagers) learned how to cope with the weighty responsibility of new parenting. Specific information on parent effectiveness trainers (PET) is given below.

Issues to Understand

There are many issues to be aware of when training parents on how to be more effective in raising children. First, many parents may be mandated to attend training, and they may be resentful at being there. Another factor is that counselors will have many teenage parents and other single parents who are struggling to meet the emotional, behavioral, and financial responsibilities of parenting. Physical abuse and neglect will likely be common among the parents in the class, and you may discover yourself struggling to "like" your students. It is fair to say, however, that many people who come to counseling, mandated or voluntary, are people struggling with the demands of their lives. Your role as the counselor is to help them manage those demands and to learn new skills that will lessen their stress level.

Parent effectiveness training usually occurs in public and private agencies as opposed to counselors in private practice. Some high schools will offer parent training to teen parents or even to high school students interested in learning about the demands of future parenting. Counselors offering PET will work from a teaching framework, with role plays, much discussion, utilizing DVDs, and open discussion with the facilitator or cofacilitators. Many couples and family counselors provide parent effectiveness training to parents as it is clearly related to their background and training as marriage and family counselors. That being said, numerous other professionals, such as social workers, ministers, school counselors, mental health counselors, caseworkers, and teachers, also teach parenting classes. The advantage of counselors (or any other mental health professionals) teaching the class is that they will better recognize anxiety and depression and can make referrals for individual counseling.

Most counseling programs will not provide parent effectiveness training as part of the curriculum, though it may be touched on in a family counseling class or on an internship. Parent effectiveness training is offered throughout all regions of the United States, and counselors can earn a certificate in parent effectiveness training, as well as in continuing education, for licensure and certification.

Best Aspects of the Job

Probably, one of the most rewarding parts of the job is the knowledge that you acquire while assisting parents and their children in establishing a healthier relationship. Many counselors also enjoy teaching as it is very different from individual counseling. Counselors who enjoy the challenge of teaching parents who may be oppositional are the optimal candidates to run parent effectiveness training.

Challenging Aspects of the Job

Many counselors offering parent effectiveness training are themselves parents, and having children will give them far more credibility than counselors who are childless. The students in the program are likely to challenge the counselors who are teaching the class, and the counselors must be able to manage class resistance without getting into power struggles with the students and without losing control of the class. Counselors will also hear painful stories of neglect and abuse when teaching this population, and few participants in PET trainings may thank the counselors for her or his efforts.

Occupational Outlook and Salary

Though the BOLS did not report statistics for this particular counseling-related job, the occupational outlook is likely to be high, because people will continue to have children at an early age, and because of the reality that some parents are not ready for parenting or are poorly suited for the multiple demands parenting requires. In most cases, mental health counselors, marriage and family counselors, and even school counselors will provide parenting trainings as a part of their overall role in their clinic or school counseling office. Salaries for counselors providing parenting training will be consistent with what has previously been reported in this chapter.

10. COUNSELOR WORKING IN CHILD PROTECTION AND FAMILY SERVICES

Though counselors are outnumbered by social workers, who traditionally staff child protection agencies, counselors often are hired to work with children and families. In many cases, the counselor provides counseling to parents and children for the purposes of reunification. Counselors may also counsel children who have been placed in foster care or those who are in residential treatment facilities. Counselors may even serve in traditional social work capacities and provide some counseling but spend much of their time serving as case managers. Some counselors in child welfare may also assist with investigations of allegations of child abuse or neglect and participate in finding the child a foster care placement.

Issues to Understand

Working with child protection services is often a very difficult job. There will be people in the community who view child protection staff as "people who break up families." Child protection staff deal almost exclusively with children who have been abused by their families, and many counselors will have difficulty maintaining a therapeutic mindset without suffering from compassion fatigue or burnout. Due to budgetary restrictions, child protection services tend to be understaffed and overworked. Thus, a counselor working in this field may have several children and families to counsel, may have to make site visits to homes and agencies, and may complete numerous reports and paperwork for tracking purposes. Counselors working in child protection will need to be highly organized to stay up with the multiple demands of the job and emotionally resilient in order to manage the trauma they will witness with abused and neglected children and adolescents. A strong core of supportive family, friends, and colleagues is also desirable as child protection workers will receive a lot of criticism.

Best Aspects of the Job

Many counselors enjoy the challenge of working with children who have suffered abuse. Counselors who can thrive in these settings will likely have a mixture of compassion, patience, and some degree of resilience as everyone they counsel is in pain. Perhaps the "best" part of the job comes with the feeling that one has made a difference in a child's life, no matter how slight or how significant.

Challenging Aspects of the Job

There are many challenges inherent with the child welfare field. As previously mentioned, child abuse is difficult for most professionals to deal with. Children who have been abused may also act out their anger on a convenient target, namely the counselor or caseworker. In every community I have lived in, there has been some political backlash against child protection services for "breaking up families." Conversely, if child protection workers do not intervene and remove a child, they may be blamed for not acting quickly enough. Clearly, it is easier to blame child protection professionals for doing their jobs than to focus on the root problems of child abuse and neglect (poverty, devaluation of children's rights, and communities that value keeping children in the home at all costs).

Occupational Outlook and Salary

The occupational outlook for counselors working in child protection is likely to mirror caseworkers and social workers and will be high (say 23%–24% growth rate). Child-welfare agencies are usually part of state government, and salaries will vary depending on the experience of the counselor and whether the counselor is line staff or manager. The BOLS states that median salary for mental health counselors in government settings is slightly higher than that for general mental health counselors, and it is $45,510.

4   Counseling the Elderly

Spotlight: Grief Counselor
Career Counseling Spotlight: Neil Mellor, A/Program Leader, Lecturer in Counseling, Faculty of Arts and Business, University of the Sunshine Coast, Maroochydore DC Qld, Australia

I have worked as a counselor for 30 years and am an accredited Mental Health Social Worker and Level 4 Practitioner with the Australian Counselling Association (ACA). I am in private practice with my wife Kathy at Altogether Psychology Services and I teach Counseling and Social Work at the University of the Sunshine Coast in Maroochydore, Queensland, Australia.

My first professional experience of the importance of grief counseling occurred in 1981 when I was a new graduate social worker responsible for running a men's community housing project. I was coordinating 8 houses with 60 residents located in the inner-city area of Melbourne, Australia's second largest city. The extent of the grief and loss issues experienced by the residents surprised me at the time, as this was not a well-understood problem in the context of welfare practice. My early social work training had provided me with only limited exposure to the "Five Stages of Grief" developed by Elisabeth Kübler-Ross in 1969 in her book *On Death and Dying*. While working in this program, I had an experience that seemed to epitomize the field as it was at that time.

One morning I arrived at one of our houses and found that a long-term resident, whom I shall call Ernie, had suffered a major heart attack and was barely breathing. I immediately called an ambulance, gave him mouth-to-mouth resuscitation, and kept him alive for 25 minutes while waiting for the ambulance. The ambulance came after 30 minutes, but sadly, Ernie had died. When I asked what caused the delay in the arrival of the ambulance, the senior officer reported that the ambulance staff knew this was a house for homeless persons and because the staff had a log of emergency service calls to these premises previously, they did not prioritize the call as urgent! As I spoke to the residents of the house and those who knew Ernie to help them process the shock of his death, I came to understand that residents who suffered from problems associated with psychiatric and physical disabilities were treated as second-class citizens by many health and welfare services, and their issues of bereavement were largely discounted. I found that death and loss were an ever-present reality in the lives of these residents, and although this was not often spoken about directly, grief was present in my daily conversation without being named. Up until this time I had mostly thought of grief as a reaction to death or to an incident resulting in serious injury or disfigurement. I soon learned that grief and sadness took many forms and were caused by a variety of phenomena, including the loss and estrangement of loved ones such as family, friends, and pets, the dissolution of marriages and de facto relationships, lost careers, and lifestyles. When I arranged Ernie's funeral, his former wife, children, and siblings chose not to attend and a Methodist Church organization was the only one who would pay for his funeral. There were virtually no services dealing with death, dying, and grief in those days, except for churches, hospitals, and funeral homes.

As I moved on in my career, I found the themes of grief and loss present in my direct client work in mental health, addiction, problem gambling, relationship, and employee assistance counseling. There were no training programs specifically dealing with issues of grief in those days as there are now, so I developed my competency through a combination of professional training and supervision in transactional analysis psychotherapy and other experiential therapies, and by spending time with those who worked closely with people who had experienced great loss and pain.

Australia now has a robust set of national, state, and locally based centers and services addressing grief, bereavement, and loss.

Many of these services are supported by funding from federal and state governments; in some cases, these centers are affiliated with universities, and are generally run by not-for-profit community organizations.

On a national level there is a specialist organization, the Australian Centre for Grief and Bereavement, which was established in 1996 to provide a range of services to those who are suffering from grief and bereavement, or for those caregivers or professionals who want training, supervision, and advice on how to work in this area. There is also the National Association for Loss and Grief (NALAG), which provides accreditation for members working in this area and which has many branches in the major states of Australia. Numerous state-based organizations are also active in this area, including state and local government health and mental health providers. In addition, several other helpful services provide a range of face-to-face, telephone, or web-based assistance.

Grief counseling is addressed in several professional-degree courses in Australia, including Counseling, Social Work, and Psychology, courses that are offered at the university with which I am affiliated (University of the Sunshine Coast). Several prominent professional associations such as the ACA offer support for members specializing in counseling in this area through publishing journals and clearinghouses of resources disseminating research, providing professional development opportunities, and maintaining standards and registers on national members. In addition, organizations such as the ACA provide a register of volunteer members who offer free telephone counseling to victims of natural disasters such as the Queensland floods (2010–2011) and the Victorian bushfires (2009).

Private practitioners in counseling psychotherapy and allied health disciplines such as social work provide grief counseling and other services to community members under several different fee-for-service arrangements and other health insurance and federal government-funded Medicare health plans. For instance, under the Better Access Mental Health Care Initiative, clients may be referred by a medical practitioner to an accredited counselor, at no cost, for problems such as bereavement disorders or posttraumatic stress disorder.

Counselors use a range of psychoanalytic, person-centered, and cognitive behavioral approaches to grief, with cognitive behavioral therapy the most commonly practiced.

11. COUNSELOR FOR THE ELDERLY IN RETIREMENT CENTERS

Counseling the elderly in retirement centers will likely become more common in the near future. With the average life span of people in the United States increasing and with services for the elderly likely to increase, counseling geriatric populations will become more popular. Though figures are hard to come by, my own experience in the counseling field is that the elderly are being underserved by the mental health field. You can expect this to change as the elderly population increases and the demand for services intensifies. Some retirement centers hold classes on academic topics, exercise classes, social outings, and many more activities. Expect counseling services to be added to the list. After all, giving up one's home, independence, mobility, and so forth and being near the end of life will likely result in depression and a desire to discuss meaning-of-life issues.

Degree Required

Master's degree.

Issues to Understand

Counseling in a retirement community will be very different from counseling in many other settings. First, the residents of the retirement community are elderly and are not in the stage of planning a career, looking to expand their family, or contemplating preparing for the next 30 years of life. The elderly are likely to be more concerned about their health, family relations, personal autonomy, and end-of-life care. Many elderly in retirement homes would have been separated from their family by long distances, or may be isolated because their family members do not visit them regularly. Depression will be very common, and loneliness is to be expected for many of the residents.

Another issue is that retirement centers will be staffed by nurses, occupational therapists, administrators, certified nurse's assistants, and other noncounseling professionals, and therefore counselors will need to work to establish good professional relationships with some colleagues who may not understand mental health issues (or may not value them as they value medical issues).

Perhaps the most challenging issue will be that many residents are dying or in serious physical and mental decline. Counselors will watch many of their clients decline and die. Some residents will decline rapidly and die in a short time span, while others may linger for months or even years. It will take a resilient person to provide ongoing services to the elderly in retirement homes.

Best Aspects of the Job

As a college student home for the summer, I spent a summer working as what was then called an "orderly" in a nursing home. The job was physically and emotionally demanding, though I enjoyed the interaction with many of the residents. I found much collective wisdom in the oldest of the residents (the residents who had not slipped into dementia) and looked forward to my daily conversations with those people. I suspect that counselors who choose to work with the elderly in retirement communities would enjoy the challenges of serving the elderly and like the personal connections with a population who have so much life experience.

Challenging Aspects of the Job

The most challenging part of the job is likely to be the emotional difficulty of observing many of your clients decline and die. Many residents will die quickly and with dignity, surrounded by loved ones. But others will die a protracted death, alone and isolated, and in many cases, their minds will have slipped into the throes of dementia long before their actual death. Then there are the residents whose families have abandoned them. These residents are lonely, depressed, angry, and confused as to why their children and grandchildren do not come to visit. (There can be many reasons for why their family does not visit, such as discomfort with retirement communities or unresolved issues with the senior family member.)

Occupational Outlook and Salary

Currently, the Bureau of Labor Statistics does not compile figures for counselors working with the elderly. At present, few counselors are working in retirement homes due to an underappreciation of mental health services for the elderly and the fact that counselors are still unable to bill Medicare. (Again, Medicare is the last "great" obstacle for counselors to overcome. It is likely that the counseling profession will overcome this obstacle within the next 10 years.) However, readers of this text can be assured that with more people living longer lives, counseling the elderly will be as common as counseling children and adolescents at some point in the future. It is likely that salaries will approximate salaries of counselors in inpatient hospitals (say, a range of $30,000 to $45,000, depending on the years of experience and the funding of the retirement community).

12. COUNSELOR FOR THE ELDERLY IN OUTPATIENT CENTERS

In addition to counseling geriatric patients in a residential setting, counseling elderly clients in outpatient settings will likely become more common. The retirement age is to be raised from 65 years to around 70 years within a decade, meaning that many senior citizens will be working. It is also likely that seniors will make use of services, and this includes counseling services. While previous generations were reluctant to seek counseling, the late baby boomer generation and those generations coming thereafter do not hold the same stigma toward counseling.

Degree Required

A master's degree in one of the counseling fields (e.g., mental health counseling, marriage and family counseling, and geriatric counseling).

Issues to Understand

Counseling the elderly will be similar to, though slightly different from, counseling people of other age groups. The elderly will struggle with depression, anxiety, troubled relationships, and so forth just as younger populations do. But the elderly know more than any segment of society that their time in life is running short and they realize a need to make the most of their remaining years. Many elderly will feel disappointed that they did not accomplish what they set out to accomplish in their lives. Others will be grappling with grief as their spouses and perhaps some of their children have died. Then there is the reality that for many elderly people, bodies do not function as well as in their younger years, and this will require many cognitive and emotional adjustments. Then there is the lingering bias by many parts in society that the elderly will not want the same things that most people want, such as an active sex life. Some elderly will have been diagnosed with a terminal illness and many wish to end their life on their own terms by euthanasia. Senior citizens have the highest suicide rates of any age group (Granello & Granello, 2007). There is a plethora of issues for counselors serving the elderly to be prepared to address with their clients.

Best Aspects of the Job

The best part of counseling seniors may be in counseling seniors. What I mean is that many counselors may enjoy counseling people with a lot of life experience under their collective belts. Many elderly people of the age 70 or older likely harbor a desire to discuss existential, meaning-of-life issues with a counselor. Counselors are required to be prepared to address spiritual or religious issues with elderly clients. Counselors who enjoy working with such weighty issues and concerns like these will enjoy counseling this population. In addition, many elderly counselors may very well enjoy the challenge of serving the very population they now represent. In fact, you can expect to see counselors who have reached their golden years being the professionals counseling the elderly.

Challenging Aspects of the Job

There will be many challenges the elderly face: declining physical and cognitive functioning, family relations, isolation, impending death, and reviewing their lives. Many senior citizens will be bitter at life's disappointments, struggling with depression, estranged from children and grandchildren, in declining health, or angry at a loss of freedom. Young counselors may especially have difficulty bridging this generational gap and empathizing with their geriatric clients. It is also accurate to stress that counseling elderly clients, many of whom may be near death, is not for most counselors.

Occupational Outlook and Salary

As previously stated, the Bureau of Labor Statistics did not yet compile figures for counselors serving the elderly. Also, as counselors cannot yet bill Medicare for counseling services, this also limits the counselor's ability to counsel the elderly in many settings. But in the near future, say, within 10 years or less, counselors are very likely to be awarded Medicare privileges. Salary for counselors serving seniors in outpatient centers is likely to be comparable with salaries for counselors working with other populations. The current median salary for outpatient counseling is $37,590.

13. COUNSELOR FOR THE ELDERLY FOR END-OF-LIFE DECISIONS

Along with counselors working with senior citizens in inpatient and outpatient centers, a topic of interest is counseling the elderly on end-of-life decisions. These counseling jobs may be somewhat distinct from counseling in a retirement community or a regular outpatient setting. In most cases, counselors specializing in end-of-life care for seniors may well be working in a private practice.

Degree Required

A master's degree in one of the counseling specialty areas (e.g., geriatric counseling, rehabilitation counseling, and mental health counseling).

Issues to Understand

There are many sensitive issues regarding end-of-life decisions. Foremost in the minds of many elderly clients is likely the topic of how they wish to end their lives. A growing percentage of seniors wish to end life on their own terms, meaning holding out the possibility of euthanasia (Granello & Granello, 2007). Currently, Oregon is the only state that allows for legal suicide, though other states may follow Oregon in the future. Regardless, many seniors end their lives each year. Euthanasia will likely be an issue for discussion for many.

Counselors counseling the elderly should be prepared to face many clients, discuss their wills, and discuss what to do with their home, land, and so forth. The counselor need not be an expert in law or real estate, but some working knowledge of these issues would be important. Elderly clients may also wish to discuss which family members they wish to "reward" and those they will leave out of their will. Because of the emotional issues involved, counselors will need to elicit the clients to discuss the stories and issues around their decisions, so the client can make an informed decision.

Best Aspects of the Job

The elderly often represent one of the most vulnerable segments of society. Counselors working with the elderly to assist them in their end-of-life decisions may be able to help protect senior clients from being taken advantage of as they can assist the client in examining the most appropriate beneficiaries for their assets. This responsibility means that counselors must ask themselves, "What is in the best interests of my client?" While all counselors must address this important ethical question, vulnerable clients with assets require sober reconsideration of this maxim by the counselor.

Another benefit of counseling the elderly on end-of-life decisions is likely to be the satisfaction of providing a safe atmosphere for elderly clients to be taken seriously and to be respected and attended to in a manner congruent with their wishes. Many elderly people in our society do not get to experience this type of consideration in significant areas of their lives.

Challenging Aspects of the Job

One reality the counselor will face regarding counseling elderly clients is that the client's wishes may differ significantly from that of her or his family. Loved ones, even those with honorable motives, may find it difficult to accept the wishes of their elderly family member. This is especially true when the issues concern money, property, religion, and how a client chooses to die. Counselors can expect angry phone calls from family members expressing hostility at the counselor for "making mom or dad give their money away," "... talking them out of a religious funeral service," or worse, and from extended family fishing to find out what their relative told the counselor. Counselors will need to be resilient in the face of intrusive efforts and maintain confidentiality.

Another challenging aspect of end-of-life counseling naturally involves how to die. Oregon is the only state that provides for legal suicide, though clients in the other 49 U.S. states and territories might commit suicide, and many others will wish to discuss this possibility. Counselors must be able to be present for difficult therapeutic conversations such as euthanasia. The tricky issue is how to have such conversations while keeping oneself from potential prosecution.

End-of-life counseling also is likely to involve an existential (or spiritual) discussion regarding a critique of the elderly client's life. Many clients may feel that they failed to accomplish what they sat out to accomplish and may be disappointed or even bitter. Other elderly clients will feel a strong sense of satisfaction at life accomplishments and feel a desire to discuss them. Some elderly clients will also see their lives as beginning to unfold in their late years, and they may desire to discuss how to make the most of remaining time.

Occupational Outlook and Salary

At this point, with the lack of tracking from the Bureau of Labor Statistics, salary is hard to estimate. For end-of-life decisions, outside of hospice services, counselors working in this area likely will be in private practice where salaries vary considerably. Occupational outlook is very poor at the moment; however, with life expectancy increasing, counseling services for the elderly are likely to become a regular part of a counselor's work in the future.

14. COUNSELOR AS DAY CARE COORDINATORS

Though counselors are primarily trained to address mental health and personal concerns and needs, some counselors have branched out into related areas. Counselors who choose to work with the elderly in residential settings may wind up "wearing many hats" in their job. Some counselors are likely to work as day care coordinators in retirement centers.

Degree Required

A master's degree in a counseling specialty area is optimal (e.g., rehabilitation counseling, geriatric counseling, and mental health counseling). Geriatric counseling or rehabilitation counseling may be the most appropriate areas to train in, though they will not be required.

Issues to Understand

The responsibilities of a day care coordinator will be different from those of a counselor. Day care coordinators are certainly concerned with the mood of the residents, though their role is not to provide counseling. They may arrange for counseling services or make a referral to the counselors or social workers providing the counseling. Additional responsibilities may involve scheduling exercise and activity classes, social outings, educational trips to museums and art galleries, concerts, and so on. The day care coordinator's responsibilities will include arranging guest speakers on a variety of topics including professors from local colleges, religious leaders, local politicians, medical experts, lawyers, and so forth. Basically, this job is a type of "catch all" position with a broad range of responsibilities.

Best Aspects of the Job

The best part of the day care coordinator's job may be in bringing services to the residents or in taking the residents out to services. Day care coordinators will be aware of the need to create productive time for a population who may have an excess of time on their hands. Creating a community where elderly residents can be challenged to make productive use of their minds and bodies, and enjoy the social activities other segments of society enjoy is likely a satisfying job. The day care coordinator may also be responsible for arranging volunteers to come into the retirement community. This may involve artists running workshops, writers reading their books or poems, and professionals bringing in dogs for animal-assisted therapy.

Challenging Aspects of the Job

Just as every job has its challenges, day care coordinators have their own. There will be both family members and fellow staff who see the day care coordinator's job as trivial or even unnecessary. Some administrators may begin to question financial expenditures for "unnecessary" expenses (trips to art galleries, plays, etc.). Residents themselves will occasionally complain that you are not "giving us the things we like" and so forth. Day care coordinators will need to be resilient in the face of underappreciation. It is also a good idea to maintain close relationship with the residents and survey them for programming they would like so as to create a communication feedback loop. The more the day care coordinator can involve residents, the more support she or he is likely to have.

Occupational Outlook and Salary

A perusal of the Bureau of Labor Statistics' *Occupational Outlook Handbook* (2010–2011) did not mention any categories for day care assistants. Such professionals are likely to go by different job titles such as "activities director" or something similar. Salaries are difficult to estimate although they depend on whether the retirement community is well funded and whether the position is full-time or part-time.

5 Counseling in School Settings

Spotlight: School Counseling
School Counseling Spotlight: Garda O'Keefe, MSEd, School Counselor, Niagara Falls, NY School District (Retired)

A school counselor's job follows the rhythm of the school year. Every September is a new start, and every June is a culmination. In between, counselors help students, parents, and staff with the yearly pace of studies, exams, course selection, and college applications. The daily focus is on resolving academic, behavioral, and social problems that interfere with learning. The old-fashioned guidance teacher has been replaced by a multitasking professional who addresses a variety of needs across the school population.

In elementary schools, the counselor can be a valuable consultant to teachers and parents. By working with a troubled child and developing an understanding of the source of the child's fears or difficulties, the counselor may provide strategies that improve behavior and strengthen learning. The middle school years are rife with uncertainty. The counselor can provide acceptance and encouragement with individual sessions, group sessions, and classroom lessons on bullying, friendship, self-esteem, and so on to promote an atmosphere of tolerance at school. The high school is a special domain. Most high school counselors have a "caseload" of 300 or more students. Each student must be seen to discuss academic progress, course selection, and career/college plans. These "routine" meetings are very often the beginning point of the counseling needed by adolescents struggling with drugs, alcohol, depression, sexual involvements, abuse, problems at home, and on and on. School is the teens' "world," and the counselor serves as a resource with unique knowledge and skills to help them resolve problems that hinder their education and peer relationships. The section below illustrates a "typical" day in a school counselor's job.

Journal Based on Entries From the Appointment Calendar of a School Counselor

7:15—Arriving at school before the students enter, several contacts set the pace:

- Meet principal regarding students returning from detention home
- Place morning announcement regarding field trip to an area college
- Consult with a team of teachers regarding students with chronic attendance problem
- Drop applications in homerooms for SAT prep class

8:30 to 3:00—Students are scheduled throughout the day to discuss academic concerns and for help with personal problems that affect them at school:

- Jill—needs help with a college application—first in her family to graduate!
- Rob—failing two courses—a change this marking period... why??
- Al—sent by the vice principal for disrupting class—no sleep at home
- Committee on special education meeting regarding Peter—attention deficit hyperactivity disorder, may need meds
- Meet with parent and Jamal regarding cyberbullying incident— parents to resolve
- Tim and Brian—want to know about an electronics elective—to visit class
- Call from parent regarding Gina and depression—set appointment, gave referral
- Karen in tears—pregnant?—meet tomorrow with student and mom

- Lunch bunch career talk with contained class—park supervisor talks
- Candy refuses to take physical education class—work on strengthening self-image
- Nina selecting courses for next year—wants to be a lawyer...or a chef!
- Call from colleague at the middle school regarding transition program
- Check e-mail contacts from the ninth-grade mentor program
- Return calls from parents and agencies about students

School counselors should have completed a master's degree in school counseling that includes training in therapeutic counseling skills, educational program development, testing and evaluation techniques, and so on. Most jobs follow the traditional 9-month school schedule with some summer work and occasional evening hours.

I have had the opportunity to work in elementary, middle school, and high school settings. Each offers unique challenges and rewards. The large numbers of students with their varying degrees of need is an ongoing challenge. We have been fortunate to have support from a range of colleagues in each setting. By wearing many hats to serve students, school counselors develop expertise in contemporary social problems, psychological counseling, and community resources, as well as career development activities, classroom presentations, and information on the wide array of college choices. The expectation for counselors to be versed in so many areas requires ongoing professional development.

The rewards of this career are both frequent and fulfilling. The success of a student turning around failing grades, the anger that is controlled before a fight, the depression that does not become a suicide, the bully making friends, the pride in the eyes of graduate and so forth are all markers for a counselor of a job well done. There are signs of gratitude as well. In elementary, they come in the form of hugs, smiles, and valentines. At the middle school, a smile and grateful nod can make the challenges worthwhile. One day at the high school, I found two "thank you" notes on my desk. One was written on a scrap of notebook paper and the other on a post-it note. One said thank you for helping her find the words to tell her mom about the baby on the way. The mother and daughter had been to the doctor and talked it out—together.

The other note said the boy was home from his first semester at college. There had been five rough years before he graduated last June, but college was great and his note said thanks for helping him make it through.

School counselors have the opportunity to influence young lives in very positive ways. It is a hard job, challenging, and often frustrating, but it is *good* work...everyday.

15. COUNSELOR IN ELEMENTARY SCHOOLS

Counseling in an elementary school is a very desirable setting for any counselor who desires to work with children. Elementary school counselors will provide both personal and academic counseling to students in need, generally from the kindergarten through third-grade levels (this varies depending on state and region). School counselors make up the largest segment of professional counselors, numbering 275,800 (Bureau of Labor Statistics [BOLS], 2010–2012). Unfortunately, elementary school counselors seem to be a small percentage of school counselors due to shrinking budgets.

Issues to Understand

Though hard figures are difficult to come by, elementary school counselors comprise the smallest percentage of school counselors overall. Elementary school counselors, like the majority of school counselors, generally work 9 to 10 months in a year and have 2 to 3 months off. Because of this and the fact that school counselors are the highest paid segment of the profession (BOLS, 2010–2012), and that school budgets have shrunk, employment in schools is competitive for counselors.

Counseling in an elementary school will be more like counseling in a middle school and very different from that in a high school. Most elementary school counselors work in public schools, though a number of them are employed in parochial school settings. Elementary school counselors must enjoy a variety of activities, including individual and group counseling; multidisciplinary committees; conferencing with teachers, administrators, and parents; and advocating for special needs children. Elementary school counselors must also understand that school is not a treatment center and thus they will be working in an environment where counseling is likely to be considered an ancillary function to education and teaching.

Best Aspects of the Job

Elementary school counselors I have trained and been around often cite assisting in the educational and social development of young children as one of the most rewarding aspects of the job. They are also likely to enjoy working in an educational setting compared with clinical setting. In this setting, counselors are unlikely to diagnose the children and will instead focus on meeting children's educational, social, and developmental needs. Many elementary school counselors will enjoy the variety of responsibilities they are required to perform, though this also requires them to be very organized.

Challenging Aspects of the Job

Some of the most challenging aspects of the job include mandated reporting issue of child maltreatment and neglect. Elementary school counselors must also be aware of playground issues such as bullying and cruelty to animals. Another factor cited by virtually all the school counselors I have helped train revolves around the fact that school administrators sometimes see the school counselor as a "quasi-administrator," where counseling is a low priority. The American School Counselor Association (ASCA, 2002) has developed a national model for school counseling to combat this tendency and to assert a lower student-to-school counselor ratio. The ASCA has also advocated for hiring more elementary school counselors, though this remains very much a work-in-process. The ASCA (2002) also recommends a 250:1 student-to-counselor ratio, though the national average is 457:1 (ASCA, 2008–2009). Urban schools likely have the highest student-to-counselor ratio due to budgets and overcrowding of schools.

Occupational Outlook and Salary

The BOLS (2010–2012) reports the occupational outlook for school counselors at a healthy 14% through 2018. However, job growth for elementary school counselors is likely much less than this reported figure. Because of scarcity of jobs, many elementary school counselors may start their careers counseling in parochial schools, which have a much lower student-to-counselor ratio but also pay substantially less salary. The BOLS reports that the school counselor's current median salary is $57,800, which is the highest for all counseling occupations. Elementary school counselors would likely be somewhere close to this figure.

16. COUNSELOR IN MIDDLE SCHOOLS

Counseling in middle school will be somewhat similar to counseling in an elementary school. Middle school counselors will run groups and provide individual counseling related to managing anxiety, addressing self-esteem, and dealing with loss (such as parental divorce), as well as providing academic counseling and coordinating testing.

Issues to Understand

Counseling in any educational environment will necessitate that the counselor be ready to address issues that community mental health counselors will not have to grapple with. First, the school environment is not set up as a therapeutic community. The middle school counselor, like a counselor in residential treatment, will have multiple roles, though schools are not set up for milieu therapy. The middle school counselor will need to address issues with classroom teachers, coaches, and of course parents and guardians. At times, the middle school counselor will be torn on what issues to bring to teachers and administrators and what to keep from disclosing. All that school counselors need to remember is that the golden rule is "What is in the child's best interest?" While the "best interest" may be debated, it is likely that including parents, teachers, and coaches could certainly be part of that.

Middle school counselors, in addition to counseling work, will also serve on multidisciplinary teams with special education teachers, school psychologists, school nurses, and, possibly, administrators. It is essential that a middle school counselor be able to advocate for the child's best interest and explain how counseling supports the child's educational attainment. Teachers and administrators will likely be more concerned with a child's behavior and academic performance and may not always understand the mental health issues behind acting-out behavior and deficient academic performance. The middle school counselor will need to serve as a bridge between the school and parents, including facilitating meetings with the parents to address a child's academic and emotional well-being.

Readers interested in counseling children in any school setting will need to be prepared to deal with abusive and neglectful parents or guardians. This means mandated reporting of issues to child protection services and a willingness to address sensitive topics with authoritarian parents who will want the counselor to side with them against the child even in egregious situations (e.g., the verbally abusive parent who insists he is doing this for the good of the child). Good negotiation skills are required, as well as an ability to deal with pressure from teachers, school administrators, and parents. Good organization skills are also a necessity because the number of students in a middle school will exceed the American School Counselor Association's recommended student-to-counselor ratio of 250:1.

Best Aspects of the Job

The best aspects of middle school counseling may lie in the variety of services and roles a middle school counselor will need to play. Middle school counselors will provide individual and group counseling, run support groups, possibly serve as advisor to a school mediation program, sit on multidisciplinary teams, assist with school athletics and other functions, and coordinate referrals to off-campus providers. One veteran middle school counselor in New York once told me, "I love the variety in my work!"

Challenging Aspects of the Job

Some of the best aspects above may also become some of the challenging aspects. For example, variety can begin to make a counselor feel stretched thin in the job. Many middle school counselors, especially those who serve as the only middle school counselor on their campus, may feel frustrated with the workload and the inability to address deeper psychological issues. Teachers are likely to give more respect to middle school counselors who also have been teachers, and counselors who never served as teachers may feel disrespected. Then there is the reality that some school administrators will view the middle school counselor as simply a quasi-administrator and offer little support for the therapeutic role. After all, high stakes testing seldom takes into account the role good emotional health plays in school performance.

Occupational Outlook and Salary

The occupational outlook for middle school counselors likely mirrors the BOLS figures of 14% growth through 2018 (BOLS, 2010–2011). Therefore, job prospects are good, provided a middle school counselor can move, as some regions of the country are expanding (the Sunbelt), while others are contracting (upper Midwest and Northeast). Salary figures are again among the highest, with a median of $57,000 (BOLS, 2010–2011). Most middle school counselors work a 10-month schedule, though others may have a 12-month contract.

17. COUNSELOR IN HIGH SCHOOLS

Counseling in a high school is likely to be very different from counseling in the lower grades. The reason for this difference lies in the reality that high schools are preparing students for college, community or technical college, the military, and so on. Essentially, high school counseling is likely to be academically and vocationally focused at the expense of personal counseling. High school counseling is covered in more detail below.

Issues to Understand

Counseling in a high school can be very rewarding provided you enjoy a variety of activities and that you expand your view of counseling. The American School Counselor Association (ASCA) (2000) has developed a model for school counselors to follow, though it is likely that many school administrators, few of whom were counselors, are not as supportive of it. The ASCA model envisions school counselors as resource professionals and supports more developmental counseling. Unfortunately, with the high stakes placed on testing currently gripping the U.S. educational system, the counselor's role is likely to be focused on testing results. A lot of work will also revolve around college preparation (ACT and SAT test preparation), college advising, vocational advising for students considering the military, technical college, or those contemplating dropping out of school.

High school counselors must also address the difficult realities of puberty and adolescence, such as sexually active teens, pregnancy, sexually transmitted diseases, dating abuse, and bullying. A frustration for counselors in many schools is that they will not be allowed to provide contraception and safe sexual practice advice to students, given the weighted political, social, and religious issues it involves. High school counselors will also need to address mandated reporting issues of abuse and neglect. Effective high school counseling involves a task-oriented counselor who is very organized and able to communicate across the teacher–counselor–administrator divide.

Best Aspects of the Job

Some of the best aspects of counseling in a high school will be similar to that in lower grades. High school counselors are likely to enjoy job variety and addressing career vocational concerns as opposed to more in-depth mental health disorders, as such students are likely to be referred to outside mental health professionals. Another positive aspect is that the majority of high school counseling positions are likely to operate 9 or 10 months, with summers off.

Challenging Aspects of the Job

There are many challenges to being a high school counselor. Most high school counselors will find they have little time to address the needs of the students in the school. School administrators are likely to place testing results over addressing mental health issues, to the frustration of many school counselors. High school counselors may be silenced from dealing with addressing gay and lesbian student concerns by administrators, local politicians, and evangelical religious leaders.

Occupational Outlook and Salary

The occupational outlook of high school counselors would be, consistent with the BOLS (2010–2012), 14% growth through 2018. This represents moderate job growth. Some areas of the United States will offer more opportunity, especially the Sunbelt. Urban areas often provide the starting point for beginning high school counselors, though urban schools often are the most overcrowded and run down. Median salary reported by the BOLS was $57,000.

18. COUNSELOR IN PRIVATE SCHOOLS

Some counselors have chosen to practice in private schools for a variety of reasons including a significantly lower student-to-counselor ratio, a desire to work in religious schools, and the difficulty in landing a public school counseling position in many areas. Counseling in a private school, whether Catholic, Protestant, Jewish, Muslim, or nonsectarian, will be similar to and at the same time very different from that in a public school.

Issues to Understand

There are many issues to understand when contemplating applying for a counseling position in a private school. First, how well do your values match that of the private school? Granted, no school, public or private, will offer a perfect fit and there will always be administrative, political, and social issues to consider. However, counseling in a Catholic high school, for example, will carry with it some particular concerns. Are you Catholic, or can you respect Church values? How do you feel about providing birth-control counseling, gay and lesbian issues, and abortion? These certainly are issues in public schools, but a public school is likely to have more flexibility than a Catholic school.

Another factor to consider is that in private schools, much more may be expected by parents who are paying large sums of money. I know of many counselors in public schools who would complain of the difficulty in getting many parents involved in their child's education or treatment. In private schools, counselors tell me just the opposite—parents may be too involved (think "enmeshed" or the term "helicopter parents" who are always hovering). Counselors will have more time to provide one-on-one service, and that may involve more personal counseling or group work than in public schools. There will also be more overt pressure on the students to perform academically, as private schools will be well stocked with exceptional students, competitive by nature or encouraged to excel by parents. Anxiety issues, depression, eating disorders, and self-injurious behaviors are common mental health concerns to be addressed.

Best Aspects of the Job

One of the best parts of the job is working with gifted, motivated students who will want your services. One former student of mine who took a counseling position in a private high school mentioned to me that she could not believe how motivated the students were. "It's worth getting less pay," she exclaimed. Private schools also, in my experience, are more likely to be supportive of the counselor providing personal counseling than their public counterparts, though small enrollments also are a part of this.

Challenging Aspects of the Job

No doubt, one of the biggest challenges of counseling in a private school is the poor pay. Though the BOLS did not provide salary figures for private school counselors, the pay will be considerably less due to the fact that private schools are not supported by tax dollars. Another challenge is that many, if not most, private schools, are religiously affiliated. Counselors who do not share the religion of the school may feel somewhat alienated or have difficulty accepting some of the religious mandates (even counselors sharing the school's religion may have difficulty).

Occupational Outlook and Salary

Occupational outlook and salary are difficult to discern given that the BOLS does not compile figures for counselors in private schools. It is likely that the demand for school counselors in private schools is less due to the reality that there are far more public schools than private schools. However, I know personally of many beginning school counselors who chose to begin their career in private schools because of the ease in getting a job. Because the salaries tend to be significantly less for private school counselors, many counselors are hesitant to take such positions, and some who do will leave for a public school job as soon as they secure one.

19. COUNSELOR IN ALTERNATIVE SCHOOLS

Counseling in an alternative school is likely to be different from counseling in most private or public schools because of the types of students the alternative schools serve. As a young counselor, I spent five summers counseling in an alternative school that was part of a large human services agency. The students, like most in alternative schools, were mostly high school students who had failed in the traditional school environment and were referred. The school also provided general educational development study and preparation for high school students and adults who lacked a high school degree. Other alternative schools exist to serve the educational and mental health or developmental needs of students with special needs.

Issues to Understand

First, alternative schools vary considerably. Many serve students unable to thrive in a traditional school environment. Others may be in therapeutic settings where treating mental health issues may be the principal focus. For example, some residential psychiatric treatment centers also have schools attached to their centers. Counselors in these schools will counsel students with a wide range of mental and emotional challenges, from developmentally delayed students to students with major depression, attention deficit hyperactivity disorder, post-traumatic stress disorder, and schizophrenia, to students who have been adjudicated through the courts, and many others.

Counseling in alternative schools can seem overwhelming due to the myriad of emotional, social, legal, familial, and academic issues. Counselors in alternative school settings will need to be resilient, patient, and able to set limits with sometimes angry and hostile students, and need to enjoy the vast challenges the setting offers. The academic aspect, though important in these schools, may actually take a "back seat" to the demanding personal and mental health issues. Counselors will need to be adept at addressing both personal and academic issues and be able to create dialogue with teachers, school officials, treatment center administrators, court officials, parents and guardians, and child protection services.

Best Aspects of the Job

The best part of the job may lie in the knowledge that you are counseling some of the most difficult-to-serve adolescents in society. The counselors I have met who were staffing alternative schools often cite this as the reason they remain in such settings in the face of great challenges. Other rewarding segments of the job cited are variability, adventure-based therapy (in some settings), a desire to start a career working with very difficult students so that they will be prepared to transition to traditional high schools where the challenges will seem less (or at least different), and a strong sense of accomplishment.

Challenging Aspects of the Job

Naturally, a significant challenge is the students attending the alternative school. Most students in alternative settings will possess significant academic, social, emotional, mental health, and legal issues. Salary is likely to be less in most alternative schools (though not in all as some alternative schools are run by the school district), and working conditions will likely be less than ideal. Alternative schools often receive less funding than their traditional counterparts, and the facilities may not be as well maintained. Some positions in alternative schools may be 12-month positions due to the reality that students are attending the school throughout the summer, especially if they wish to return to a more traditional school in the fall.

Occupational Outlook and Salary

The Bureau of Labor Statistics does not compile statistics on alternative schools. Salaries are likely to be less than that in traditional schools, and occupational outlook is difficult to predict. It is possible that the demand for counselors in alternative schools will increase, though this is far from certain.

20. COUNSELOR IN RESIDENTIAL SCHOOLS

I have separated this section from the section "Counselor in Alternative Schools" because many residential schools are not alternative schools.

The U.S. educational model was initially influenced by the British educational model, where young children were often separated from their
parents and sent off to boarding school from grade school through high
school. Though the U.S. system is vastly different and most American
students do not attend boarding school, some do. There are some famous
elite boarding schools such as Phillips Exeter Academy. Some residential
schools have a religious component, while others are entirely secular. A
perusal of the Internet will also reveal a number of military boarding
schools, which will differ vastly from other private residential schools.

Issues to Understand

Counseling in a residential school may be the most unusual job described
in this entire book. First, few students in our society are given the privilege of attending boarding schools. Most boarding schools will be very
expensive due to the cost of purchasing, staffing, and maintaining such a
facility. Students attending a residential school are likely, of necessity, to
come from upper middle class to wealthy families. I have had a few students complete their internship in residential schools where the annual
tuition cost exceeded $30,000!

Given the exorbitant cost in residential education, parents who
send their children to such schools are likely to expect a lot in return.
Counselors will provide career services (focused on getting the student
into an elite private or public college) and personal counseling. Because
most residential schools will have a low student-to-counselor ratio (likely
under the 250:1 ratio that the American School Counselor Association
recommends), counselors will likely be able to provide a lot of one-on-
one counseling. In many of the residential schools that I have visited,
counselors have the opportunity to use therapy in creative ways. Many
residential schools, especially those located in rural areas, may make
use of wilderness-based therapy (or wilderness-based education, which
likely has a therapeutic component). Counselors may also use challenge
courses, ropes courses, climbing walls, and other creative venues to
address developmental issues.

Counselors interested in working in residential schools will need to
be prepared to address a plethora of issues related to removing adolescents from their family home and placing them in schools that may be a
long distance from their home (many such schools will have a high number of international students). Depression, anxiety, homesickness, verbal
taunting, homophobia, physical abuse, and eating disorders (for females)
are all common issues. In addition, pluralistically oriented counselors may
find it challenging to come to grips with the enormous wealth involved in
many residential schools. Parents of students in residential schools may

be less available for the counselor to dialogue with them regarding their children due to distance and time constraints.

Best Aspects of the Job

Counselors working in this environment may well have more resources than any segment of the counseling profession. Because many residential schools are costly, counselors will have a number of resources at their disposal that most counselors will lack (e.g., adventure-based therapy, challenge courses with the very best equipment, low student-to-counselor ratio, and motivated students). The students attending residential schools are likely to be very bright and motivated on average.

Challenging Aspects of the Job

There is an old adage that goes, "When much is given, much is expected." This is definitely true with regard to residential schools. Parents spending more than $30,000 on a child's education will expect the very best of everything. Counselors may feel overt pressure from administrators and parents to provide a high level of services. Issues of confidentiality can be challenging on a residential campus where everyone—students, faculty, and staff—live in a "fishbowl" environment.

Occupational Outlook and Salary

Counselors interested in working at a residential boarding school will find it competitive to land such a job because residential schools are few in number. No official statistics are available on job outlook or salary. Counselors interested in working at a residential school would be wise to serve an internship at such a school during their graduate school years or look for a way to provide some services to such a school while working at another counseling position. My own experience is that counselors at residential schools will have a number of roles and functions. It would be important to be well versed in academic and career counseling (especially college placement) and wilderness and adventure-based therapy, and have experience or willingness to run groups.

21. COUNSELOR IN SCHOOL-BASED FAMILY SERVICE CENTERS

School-based family service centers are relatively new phenomena in the public schools. Many family service centers operate in conjunction with the school counseling office. School counselors may help staff the family service centers, though much of the counseling services will be provided by external counselors working in the afternoons and evenings. School-based family centers are often located in urban or suburban areas.

Issues to Understand

Family service centers often serve underperforming students and their families. One of the family service centers, where my students interned, worked from the philosophy that counseling, whether individual, couple, or family counseling, is to assist the student in academic achievement. Many students presenting for counseling will come from impoverished, single-parent families. Such students will often have a number of challenges such as academic underperformance, legal difficulties, school suspensions, drug and alcohol issues, and teen parenting. Essentially, a counselor will need to be prepared to address a wide array of personal, social, educational, vocational, legal, and familial issues. It is worth admitting that all counselors in all settings will address these issues, but counselors in family service centers will need to be facile in academic counseling (placement testing, planning for life after high school, etc.) and the broad spectrum of mental health issues.

Counselors in family service centers will need to develop a strong relationship with the school counseling office, school social workers, school psychologist, nurse, teachers, and the principal. Administrators and teachers will likely expect the counselors to reduce acting-out behavior over all other issues. This may cause some friction between counselors and other school personnel, given that the issues with many of the students are so ingrained and that students referred to family service centers often have a number of personal issues. Counselors will also need to address alcohol and drug use, violence, gang activity, risky sexual behavior, and many more issues.

Family service centers also provide family counseling given that the family unit may well be one of the difficulties the student is facing. I have placed a number of graduate counseling students in family service centers, where virtually all clients came from single-parent families, where the father was uninvolved and the mother and children lived at the poverty level. Often, requests for family therapy went unanswered, though many mothers and some fathers did participate in family therapy.

Best Aspects of the Job

Counselors who enjoy the challenge of addressing a number of personal, developmental, family, educational, and social issues will like this setting. Counselors in the family center will provide individual, group, and family counseling. In many family centers, cotherapy is the model practiced. Therefore, two counselors might provide family therapy or run a group. In addition, there may be graduate interns and additional counselors watching from behind a two-way mirror, who will occasionally call in and provide suggestions. This team-oriented approach is very common in many family service centers.

Challenging Aspects of the Job

Readers of this book have likely figured out that there is no such thing as "easy" counseling work. Family service centers certainly do offer a challenge on a number of levels that have been noted above. The students and families will most often come from the lower middle class and below. Students will be struggling with multiple issues, including legal charges. Even the school that hosts the family service center may not always understand or be supportive of the work the counselors are providing. Providing a safe environment for gay and lesbian students, birth control information, and so forth are always "hot" topics in many schools.

Occupational Outlook and Salary

Once again, hard figures are difficult to report due to the lack of tracking by the Bureau of Labor Statistics and the fact that family service centers are still few in number. Currently, jobs at such centers are also few in number, though family service centers may become more popular over time. Such centers are more likely to be located in less-affluent school districts, or run by public alternative schools. Salaries are likely to be more in line with that of mental health counselors (median salary $36,810) as opposed to school counselors (median salary $57,000).

22. COUNSELOR IN AFTER-SCHOOL PROGRAMS

After-school programs have been in existence for a long period of time. Counselors have more recently become a part of after-school programs, especially in providing group counseling and teaching psychoeducational groups for students (grief support group, divorce support for children, conflict resolution, etc.).

Issues to Understand

Counselors working in after-school programs can expect to provide an array of intervention services focused at reducing risky behavior (addiction, delinquency, dropping out, career preparation, etc.). Most often, the counselor will be working with students referred to the program from teachers, school counselors, school psychologists, coaches, pastors, and parents. The counselor is likely to be either in private practice and contracting with the school district or working in an agency that has a contract with the local school district.

The students in the after-school program can range from elementary to high school, and the concerns they bring can be divorcing parents, behavioral issues, "latchkey" students (those lacking proper adult supervision at home), gang activity, and isolated students in need of friends. (This latter category may be one of the most important as isolated adolescents are the most likely to contemplate suicide.) Counselors will perform individual counseling, though more likely group counseling, educational activities, mediation training, life skills (grooming, peer relations, dealing with peer pressure, etc.), and for older adolescents, job preparation.

Best Aspects of the Job

Some counselors enjoy working in after-school programs because it involves developmental guidance that may differ from more traditional mental health work. The counselor's role is somewhat a cross between traditional guidance activities and more standard mental health work. Counselors in this job will do a lot of modeling and teaching to students in groups. Many counselors may report that they enjoy more freedom as they do not have to label the students with mental health diagnoses in order to access services.

Challenging Aspects of the Job

After-school programs may fall into an "in-between" position with regard to educational and social services. Counselors in after-school programs may be working alone or with a small number of other professionals and could potentially lack the organizational support counselors in agencies and schools possess (though this depends on the after-school program and its level of funding). Counselors would need to be interested in applying psychotherapeutic knowledge in ways different from traditional one-on-one counseling. Group approaches, whether therapeutic groups, support groups, or psychoeducational groups (i.e., teaching students how to manage stress, anxiety, turn down drugs, etc.), will likely be the more prevalent type of activity the counselor provides.

Many students involved in the after-school program may be mandated by a parent, coach, school counselors, or someone else and may not have an ideal level of motivation.

Occupational Outlook and Salary

Most counselors working in after-school programs are likely to be in private practice and contracting with the local school district, or working in an agency that contracts with the school district. Agency counselors are likely to earn somewhere in the neighborhood of mental health counselors (median salary $36,810). Figures for counselors in private practice were not reported, so salary estimates are difficult to estimate, though they may approximate that of agency counselors depending on whether the counselor works full time or part time. The occupational outlook for mental health counselors is very strong, with a 24% growth rate estimated by the Bureau of Labor Statistics (2010–2011).

However, only a small percentage of mental health counselors work in after-school programs, so counselors interested in this type of work should target agencies that provide this service or plan to transition into after-school programs as part of a private practice providing a contractual service.

6   Counseling in College and University Settings

Spotlight: Professor of Counselor Education
Counselor Education Spotlight: Shannon Hodges, PhD, LMHC, NCC, ACS, Associate Professor of Counseling, College of Education, Niagara University, Lewiston, NY

I completed my doctorate in counselor education from Oregon State University in 1995. I worked in community mental health and in university counseling centers before becoming a professor of counselor education in 2000. A significant part of my job has been teaching, supervising, and mentoring future counselors-in-training. Being a professor, I am also involved in scholarly activities such as publishing in professional academic journals, writing books and book chapters, serving on the editorial boards of professional journals, and actively participating in organizations such as the American Counseling Association (ACA) and the American Mental Health Counselors Association (AMHCA). As a professor, I am expected to make annual presentations at conventions such as ACA, AMHCA, and similar professional associations. Each year, I publish two to three articles in scholarly venues, and I am often writing a book or making a book proposal to a publishing company. Naturally, writing and rewriting articles and books takes a lot of time and effort.

Professors also are charged with evaluating applicants for graduate counseling program. As professionals who train future counselors, we are expected to serve as "gate keepers" for the profession.

That is, we are to recruit and admit students who we believe are good candidates for the profession. One of the realities in this current era is that because of increased competition (more counseling programs, web-based programs, etc.) and declining budgets, a dynamic tension exists between accepting qualified students and pressure to admit less-qualified applicants due to financial concerns. My own experience is that a professor's primary consideration centers on quality, while an administrator's first priority is finance. While both of these issues are important, they sometimes are at odds with each other.

Some of the other realities of scholarly life lie in grading (one of my least favorite activities), attending meetings (there are many of these), chairing committees, and even serving as department chair. Prior to becoming a professor, I never realized just how much time and energy went into department, college, and university committees. Committees have a way of multiplying responsibilities for members, it seems! For the most part, committee meetings and grading are what I like least about being a professor.

What I like best about being a professor is the opportunity to disseminate knowledge to future counselors, whether in an actual classroom or via a virtual classroom. I especially enjoy engaging small classes (say, 10–20 students) as this size is intimate enough to promote more active engagement in the topic of interest. The structure of the classroom also provides the opportunity to reach diverse learners in a variety of ways: through traditional lectures, role plays, and breaking students into dyads and triads for small group discussions. Role plays are one of my favorite tools as they bring theories to life and can be downright interesting and occasionally fun.

After many years as a professor, I find that I still enjoy teaching, mentoring, and scholarship. Though the field of higher education is evolving rapidly, with the Internet revolutionizing higher education much in the way the internal combustion engine revolutionized transportation, I still enjoy vocational life lived within the margins of the scholarly life. If I had the choice to make all over again, I still would choose to be a professor. I like teaching, writing, advising and mentoring students, and working in a global community of scholars. I look forward to continuing my career and being part of the further evolution of higher education.

23. PROFESSOR OF COUNSELOR EDUCATION

Some counselors in the field who go on for a doctoral degree in counselor education will teach in graduate counseling programs (usually called "counselor education"). Professors of counselor education train graduate students to become professional counselors in master's and doctoral degree programs.

Degree Required

Tenure track (or full-time) professors of counselor education are required to have a doctoral degree. Earlier, most professors in graduate counseling programs held doctoral degrees in counseling psychology, though now with counseling as a distinct profession from counseling psychology, the doctoral degree in counselor education is preferred; for CACREP-accredited programs, a doctorate in counselor education is required. The preferred counselor education doctorate is a doctorate of philosophy (PhD) in counselor education, though the traditional doctorate of education (EdD) in counselor education is still offered.

Issues to Understand

Traditionally, the professor's job was more about research than about teaching, though teaching was always important for advancement. In today's higher education world, the "teaching–scholarship" ratio depends on the type of institution at which a professor works. For large research institutions with doctoral degree programs in counselor education, research is very important, and professors will need to spend a lot of time conducting research and publishing books, journal articles, and the like. For master's degree programs, some research is required for tenure and promotion, and teaching ability will be more emphasized than it is at large, doctoral-granting universities. In addition, there are now virtual institutions, such as Capella University and Walden University, that offer CACREP-accredited counseling programs. These institutions usually hire only part-time faculty, many of whom hold only a master's degree. Research is not important at these institutions, and the number of classes professors teach depends on their contract. At such institutions, almost 100% of the classes are virtual.

Best Aspects of the Job

Some of the best parts of being a professor are love for research, fulfillment in training future professionals, tenure, and the freedom that traditional academia provides. Though higher education does not pay as well as many would imagine, the benefits can be very enticing: a 9-month contract for most faculty, an occasional sabbatical for 6 months to 1 year, working with gifted students, being paid to think and express yourself, and regular breaks.

Challenging Aspects of the Job

The world of higher education is rapidly evolving, mostly due to the impact of the virtual age (Freedman, 2004). As noted above, distance education has exploded, and more and more graduate students are earning advanced degrees without leaving their homes. While this may be good for students (now called "consumers" in many institutions), traditional faculty are less enthusiastic about the changes. As a faculty member hired at the onset of the virtual institution boom, I can see both sides of the issue. The most likely future is the one where counselor education faculty will teach more online courses and less in-person classes.

Tenure is also on the decline. In the future, it is likely that tenure will be reserved for faculty at elite colleges (e.g., Ivy League, elite private institutions, and large doctoral institutions), while master's-level institutions, state colleges, and virtual institutions will offer 3- to 5-year renewal contracts. Research will continue to be heavily emphasized at elite institutions and less so at other types of institutions.

Occupational Outlook and Salary

The Bureau of Labor Statistics (BOLS) does not separate counselor education from other fields in higher education, but we can draw some fairly accurate conclusions from the general data. As a professor who makes a weekly perusal of *The Chronicle of Higher Education*, I can attest that counselor education faculty positions have remained healthy regarding faculty openings. BOLS estimates a 15% job expansion for all university faculty positions through 2018 (BOLS, 2010–2011). Now, that figure included everything from astronomy to zoology, with counselor education in between. BOLS also reports a mean salary of $62,300 for faculty (BOLS, 2010–2011). Salary will depend on the type of institution: doctoral versus master's level, public versus private, and traditional versus virtual institution. So, readers interested in a career in counselor education can feel good that the future looks healthy, but they should be aware that the field is dynamic and changing rapidly.

24. COUNSELOR AS DEPARTMENT CHAIR

Many professors of counselor education will eventually rise to becoming department chair at their institutions. It is fair to say that for some counseling faculty, serving as department chair is a step on the road to academic administration (assistant dean of the college, dean of the college, assistant vice president of academic affairs, etc.), though for most, they are simply taking their turn as a quasi-administrator who also teaches.

Degree Required

The required degree is a doctorate in counselor education, and the preferred type of doctoral degree is PhD, though the EdD remains in many doctoral programs.

Issues to Understand

As has been previously mentioned, higher education is evolving rapidly due to the Internet age. Today's department chair needs to be a seasoned (associate professor or above) and well-organized faculty member and a good communicator and should have a calm demeanor in order to resolve interdepartmental conflicts and neutralize pressure between dean and faculty and between faculty and students. The department chair is also required to be able to dispense difficult news to students (such as suspension from the counseling program), faculty ("No, we're not supporting you for tenure"), and administrators ("We cannot take that many students if we wish to retain our CACREP accreditation").

The previous paragraph mentions some of the issues an aspiring department chair needs to understand in order to be effective. As a former department chair and longtime professor, my experience is that most counseling faculty are not interested in becoming department chair as it impeded their research time and, in many cases, requires a 12-month (as opposed to 9-month) commitment. Department chairs typically get a reduction in teaching load (say, from three courses per semester to two courses) and a small increase in salary (though large institutions will provide a larger salary increase). It is also fair to say, from my experience, that few professors of counselor education move up the academic administration ladder to become dean of the college and even fewer become provost. Simply put, most department chairs in counselor education will take the job for 3 to 5 years and then step aside for a colleague.

Best Aspects of the Job

Many department chairs may enjoy their opportunity to make a more significant impact at their institution. A department chair would be in a better position to advocate for their counselor education program than would a line faculty. The department chair is in a position to dialogue with the dean of the college and, in fact, may meet with the dean regularly. In some institutions, being selected as a department chair by one's colleagues is a recognition that the faculty member has garnered the respect of his or her colleagues.

Challenging Aspects of the Job

There are many challenges (facets) in the job as department chair. (And I speak from experience!) The department chair is "caught" between the faculty and the dean of the college (usually the College of Education), and this can at times be a precarious position with the faculty seeing you as too cozy with the dean and the dean viewing you as too "pro" faculty. Though you will receive a salary increase, it will often be slight. You will get reduction in teaching time (most often, reduction of one course), but this may be offset by the increased workload. A department chair is part professor, part administrator, ombudsman, advisor, mediator, "priest" (there is a type of confession-like role at times, though a secular one), disciplinarian, and, occasionally, friend. These different roles likely will put a department chair in the role of addressing challenging issues, such as tenure decision, student discipline, negotiating with the dean, and mediating between faculties.

Occupational Outlook and Salary

The BOLS does not report salary figures or occupational outlook for department chairs, but you can look at the mean salary reported for professors and get some idea. For example, if Mid State University (master's degree–granting institution) pays $57,000 for an associate professor, you could probably add another $1000 to $3000. Regarding occupational outlook, there will be far fewer department chairs than faculty as there is only one department chair for a counselor education department at a time.

25. DIRECTOR OF A COLLEGE OR UNIVERSITY COUNSELING CENTER

Some counselors will make a career in higher education as director of a college or university counseling center. With some 4000 community colleges, colleges, and universities, there are a number of positions available. However, competition for directing a college or university counseling center is very competitive. Many counselors would like the opportunity to counsel college students and to have the regular breaks of an academic calendar.

Degree Required

Any counselor planning to become a director of a college or university counseling center should earn a doctoral degree. The preferred doctoral degree is the traditional PhD in counseling or clinical psychology, though counselors holding a doctorate in counselor education have made gains, especially at smaller institutions (say, 5000 full time equivalent [FTE] and below). There are master's-level counselors serving as directors of college and university centers, though they mostly work at the community colleges and small colleges.

Issues to Understand

Becoming a director of a college or university counseling center requires planning your career in a strategic manner. Students in master's or doctoral degree programs interested in directing a college counseling center should serve internship at a college counseling center. Most college and university counseling centers prefer counselors who have previous experience working in college counseling centers. Directors of college counseling centers usually have spent several years working in college counseling centers before becoming directors. Therefore, it is likely that you will need to earn a doctoral degree, serve an internship in a college counseling center, and then get hired and work several years in a college counseling center before becoming a director. Sometimes, roles such as training director or assistant director are prerequisite for becoming a director.

Most college counseling centers still prefer directors who hold a doctorate in counseling or clinical psychology (particularly large institutions), though doctorate-level counselors have made inroads into university counseling centers, particularly at smaller institutions and community colleges.

Directors of college counseling centers will need to be well versed in crisis counseling (witness the tragedies at Virginia Tech and Northern Illinois), sexual trauma, anxiety and depression, addictions, eating disorders, and major mental illness, in addition to traditional issues of homesickness, career development, and running counseling groups.

Best Aspects of the Job

Some of the best aspects of directing a college counseling center are the satisfaction of working with bright, motivated, creative clients. These clients, however, will struggle with the same types of mental health issues as clients in other settings, though they will be more optimistic due to their level of education and the fact that they are more excited about their future compared with the average client at a community mental health agency.

Directing a college counseling center also puts the director into organizations that can provide a lot of support and consultation. The Association of College and University Counseling Center Directors is composed entirely of college counseling directors and holds an annual conference. The American College Counseling Association (ACCA), a division of the ACA, is open to all college counselors (and in fact any counselor), and this organization holds a conference every 2 years. Both organizations operate list-serves, and ACCA publishes a journal twice a year. Directors of college counseling centers should join both these organizations.

Challenging Aspects of the Job

Veteran directors (those who have been in the field for 15 years or more) will likely tell you that their jobs have gotten more difficult, given the apparent increase in mental disorders among college students (Kadison & DiGeronimo, 2004). In the previous era, counselors could focus on developmental issues such as college adjustment, test anxiety, career indecision, and basic depression (certainly suicide prevention has always been a concern). Today's campus seems more volatile with crisis intervention a regular issue. Sexual trauma seems commonplace, and anxiety and depression appear to be the norm in students presenting for counseling at college centers (Kadison & DiGeronimo, 2004).

Directors of college counseling centers will also be asked to provide detailed statistics of their effectiveness, number of clients counseled, presenting issues, and so on. Staff at many college counseling centers will also be required to serve in an evening and weekend on-call capacity and will at times require after-hours work on the phone or going out to counsel a client in person.

Occupational Outlook and Salary

BOLS does not report figures for the number of directors of college and university counseling centers. However, given that there are some 4000 colleges and universities in the United States, the readers can get some idea of the number of director positions available (very small). Salary figures also are not reported, though we know larger institutions will usually pay better than smaller ones (wealthy, small, private colleges are an exception). Competition for a director position will be stiff, depending on the location of the institution. A director position at a good-sized university in a desirable area of the country will garner more applications than at a small, state college in an isolated part of the country.

26. COUNSELOR IN A COLLEGE OR UNIVERSITY COUNSELING CENTER

Counseling in a college or university counseling center will mirror the category of directors of college counseling centers with the exception that there will be far more positions available for line counselors. Still, competition for a college or university counseling center position will be stiff.

Degree Required

The preferred degree for college counselors is a doctorate in counseling or clinical psychology. But my experience is that counselors with doctoral degrees in counselor education, or master's degree in various counseling fields (e.g., mental health counseling, addictions counseling) also are getting hired, particularly in smaller institutions (5000 FTE or less) and in community colleges where counselors are likely more numerous than psychologists. There are master's-level counselors who staff college counseling centers, usually in small public and private colleges that pay less than their larger counterparts.

Issues to Understand

Readers interested in a career in college or university counseling should plan on earning a doctoral degree. Counselors should also serve an internship in a college counseling center since this is often a prerequisite for being hired into a college counseling center. As competition for such positions is stiff, counselors who are free to relocate to any part of the country will have a better chance of getting hired. Many college counselors take whatever initial college position they can find, work a few years, and then try to land a job in a more desired location.

Counselors with a background in addictions, depression and anxiety, *Diagnostic and Statistical Manual of Mental Disorders* diagnosis, and trauma, and who have experience working in a college counseling center, will be more desirable candidates. Many college counselors will also have a background working in college residential living or the dean of students' office, both of which are advantageous, though not required.

Best Aspects of the Job

College and university counselors will generally get to work with bright, motivated, creative people, who for the most part are excited about their future. This will likely be more the case among college students than say, your typical community mental health clinic. College counselors also can join organizations such as the ACCA, which offers a listserve, a professional journal, and a conference every 2 years.

Challenging Aspects of the Job

College and university counseling has likely become more stressful in the past decade, with college students apparently more stressed and anxious (Kadison & DiGeronimo, 2004). With high-profile tragedies at Virginia Tech and Northern Illinois University, counselors must be acutely aware of the potential for explosive violence. Due to budgetary contraction, many college counseling centers are likely to be understaffed, putting more stress on the counselors.

Occupational Outlook and Salary

The BOLS did not report figures for salary or occupational outlook for the post of college counselors. In my experience as a former college counselor, for director of a college counseling center and a professor who has placed graduate counseling students in college counseling centers, landing a job in this counseling field is competitive, though possible. Salaries will depend on the type of institution (large vs. small, public vs. private, 4-year vs. community/technical college).

27. COUNSELOR IN A LARGE-UNIVERSITY COUNSELING CENTER

Counseling in a large-university counseling center means working in a large-university setting. For practical purposes, I will consider that "large" means university enrollment of 15,000 FTE or higher. Large institutions usually have more counseling staff (usually 10 or more counselors), though there is much variation among counseling centers.

Degree Required

In large institutions, the requirement will be some type of doctorate, typically a PhD in counseling or clinical psychology, or any another doctoral degree (MD in psychiatry, EdD in psychology, PsyD in psychology, and, occasionally, PhD in counselor education).

Any counselor interested in working in a large-university counseling center should plan on earning a doctoral degree in counseling psychology or clinical psychology. Many of the larger university counseling centers also require a postdoctorate in an American Psychological Association (APA) accredited university counseling center (usually, a 1-year paid experience).

Issues to Understand in Large-University Counseling Centers

Working in a counseling center at a large university is likely to be very different from that in small colleges and community colleges. Counseling center staff at large institutions will be, with few exceptions, composed of doctoral degree staff including a psychiatrist for medication issues. The counseling center will often be APA accredited (sometimes accredited by the International Association of Counseling Services) and composed almost entirely of psychologists, with occasional doctorate-level social workers and counselors. Some large centers will hire master's-level counselors, though this currently is the exception at large institutions.

Many large universities will also have a medical school, and faculty may hold appointments in the medical school or the psychology department, and doctoral students in psychiatry and psychology will serve graduate internships in the counseling center. Because of the nature of large counseling centers where almost all staff holds doctoral degrees, where doctoral students serve internships, and where a psychiatrist may be employed full time, treatment may resemble more an outpatient treatment setting than treatment at the traditional developmental college counseling centers. Diagnoses using *the Diagnostic and Statistical Manual of Mental Disorders, Fourth Edition-Text Revision (DSM-IV-TR*; APA, 2000) is likely to play a big role, and treatment planning will be evidence based and measurable.

A large counseling center will focus more on psychotherapy and much less on career counseling and advising. Psychological assessment using instruments such as the Minnesota Multiphasic Inventory-2 and other tests will be a large part of the services provided as well. In essence, counseling in this setting is likely to be based on the traditional medical model. Students may even be referred to as "patients" as opposed to the traditional "clients" in many other collegiate settings.

Best Aspects of the Job

Working in a large-university counseling center will mean working alongside a highly trained professional staff many of whom are graduates of top ranked programs. The standard of care and performance is very high, and there may even be an expectation that the staff publish scholarly articles and books (especially, if the staff hold appointments in psychology or psychiatry departments). The staff are likely to be very professional and creative, and some may be leaders in their professional associations (APA, Association of College and University Counseling Center Directors, American Psychiatric Association).

Students at some large universities will represent some of the brightest students in the country and are likely to be highly motivated and goal oriented, though this will vary among individual students. The student population at large institutions will be more multicultural and have a greater age range (because of large graduate enrollments); the counseling center will likely be a very busy place also due to the level of stress among the students in competitive programs, such as medicine, graduate, and professional programs (e.g., engineering, doctoral programs in the sciences).

Challenging Aspects of the Job

Working in a large, high-volume university counseling center at a large campus is not for everyone. Counselors at this setting will deal with a large number of suicidal students; diagnosis and medical therapy will be the driving forces, and the staff are likely to be very busy and feel a higher level of stress. Despite the apparent need for additional on-campus psychological services, counseling centers are often not staffed to meet the demand (Kadison & DiGeronimo, 2004). Readers interested in working in a large-university counseling center would need to earn a doctorate in clinical or counseling psychology and work a 1-year postdoctorate in an APA-accredited counseling center. Counselors should also serve an internship in a large-university counseling center during their master's and doctorate programs.

Occupational Outlook and Salary

Getting hired in a large-university counseling center is likely to be very competitive due to the setting. Though exact figures are difficult to come by due to the BOLS grouping all college counselors together, the median salary is $43,980, with larger centers paying higher salaries. It can be assumed that the growth rate of university counseling centers is not expanding at an appreciable rate due to budget constraints. Salaries will likely be higher than at community mental health centers because university counseling centers mostly are composed of doctoral degree staff and the probability that some staff also hold academic appointments in psychology or psychiatry. The BOLS projects the growth rate at only 2% for the next several years.

28. COUNSELOR IN A MEDIUM-SIZE UNIVERSITY

Counseling in a medium-size university will somewhat follow the standards and practices in a large university, though with some differences. Here, we will consider the medium-size universities to range from 5000 to 15,000 FTE.

Degree Required

Most counseling center staff in this college category will hold a doctoral degree. PhD in counseling or clinical psychology will be the most common degree although staff holding a PhD in counselor education are not unusual. For "smaller" medium-size institutions (5000–7000 FTE), master's-level staff are common and staff will consist of master's-level counselors and social workers holding the master's in social work (MSW) degree.

Issues to Understand in Medium-Size College Counseling Centers

Readers interested in counseling at a medium-size college or university should serve an internship at a college or university counseling center during their master's and doctoral degrees. College and university counseling centers prefer to hire staff with a background in college counseling. Counselors who also have training and experience in addictions counseling, trauma counseling, medicine (e.g., a degree in nursing), and career counseling (as some centers will also provide career counseling), and experience working in the residence halls as a resident director (RD) or resident advisor (RA) will have an advantage in getting hired.

Counselors at a medium-size institution will deal with the same types of issues as their colleagues in large institutions, though with reduced staff and less doctorate-level staff. Many medium-size institutions have counseling centers that will use the *DSM-IV-TR* to diagnose, though they may not use it as a rule. Medium-size counseling centers may also provide career counseling as part of their service to the campus. It is likely that most of the counseling center staff will not hold an academic appointment and will not be expected to publish. The composition of the staff will largely be made up of psychologists (PhD and PsyD), though counselors are not uncommon, and most typically at the master's degree level. The staff at medium-size universities will also spend a lot of time addressing anxiety, depression, trauma, suicide prevention, medical issues, career concerns, roommate issues, family issues, homesickness, and other developmental concerns. Medium-size counseling centers may also provide outreach to the campus community in the way of psycho-educational trainings on eating disorders, sexual orientation, managing stress, and so forth.

Best Aspects of the Job

For anyone working in a college or university counseling center, one of the best benefits is counseling a mostly motivated, optimistic population. While counselors at the college level will address many of the same issues as in community mental health settings, they are likely to have a higher success rate due to a more functional population (better education, more resources at hand, and an idealistic time of life for many students, etc.). Most counselors at medium-size institutions will have a 9- to 10-month contract and have ample time off for recreation.

Challenging Aspects of the Job

Students at all institutions will deal with a good amount of stress due to academic, career, personal, family, and health concerns. Depression, anxiety, and addictions are the "big three," as many in the field of college counseling call them. Suicide prevention is also a reality for anyone working in college counseling, as are eating disorders, self-mutilation, and loneliness. Virtually all college counseling centers will struggle with inadequate staffing needs, as demand will usually exceed supply, meaning a waiting list to see counselors.

Occupational Outlook and Salary

The occupational outlook and salary are difficult to discern as all counselors in collegiate settings are grouped together, but a perusal of the student affairs section of the BOLS *Occupational Outlook Handbook* (2010–2011) indicated a growth rate of only 2% for all college counselors. This translates into it being very competitive to land a job in a medium-size college counseling center. Salaries have a median of

$43,980 (2010–2011) and will likely range from say, low $30,000 to the mid $50,000. Once again, readers interested in working in a medium-size college or university counseling center should plan their career strategically by serving an internship in a college counseling center during graduate school.

29. COUNSELOR IN A SMALL-COLLEGE COUNSELING CENTER

Counseling in a small-college counseling center will bear more of a resemblance to that in a medium-size institution than a large university. Small colleges will be defined as those with an enrollment of 5000 FTE and less. Some small colleges will have enrollments of less than 1000 FTE and will likely have one or two counselors.

Degree Required

Though a doctoral degree is an advantage, there are several master's-level counselors staffing small-college counseling centers. In small-college counseling settings, counselors are commonly psychologists. Their degrees may include PhD, PsyD, or EdD in counseling or clinical psychology; PhD or MS (or MA) in counseling (mental health counseling, college counseling, etc.); or the MSW in social work.

Issues to Understand

Counselors working at small-college counseling centers will deal with the same types of mental health issues as their colleagues at medium- and large-size institutions, though some issues will be fewer in number. Like all collegiate settings, the "big three" of depression, anxiety disorders, and addictions are the most common issues. Suicide prevention will be a significant concern, as will the eating disorders, sexual assault trauma, and traditional issues such as loneliness, roommate conflicts, and academic and career issues. Many small-college counseling centers will also serve as the career center, and some may operate jointly with the health center (though a much smaller percentage).

Because at small-college settings faculty and staff will serve many roles (on various campus committees such as academic honesty, student activities board, and judicial board), dual relationships will be more of a concern compared with larger institutions where there is more social distance. Counselors must prepare themselves and their clients to face the reality that they will see one another in settings outside the counseling center. At small, elite private colleges, parents may not understand matters of confidentiality in the light of the fact they may be paying $30,000 to $40,000 a year in tuition and fees. In religiously affiliated institutions, the vast majority of which are small colleges having under 5000 FTE, there may be pressure to refrain from counseling on safe sex, birth control, gay and lesbian issues, and more.

Best Aspects of the Job

Like medium-size and large universities, counseling in a collegiate setting has many advantages: College students will generally be more motivated, optimistic clients who are excited about their future as a doctor, lawyer, engineer, teacher, business executive, religious leader, and so forth.

Counseling in a small-college setting also can be very rewarding because you know many of the students, faculty, staff, and coaches. Many faculty, staff, and coaches will serve as referral sources for the counseling center, and the distance between academic majors, student affairs, and classified staff will be significantly less than in larger settings. There may be more of a sense of community at a small college.

Challenging Aspects of the Job

There will be plenty of challenges for counselors at a small-college setting. The pay will be lower than at larger settings (elite small colleges are exceptions to this rule), and in some cases, the salary will be very low. As previously mentioned, religiously affiliated small colleges may set barriers to what may be discussed in counseling (e.g., abortion, birth control, and gay and lesbian issues). Small colleges, more than larger institutions, will require counselors to "wear many hats." Counselors may also provide career and academic advising, advise student organizations, be expected to serve on campus committees, be actively involved in training of residence hall staff, and so forth. Counselors at small colleges will need to be well organized and good at multitasking.

Many small-college counseling centers will also require the staff to serve as evening crisis counselors (larger institutions will often contract this service out or split the evening work among various staff). This can create a real strain on counselors, especially during midterm and near-finals when stress is at the highest.

Counseling centers at small colleges are also usually understaffed. In institutions having less than 1000 FTE, there may be only one counselor for the entire campus. In such cases, isolation is a real concern, creating the need to stay connected to professional organizations such as the ACCA, which operates a list-serv and publishes a professional journal. Consultation with other counseling professionals, standard at most college counseling centers, can be very challenging in many small-college settings, particularly those with only one counselor on staff.

As with large-university counseling centers, a background in college counseling is advantageous for getting hired. Readers interested in small-college counseling centers should serve an internship in a college counseling center during their graduate program.

Occupational Outlook and Salary

Though only a few statistics are reported, salaries will vary considerably from low $30,000 to high $50,000, with the median reported at $43,980 (BOLS, 2010–2011), depending on the affluence of the college. Small state colleges and nonelite private colleges will likely pay the lowest salaries. Occupational outlook is challenging, though in some cases, it is less so than in larger collegiate settings due to lower salaries.

30. COUNSELOR IN A COMMUNITY OR TECHNICAL COLLEGE

Counseling in a community or technical college has traditionally been radically different from counseling in 4-year institutions. The community and technical college movement mostly evolved in the 1960s as a means of offering 2-year transferrable degrees to 4-year colleges and to provide short-term certificate training in industrial and health care professions (e.g., welder, electrician, cosmetology, and nursing). For these reasons, that is, a focus on professional training as opposed to "education for education's sake," counseling in 2-year colleges has traditionally been career focused.

Degree Required

The vast majority of counselors in community and technical colleges will hold master's degrees in counseling. Some counselors at community/technical college settings will have a doctoral degree, though they are a minority.

Issues to Understand

While the population at community and technical colleges is evolving, students at community colleges are older, are more likely to have children, are more likely to be single parents, have greater financial constraints, and are more likely to drop out of college (Chen, 2005).

Few community and technical colleges have residence halls; so, the campus tends to be commuter oriented. Community and technical colleges also will scarcely resemble their 4-year counterparts, as the campus may be a few buildings that more resemble a mall than a collegiate setting.

Counselors at community colleges will spend the vast majority of their focus on career, vocational, and academic advising. A small part of the job will involve addressing personal issues, but the principal counseling focus is to assist students in transfer to a 4-year college, to assist completion of their certificate in welding, bookkeeping, nursing, and so on, and to assist with job placement. The counselor in this setting may make extensive use of career and vocational testing (e.g., Strong Interest Inventory, Campbell Interest and Skills Survey, and Self-Directed Search).

Counselors should also be prepared to see many, if not most, of their clients drop out of college due to financial issues, day care concerns, health issues, and the stress of trying to attend college and be a single parent at the same time. Counselors will need to work closely with academic advisors, financial aid staff, and faculty in order to retain as many students as possible. There is little doubt that counselors at community and technical colleges will be very busy, especially because they will also have to serve on campus committees.

Best Aspects of the Job

Counselors at community and technical colleges generally are paid well, and in many cases, better than their counterparts in 4-year colleges. Many counselors will work a 12-month contract, though some will have 9- and 10-month contracts. Community and technical college counselors will focus on career and vocational concerns and refer students with more serious personal issues out to community mental health clinics; thus, there will be less dealing with serious mental disorders.

Challenging Aspects of the Job

Community and technical college enrollments have risen dramatically perhaps due to a more affordable cost. This means counselors at 2-year colleges are likely to be understaffed and overworked. Counselors at 2-year colleges will have a steady stream of students coming through their door for career, academic, job placement, and personal issues.

The community college counseling center, like most of the campus, may resemble a large high school with modern, low-rise buildings and very few classical, ivy-covered, stately architecture designs evident. The high drop out rate has been previously noted, and the student population will have many personal, financial, and social needs that far exceed a counselor's time to address.

Occupational Outlook and Salary

Though statistics for community and technical college counselors were reported by the BOLS, the growth rate for all higher education administrators is projected as only at 2% (2010–2011). Now, it is likely that the growth rate for community college counselors would be higher given the expansion of community colleges. Median salary for all college counselors was $43,980 (BOLS, 2010–2011), though again, the median salary for community and technical college counselors may exceed this.

Counselors interested in working in community or technical college settings should complete an internship at a 2-year college. Community and technical college counselors should also have a strong background in career counseling and assessment and should have worked extensively with older students and understand their needs.

31. COUNSELOR IN A COLLEGE CAREER CENTER

Counselors working in a college or university career center will have a very different role compared with counselors providing mostly personal or mental health counseling. Collegiate career centers, in my experience, tend to operate on a philosophy different from that of college counseling centers for a variety of reasons.

Degree Required

Most career counselors staffing college career centers will hold a master's degree as opposed to a doctorate. Counselors in larger universities may be required to have a doctorate in counselor education, education administration, college student personnel, or other related doctorates. For most institutions, the master's is the entry degree.

Issues to Understand

Counselors in college career centers will likely do more advising, testing, and placement work than counseling. Many career centers have the title of "Career Planning and Placement Center," meaning that a large part of their job is assisting students land jobs after graduation. This means that much of the staff will come from fields outside counseling such as business, marketing, and so forth. Placement work requires spending a lot of time bringing recruiters to campus to interview students for potential jobs. Counselors will also spend a lot of time teaching students how to write effective resumes and cover letters, and practicing interviewing skills. Career centers will also provide career assessment to undecided majors in the way of career aptitude and interest testing, utilizing the Strong Interest Inventory, Self-Directed Search, Career Ability Placement Survey, Armed Services Vocational Assessment Battery, and many more. Counselors working in career centers will need to be highly organized, able to balance multiple tasks, and enjoy advising undecided majors.

Best Aspects of the Job

Like many collegiate jobs, the opportunity to work with motivated (mostly), idealistic people excited about their future is likely the most rewarding part of the job. College career centers also tend to work on "positive" attributes, as opposed to having to provide crisis intervention, diagnose, and serve evening and weekend on-call responsibilities. Though we have seen tough economic times resulting in concerned college students wondering if they will land a good job, my experience is that career advising and placement is generally exciting work. Helping undergraduates and graduate students get started in their careers is rewarding work, and most students tend to be appreciative.

Challenging Aspects of the Job

College career centers tend to be a "catch all" for the campus. Career center staff are expected to provide career counseling, testing, advising, and placement services; serve on campus committees; do outreach work with industry; and do multiple other tasks. Smaller career center staff will likely feel spread thin by these broad expectations. Another challenging factor is that career centers serve a wide range of students and majors. The needs of a student in, say, chemical engineering are vastly different from those in theology.

Occupational Outlook and Salary

Because the BOLS does not break career center staff into a distinct category, job growth rate and salary are difficult to determine. Based on my experience in college student affairs, I say that career center staff sometimes outearn their counterparts in the counseling centers. Salaries for full-time career counselors will range from the low $30,000 to above $70,000 a year (or higher), depending on the size of the institution and position (e.g., line counselor, assistant director, director). Though overall job growth for student affairs administrators is a paltry 2% (BOLS, 2010–2011), career center positions may fare better due to the fact they deal with job placement. A growing number of career counselor positions are likely to be in community colleges because they are the fastest growing institution.

32. COUNSELOR IN A COLLEGE OR UNIVERSITY RESIDENCE HALL

This is a relatively new position in college counseling. Traditionally, counselors worked in the counseling center, providing occasional outreach to residence halls for programming on health and safety (e.g., stress management, suicide prevention, dealing with roommate conflicts). In recent years, college counseling centers, particularly on large campuses, have begun to place counselors in the residence halls to provide available, brief counseling and assessment, and referral. Though this appears to be a small, nice job market for counselors, it may grow. (Counselors in residence halls are providing a different service compared with counselors hired to serve as residence hall directors.)

Degree Required

Because counselors in residence halls are likely to be employed at large universities, the doctoral degree may be preferred, though a master's degree may be acceptable. On some campuses, doctoral students in the counselor education or counseling psychology program may provide this service.

Issues to Understand

Counseling in a residence hall will be very different from counseling in the counseling center due largely to the reality that the counselor is working in the student's environment. Because of the availability of the counselor, the counselor may get more "drop-in" student sessions than in a counseling office across campus or located in an administration building. Counselors in this setting will do several basic screening and minicounseling sessions (say 15–30 minutes) and prepare students with greater needs for a referral to the counseling center. Counselors in the residence hall are also more available to the residence hall staff and can consult with RDs and RAs on the floors.

Counselors working in resident halls must be able to set clear limits with both students and the residence hall staff. Students will need to know that what they tell the counselors is confidential and not something the counselor will tell the residence hall staff. This is particularly important as issues of alcohol and drug abuse, conflicts with hall staff, and violations of campus policies and procedures will be discussed.

Best Aspects of the Job

Many college counselors got their start by working in residence halls as an RA or RD, and the opportunity to return to residence halls as a counselor (as opposed to having to live in the hall and enforce rules) can be both nostalgic and an opportunity to work on familiar grounds. The counselor in the residence hall will also provide short-term counseling, thus having the ability to refer difficult clients needing more in-depth work to the counseling center. The position is ideal for counselors who have previously served as RAs and RDs because of the reality that they understand the difference in counseling in a center and in the place where the students reside.

Challenging Aspects of the Job

Counseling in this setting certainly has its challenges. As previously stated, counselors in the residence halls need to establish the ability to network with RAs and RDs and, at the same time, to set boundaries with hall staff. Counselors in this setting must earn the trust of the students residing in the hall and clearly demonstrate they will not violate confidentiality by informing the hall staff of violations they hear in counseling (provided what they have heard is not a suicide plan or a plan to harm another resident). The facilities in the residence hall may not be equivalent to that in the counseling center, and privacy may be more difficult to establish due to the location of the counseling office. There is also the matter of all the distractions and noise inherent in working in a setting where people (especially young students) live.

Occupational Outlook and Salary

It is difficult to report exact statistics on what is a new occupation for counselors. The BOLS reports the median salary for college counselors to be $43,980. Counselors in the residence halls are likely to be paid less because they may be beginning their careers, as opposed to counselors in the counseling center, many of whom are seasoned veterans. Occupational outlook is likely very low as this is currently a small niche market for college counselors at larger institutions.

33. COUNSELOR IN STUDENT AFFAIRS (NONCOUNSELING POSITIONS)

Many professionals holding counseling degrees work in related fields such as college student personnel services. Some graduate counseling programs even offer degree programs in college counseling or counseling and college student services administration, as a degree option along with traditional programs in school counseling, mental health counseling, rehabilitation counseling, and so forth.

Degree Required

The required degree for most student affairs positions in the dean of students' office, student activities center, student union, residence halls, and so forth is likely to be a master's degree. Director and assistant director positions, however, especially at larger campuses, will likely require a doctoral degree in counseling, college student services, adult education, or a related degree.

Issues to Understand

A counseling background is an advantage for anyone working in college student affairs. Given the ubiquity of mental health issues in today's collegiate population, training in recognizing and understanding mental health issues and making a timely intervention may head off student struggle and even tragedy (Kadison & DiGeronimo, 2004). However, counselors working in student services settings, such as the dean of students' office, student activities, and residential life, must understand that counseling is not part of their job description. Because counselors are specially trained in empathetic communication, conflict resolution, and providing feedback, they may have an advantage over general student affairs professionals educated in programs other than counseling. A larger part of student services administration will involve good management and budgetary skills and the ability to plan and train students and professional staff. Many student affairs positions (such as dean of students' office) may involve disciplinary hearings and sanctions, something in which counselors would receive little training. Student affairs professionals, especially assistant directors and directors, are likely to be heavily involved in management and staff supervision, leaving little time for assisting students with personal growth work.

Best Aspects of the Job

As a veteran of student affairs work in numerous departments during my baccalaureate, master's degree, and doctoral study, my sense is that many student affairs professionals are drawn to the field by a desire to assist students in their growth and maturation. Student affairs professionals, particularly those serving the front lines, will have a lot of contact with college students (e.g., program advisor in student activities, hall director, and greek advisor). Many student affairs positions also hold 9- or 10-month appointments, thus providing them a natural summer break. Directors and assistant directors will usually hold 12-month appointments.

Challenging Aspects of the Job

For many student affairs professionals, the work will require more managerial skills than counseling skills. Directors and assistant directors will supervise staff; help recruit, hire, and fire staff; prepare budgets; and discipline students. Many of these responsibilities are ones counselors may not prefer. It has also been my experience in some 30 years in higher education that there remains a class distinction between faculty and student affairs professionals. Many faculty (though not all) will view student affairs staff as nonessential, if not unnecessary. Even student affairs professionals holding the doctoral degree will not get the same level of respect as faculty. As a professional who came up through the ranks of student affairs then switched over to the faculty, I was acutely aware of the class distinction between these disparate professions. This faculty–administration divide can create an uncomfortable (and unnecessary) division on college campuses.

Occupational Outlook and Salary

Student affairs jobs are still available on college campuses. The BOLS reports general salary statistics, most of which are targeted at director positions, where the median salary is very high. But as there are some 4,000 colleges, universities, and community colleges in the United States, most student affairs positions will usually be entry-level positions, and salaries will vary considerably depending on the type of institution (small college, community college, large university). Student affairs staff can expect a wide range of salary, with entry-level positions being in the $30,000 to $40,000 range. Directors and assistant directors can earn up to near $100,000, though such positions are rare, and usually more in the range of $60,000 to $75,000. The BOLS estimates a near flat growth rate of 2%, meaning the field is not expanding. Given the popularity of online degree programs, many student affairs may experience contraction in the future (especially in residence life).

34. COUNSELOR IN ACADEMIC ADVISING

Many counselors may discover that they enjoy academic advising as much as counseling. For counselors who enjoy career counseling, academic advising may be a natural career fit. Although faculty naturally will serve as advisors to students in the academic programs, many colleges and universities will employ academic advisors to provide services faculty simply does not have the time to provide.

Degree Required

Most professionals working as academic advisors are likely to have a master's degree. Counselors, with their strong training in personal and career counseling, are natural professionals to work as academic advisors.

Issues to Understand

Academic advising work is closely related to counseling in that it requires patience, good listening skills, nonjudgmental attitude, and ability to be good with details and highly organized. Academic advisors at campuses where I have worked have been responsible for advising, coaching, and monitoring large numbers of students. Academic advisors will need to stay apprised of academic programs and maintain good communication with academic departments and individual faculty. The academic advisor's role is to assist students in retention and completion of their academic degree.

Academic advisors will also need to liaison with services such as counseling, as many students facing academic difficulty and suspension are likely to be very stressed and anxious. Academic advisors need to work closely with career services as many students are likely to change majors and need career assistance. Academic advisors also work with students on academic probation to enhance their study skills. Professionals working as academic advisors may also serve on, or work closely with, committees that determine academic suspension.

Best Aspects of the Job

Professionals working in academic advising will likely enjoy being a part of students who are transitioning through college on their way to graduation and a career. Academic advisors also will likely enjoy assisting a wide range of students (from many cultures, countries, majors, etc.) and learning about their program of study, their lives and interests, and helping them navigate through their academic struggles.

Challenging Aspects of the Job

Because the volume of students served is high and the range of student majors very broad, academic advisors will be pressed to learn many details and to be able to manage multiple skills, details, and tasks. Though my knowledge of academic advising offices is not comprehensive, most academic advising professionals I have met comment that the most challenging part of their job is that they are expected to meet a wide array of needs while being short on staff.

Academic advisors also will spend much of their time advising and assisting students in academic difficulty. Students in academic jeopardy are likely to require a disproportionate amount of the advisor's time. Academic advisors may also play a role in academic suspensions, either serve on the committee that is charged with this unpleasant task or provide information to the committee about students in question.

Occupational Outlook and Salary

The BOLS did not list academic advisors as a distinct category in the *Occupational Outlook Handbook*, but a perusal in the job advertisements listed in *The Chronicle of Higher Education* over the past few editions shows salaries from $33,000 to $45,000. This range of salaries likely would target beginning advisors and those with a few years experience. Directors and assistant directors of academic advising would earn considerably more. Occupational outlook was also not reported, though in my long experience in higher education, academic advising positions are fewer in number than, say, positions in residence life, counseling, and so forth. Therefore, competition will likely be stiff when jobs do come open.

35. COUNSELOR AS CAMPUS OMBUDSMAN

Mediation and conflict resolution have become very popular in community settings, and some colleges and universities have created ombudsman positions. The ombudsman has many functions, and chief among them is serving as a mediator in faculty–administration disputes, faculty–faculty disputes, student–student disputes, and so forth.

Degree Required

No one degree is required to be an ombudsman. Though a law degree would seem to be a natural fit, it could be argued that counseling is another viable degree. Because ombudsmen are mediating disputes, they must be able to elicit a two-way dialogue and be able to entice both parties to compromise; the types of communication techniques taught in counseling programs would seem good training. Marriage and family counselors are especially trained and adept at facilitating dialogue between spouses and partners, and the same set of skills can be applied in mediation. I would recommend additional training and possible certification in mediation. Mediation training is offered in some degree programs at 2- and 4-year colleges, and by private professionals. Counselors can often earn continuing education units needed to maintain licensure and national certification.

Issues to Understand

Mediation is similar to, though very different from, counseling. While the goals of both are similar—more open communication, teaching compromise, providing a venue for disputing parties to address their complaints, and so forth—the ombudsman is only concerned with dispute resolution and not addressing underlying psychological issues. The ombudsman provides a neutral part to campus parties enmeshed in conflicts they have been unable to resolve on their own. Some common types of disputes are money matters, conflict within student organizations, conflict between two faculty members, disputes between a department chair (or dean) and a professor, and so on. Essentially, the ombudsman provides a means of resolving conflicts that might escalate to expensive litigation or fester into poisonous relations between different campus factions. Anyone interested in becoming an ombudsman must be comfortable in addressing conflict. My own experience as a mediator both in higher education and in community mental health is that most people struggle in addressing conflict. The ombudsman must come to see her or his role as simply the instrument between the conflict (or conflicts) and be able to refrain from taking sides (Barsky, 2007).

Best Aspects of the Job

One of the most rewarding parts of mediation is the realization that you are assisting people in resolving conflicts that would otherwise escalate into larger and more damaging conflicts. My own experience is also that ombudsmen feel a sense of pride and accomplishment in providing a service that most professionals would likely shy away from. Ombudsmen who demonstrate effectiveness will also be very much in demand, as campuses by their very nature (a large number of people holding diverse opinions, values, and ideas) will naturally have many conflicts. Fortunately, most conflicts do not escalate into needing the services of a professional mediator, but some will.

Challenging Aspects of the Job

There are many challenges to the role of ombudsman. First, you are working with people in distress and they may be very angry and project that anger onto you, the professional. Effective ombudsmen will need to be able deflect and redirect anger in appropriate directions so that it can facilitate a reduction in animosity. Ombudsmen will also be subject to allegations of showing favoritism by one or even both parties in a dispute. The ombudsman also needs to be very skilled at moving dialogue along when it becomes bogged down and countereffective.

Perhaps the most challenging part of the campus ombudsman's job lies in the fact that he or she works in an enclosed system (the campus) where there are so many intertwined relationships. You may be called upon to mediate a dispute between your boss's spouse and another faculty member, or perhaps you find yourself mediating an ugly dispute between two faculty members you have worked with on campus committees and whom you respect. Ombudsmen will also have to grapple with very challenging and destructive accusations of racism, sexism, homophobia, and so forth. It is no stretch to state that the ombudsman role is one few counselors or other professionals are eager to take on.

Occupational Outlook and Salary

As no statistics are listed by the BOLS, I would counsel interested readers to contact a campus ombudsman. (This position may be called a "campus mediator" on some campuses.) Campus ombudsmen are likely to be employed at larger campuses (say, 10,000 FTE and above), though it should be mentioned that the human resources office on many campuses may designate staff members to serve in this role, though their job title may be something like assistant director or mediator. For an estimate on salary, it is likely the range would run from $35,000 to $55,000 depending on the size of the institution and the experience of the ombudsman.

36. COUNSELOR AS ACADEMIC DEAN (OR ASSOCIATE DEAN OR ASSISTANT DEAN)

Because most counseling programs are located in Colleges of Education, it is likely that relatively few professors of counselor education have become deans of the college. As Colleges of Education are dominated by undergraduate and graduate programs related to the different teacher education programs, counseling faculty will be both outnumbered and likely have less political clout within the College of Education. Having made this statement, however, I have known some counselor education faculty who have become college deans.

Degree Required

To become a dean, you will need to have earned a doctoral degree (PhD, EdD) in counselor education, achieved tenure, and moved up the rank system from assistant professor, to associate professor, and in most cases, to full professor. (There are some exceptions to this.)

Issues to Understand

Because deans are high-ranking and well-paid administrative positions, there are many issues and challenges to be aware of. First, as all readers must surely know, you would not be entertaining the notion of becoming a dean anytime soon, given the long years needed to earn a doctorate degree, then climb the tenure and promotion ladder, and finally the competition to become a dean. A college dean is also a political position, and no matter how experienced and well qualified the dean, many faculty and staff will grumble at the successful candidate. Deans must also chart the direction of the College of Education (or other college), enforce tenure and promotion requirements, recommend or not recommend faculty for tenure, settle disputes, assist in the discipline of students, help recruit faculty, and ensure compliance with all the accreditations their college holds (e.g., CACREP, NCATE). Unlike most college faculty who will have a more flexible schedule, deans will work far more than 40 hours a week.

Best Aspects of the Job

Though I have never been, nor ever will be, a dean, I have worked under some and had the opportunity to observe and get to know several. I recall asking my own dean a few years ago what she thought was the best part of her job. She answered that it was the satisfaction in charting a course that could determine the future success of the College of Education. She went on to state that this knowledge helped when things became mired in conflict and her vision became clouded.

Challenging Aspects of the Job

There will be many challenges to the job of dean of a college. First, professors, who have been trained to question and critique ideas, have the reputation of being difficult people to supervise. In fact, the very word "supervise" would likely draw much faculty ire. (I speak as a long-time professor!) The dean must also determine which programs will be expanded and which programs may be cut. As this involves people losing their hard-earned jobs, you can imagine how fraught with conflict this would be. Deans also are actively involved in communicating with vice presidents and presidents and serve the role of advocating for their college and the programs within that college. Deans also must compete for resources against deans of other colleges, as budgets tend to favor revenue-producing programs. Basically, being a dean is a demanding job on many fronts, but effective deans are worth a lot of money.

Occupational Outlook and Salary

Despite the degree of difficulty and the numerous challenges the job entails, many faculty will be interested in becoming deans. Because there are a lot of faculty and few deans, competition is very stiff. The road to becoming a dean is moving from assistant dean to associate dean to dean. The BOLS (2010–2011) reports a growth rate of 2% for academic administration, and it is likely less for deans. The BOLS (2010–2011) also reports a median salary of $128,550 for deans in the College of Education.

7   Career and Vocational Counseling

Spotlight: Career Counseling
Career Counseling Spotlight: Cheri Butler, PhD, LPC, NCCC, MCC, Associate Director of Career Services, Past President, National Career Development Association, University of Texas, Arlington, TX

I came to my current profession as a career counselor in a very circuitous way. I was a traditional undergraduate, beginning my college work right after high school and taking my place in the workforce as a teacher after obtaining a BS in education. At the time, teaching and nursing were the only "respectable" occupations for females to pursue with a college degree. It took me only 1 year as a teacher to realize that I wasn't well suited to the bureaucracy of public education. However, I enjoyed teaching, so I went in the direction of training adults.

Since I had never really sat down and explored what matched my motivated skill set and my personality style, and as a result of making moves with my husband's work, I never had identified a true career path. I fell into jobs that I could do fairly well. I had also had the desire to pursue eventually an advanced degree. I just didn't know which discipline suited me best. At one point, I took an interest assessment based on the Holland codes, and one suggested occupation was funeral director. I was pretty clear that was not a fit for me.

Another suggestion from that same assessment was human resources. I learned that John F. Kennedy University offered an MBA program in a town near where I lived in northern California, and I attended an open house. It so happened that their school of management also offered an MA in career development. The more I learned about the program, the more fascinated I became. I spoke with the chair of the department, and I was hooked.

I enrolled in that program, and the further along in the coursework that I progressed, the more certain I was that I had found my calling. It was a unique mixture of classes since it was housed in the school of management, although I did have required coursework from the school of psychology. Included in my classes were the history of work, careers in organizations, and macro economics in which I studied how the economy affects the labor market. Now, after 20 years in the profession, I am still passionate about being a career counselor. Because I didn't come to my true profession quickly, I have as my mission to help students and clients find their true path. My tag line is "Helping people to find joy and success in work and life."

When I moved to Texas shortly after finishing my MA in career development, I quickly learned that the only credible way to pursue my career in Texas as a career counselor was to become a Licensed Professional Counselor (LPC). I had my transcript reviewed by the board, and I identified the four additional courses that I would have to take in order to be eligible to do my supervised hours and sit for the LPC exam. Over a 1.5-year period, I was able to take the courses, finish my supervised experience, and successfully pass the exam.

Over the 20 years in the profession, I have had the privilege of working in many venues as a career counselor. I have worked with displaced workers in the one-stop environment. I have worked in vocational rehabilitation assisting clients in identifying alternative work after being physically or emotionally unable to continue in previous employment. I have worked in the employee development center within corporations assisting employees to define new paths to pursue within the organization. I have worked in career transition centers for corporations required to implement large layoffs to assist former employees to obtain work in another organization. I am now working for the second time in a university setting helping to prepare students to successfully transition from backpacks to briefcases.

In the last 10 years, I have also been very actively involved in training paraprofessionals in career counseling competencies, as well as training instructors in the same curriculum. Now I am able to pass my knowledge and experience on to the next generation of career professionals.

I have also been very active in my professional organization, the National Career Development Association (NCDA). NCDA is a 5,000-member organization of career practitioners representing the many venues mentioned above in addition to career counselors in K-12 schools. I have had the privilege to serve as the president of that organization from October 1, 2010, through September 30, 2011. In that capacity, I had the opportunity to travel nationally and internationally to attend conferences, be a speaker on career topics, and represent my U.S. colleagues. This past year I added Lima and Trujillo in Peru, Ottawa in Canada, and Cairns in Australia to the list of cities around the world that I have visited on behalf of NCDA. Previously, I also traveled to Sharjah in UAE and Beijing in China.

As I look back over my years as a career counselor, I am reminded of so many students and clients who came to me clueless and I was able to help them "peel the onion" to find their true path. I don't have the answers, as my job as a career counselor is to help them find their own answers.

37. CAREER AND VOCATIONAL COUNSELORS IN AGENCY SETTINGS

A large number of counselors work in community or governmental agencies. Many counselors work in state employment departments and in federally funded position created by the Jobs Training Partnership Act. I spent five summers counseling and advising youth and unemployed adults in a large agency in Oregon.

Degree Required

BA/BS and master's degree in counseling for career mobility.

Issues to Understand

Before I began providing career and vocational counseling to the unemployed, my image of career counseling was that it was a low-stress job and a "fun" type of counseling. I had provided career counseling in a college setting to traditional age students who were excited about their careers. Their excitement was in part due to their being on the front end of their work career. Many unemployed adults in their mid-30s to mid-50s who had experienced downsizing, being fired, and a low wage/no-benefit job had a very different perspective.

As a career or vocational counselor, you will encounter people who are either unemployed or underemployed (working below their education, training, and experience level), and those unhappy in their career for other reasons. Career dissatisfaction can lead to depression, increased anxiety, and a decreased sense of life fulfillment (Krumboltz, 1992). Career counselors are then, in effect, providing a type of mental health counseling.

Best Aspects of the Job

Effective career and vocational counselors are professionals who enjoy their job and see themselves assisting people to have more enjoyable, fulfilling work lives. Career counseling can also be very creative and involve the use of helpful assessment instruments such as the Self-Directed Search, Armed Services Vocational Assessment Battery, Campbell Interests and Skills Survey, and many others. Assessment, counseling, and collaborating with clients can help counselors craft a holistic approach to career counseling. Some clients, especially young, well-educated ones, will enthusiastically engage in counseling and assessment and will have success in their job search.

Challenging Aspects of the Job

My first significant task as a career counselor was to assist my more experienced colleagues in interviewing some 300 people who had just lost their jobs when a timber mill had closed. While interviewing scores of these displaced workers, I found there were naturally divergent views among them: A few were excited by the opportunity to do something different; several, especially those close to retirement, saw it as an opportunity to work part time and do volunteer work; and most seemed to be very anxious over their sudden unemployment and felt pessimistic at being able to land a job that paid as well. Career counselors will often work with people who feel defeated by life circumstances, betrayed by employers, and jaded from having bounced from one low-wage job to another. Some unemployed people will actually project their anger and frustration onto the counselor, viewing the counselor as a symbolic representation of "the system."

Occupational Outlook

Though the Bureau of Labor Statistics does not compile statistics on career counselors, my experience is that this is a viable field. State, federal, and private human service agencies frequently hired counselors as counselors are natural professionals when it comes to working with the unemployed and underemployed. Regarding salary range, my best estimate would be low $30,000 to mid $40,000, depending on education, experience, and agency. Management and supervisors will likely exceed this general salary range.

38. EMPLOYMENT COUNSELOR

Employment counseling has become a "new" type of counseling, though in reality, it has been around for several decades. Employment counselors are counselors whose primary job responsibility is to assist unemployed people find work. In reality, this segment of the counseling profession differs only slightly from career and vocational counselors. After all, career and vocational counselors also assist the unemployed in finding work. One difference, in my experience, is that I have met many employment counselors who have come from outside the counseling profession (e.g., business and industry, and education).

Degree Required

BA/BS degree. Master's degree in a counseling field offers more vocational range and mobility.

Issues to Understand

Employment counselors, like their close relatives, career counselors, will work in government and private human service agencies. The employment counselor will focus primarily on assisting unemployed people find jobs and in marketing unemployed clients to potential employers. Employment counselors will need to spend quality time establishing networks with business owners, educational organizations (P-12 schools, community colleges, etc.), and religious and civic groups in order to create a network of assistance for their clients. Many unemployed clients, especially during a serious recession like that of the past few years, face loss of their homes and potential homelessness.

Some employment counselors, like career and vocational counselors, will go into private practice and offer career advice, career coaching (a recent phenomenon), and consultation to individuals and corporations. The number of employment counselors able to make a living from private practice is likely very small (though some professionals are able to do this).

Best Aspects of the Job

Employment counselors help unemployed people find work and this can have profound implications for their client's mental health, ability to provide for their family, and keep their homes.

Challenging Aspects of the Job

Many unemployed clients, especially the chronically unemployed and those who have a lack of education and relevant training, poor work history, addictions, and difficulty getting along with others, will struggle to find meaningful work. This segment, in my experience, will be the population of clients the employment counselor will find challenging and at times downright frustrating.

Occupational Outlook and Salary

Again, while no official governmental statistics are kept for employment counselors, my sense is that this is a viable field. After all, we will always have unemployed and underemployed people (sadly). Salary range would likely be similar to that of career/vocational counselors ($34,000–$45,000 per year depending on BA/BS or MS degree and experience).

39. COUNSELOR AS CAREER COACH

I could easily be accused of "splitting hairs" in this section of the text. Career and vocational counselors, employment counselors, and career coaches likely have far more in common than differences. But due to the fact that there are some interesting differences, I have maintained a division between them. This separation is more pro forma than real, but I have maintained it, nevertheless.

Degree Required

BA/BS degree. A master's degree in a counseling field is recommended as it provides the greatest degree of latitude regarding training, use of career assessments, and licensure. There are some organizations offering certificates in professional coaching, though none of these organizations are part of the counseling profession.

Issues to Understand

Career coaching is a very recent occupation encompassing a wide range of backgrounds, careers, training, and credentials. I know of many career counselors who have rebranded themselves as career "coaches." The biggest problem as I see it is that there is no agreed-upon educational and training program, no agreed-upon credentialing, no code of ethics, and no laws to protect the public in the way of licensure and national certification. I do see career coaching as a viable service if not career. I also will advocate that professionals such as counselors are the best equipped to engage in career coaching due to education, training, ethical code, and licensure. Whether career coaching is an actual "career" or simply another service the career counselors provide, I have listed it separately due to its ubiquity.

Best Aspects of the Job

I have spoken with career coaches, and they cite satisfaction that seems consistent with career counselors (in fact, many of these career coaches were trained as counselors). Coaches I spoke with mentioned the creativity of their work, the positive nature, and the ability to mentor clients emerging in careers.

Challenging Aspects of the Job

Here is what I have discerned as being challenging for career coaches: Who and what are you? Are you a professionally trained counselor? Are you professional in business and marketing? Are you former educator? Are you in all the previously mentioned categories? Also, what precisely is career coaching and how does it differ from career counseling? What education, training, and credentials qualify one to be a career coach? These are weighty and largely unanswered questions.

Occupational Outlook and Salary

More than any career in this text, career coaches are the most difficult to make projections about. I was unsuccessful in uncovering any hard facts regarding employment figures. I expect that many career coaches also are counselors who offer coaching as another service (my wife, a trained counselor, does this). Occupational outlook and salary would be a wild guess. My advice for readers interested in this field would be to find a career coach and interview that person. I maintain that career coaches should best be counselors due to (1) education, (2) graduate training, (3) an existing ethical code, and (4) existing licensure and credentialing that protects the public.

Counseling in Community Mental Health Settings

40. COUNSELOR IN OUTPATIENT CLINICS AND AGENCIES

It is likely that most counselors work in outpatient settings. The reason for this is that outpatient treatment is significantly less expensive than an operation that lasts for 24 hours a day, 7 days a week, and 365 days a year. Many outpatient agencies will pay their staff better than those in inpatient settings, though there are exceptions to this depending on the funding of the agencies involved.

Degree Required

The entry-level degree for counselors in outpatient settings is, of course, the master's degree. Because of licensure requirements, the primary degrees should be in mental health counseling, community counseling (note that, in many graduate counseling departments, this degree has been eliminated in favor of mental health counseling), rehabilitation counseling, and addictions counseling.

Issues to Understand

Readers skimming through this book will certainly have noticed that there are always "issues to understand" in all types of counseling. In outpatient settings, counselors will generally spend one hour counseling individual clients and 90 minutes with groups, couples, and families. Then, the client (or clients) leave the building and return after one week. Outpatient settings create clear boundaries between the counselor and the client, unlike inpatient settings, where the counselor may interact with the client several times in an 8-hour shift. For most counselors, clear, distinct boundaries are an advantage as they maintain a therapeutic-only relationship, as opposed to residential milieu treatment, where the counselor counsels, watches a movie with clients, plays chess, and so forth.

Outpatient clinics likely attract a wider variety of clients than do inpatient centers. Inpatient treatment tends to get the most challenging clients (or, more accurately, "patients") because their behavior is such that they temporarily cannot function in society due to addiction, mental illness, suicide attempt, and so forth. Outpatient clinics will also get clients from an inpatient unit or those who will transition to an inpatient setting, though most clients will never be placed in an inpatient center. Typical issues in outpatient treatment are depression, anxiety, numerous *Diagnostic and Statistical Manual of Mental Disorders, Fourth Edition-Text Revision* Axis I clinical issues, sexual abuse, addictions, people dealing with divorce, and death of a loved one.

Best Aspects of the Job

As a counselor who has worked in both inpatient and outpatient settings, I find that one of the advantages to outpatient counseling is the clear one-hour session, in which the client leaves the clinic when the session is completed. This type of structure minimizes the issues of dual relationships with the client. The more a counselor can limit the relationship with a client, that is, the therapeutic encounter, the less complicated therapy will be. Counselors in outpatient settings often, in my experience anyway, outearn their colleagues working in residential settings. Residential settings have many more costs to pay for, and salary reduction is a sad reality for residential treatment centers.

Challenging Aspects of the Job

Like counseling in any setting, outpatient counselors work on a daily basis with people who are struggling with some aspects of their lives. Many of your clients will welcome your intervention; it is also accurate to state that some will not. Some clients, particularly court-mandated clients, may be angry, hostile, and unwilling or unable to understand how they have contributed to their issues. In many cases, you as the counselor will be forced to write a report to the judge, probation officer, child protection services, or another official at an agency, outlining how the mandated client did not achieve her or his treatment goals.

Salary will also vary considerably in outpatient treatment. How much a counselor earns is dependent on several factors such as years experience, licensure, whether he or she is a supervisor or line counselor, and the agency's level of funding.

Occupational Outlook and Salary

The Bureau of Labor Statistics' (2010–2011) occupational outlook for counselors continues to be very strong, with a growth rate estimate of 24% for mental health counselors, 21% for addictions counselors, and 19% for rehabilitation counselors, the principal types of counselors employed in outpatient agencies. Salaries vary; the median salary is $36,810 for mental health counselors, $37,030 for addictions counselors, and $30,930 for rehabilitation counselors. Again, more experienced counselors and supervisors will earn more.

41. COUNSELOR IN INPATIENT SETTINGS

Counseling in inpatient settings can differ greatly from that in outpatient settings. Inpatient psychiatric treatment usually involves short-term (acute) stays (say 6–12 days for most patients). Inpatient wings attached to hospitals will primarily focus on medical stabilization of the patient before she or he is released back into the community. The social worker will then make an outpatient plan for continued treatment with an outpatient provider.

Degree Required

Most counselors working in an inpatient ward will have a master's degree in mental health counseling, rehabilitation counseling, or another similar degree. Counselors with a medical background also will have an advantage (e.g., counselor who is also an RN). Boston University's mental health counseling program is located within their medical school and actively prepares its students to work in hospitals and other medical settings.

Issues to Understand

Counselors interested in inpatient settings must understand that psychiatric inpatient hospitals will likely provide less counseling compared with outpatient clinics. Inpatient units will focus more on getting the patient back on medication, as cessation of medication often precipitates a patient's return to the hospital. Most counseling in residential psychiatric hospitals will revolve around group counseling. Individual counseling will be much less emphasized, though staff is encouraged to have individual check-ins with the patients for wellness purposes.

Best Aspects of the Job

Counselors working in psychiatric hospitals will need to enjoy the challenge of assisting patients stabilize their moods. Most counselors will also find a sense of fulfillment on seeing patients improve and be discharged from the hospital.

Challenging Aspects of the Job

There will be many challenges to counseling in a psychiatric hospital. As mentioned previously, stabilization through medication will be emphasized over counseling. Counselors may likely feel less valued than the medical staff as a hospital setting is primarily set up for medical staff. Finally, as patients tend to stay in the hospital for brief periods, establishing relationships can be difficult.

Occupational Outlook and Salary

The Bureau of Labor Statistics lists salaries for residential addictions treatment settings but not for counselors working in inpatient psychiatric treatment settings. This may be because only a small number of counselors work in psychiatric hospitals. The same dearth of information is applicable to the occupational outlook, though it is likely that the numbers of counselors working in psychiatric hospitals may increase. Counselors have now been approved to be hired in Veterans Affairs (VA) hospitals, and the VA includes psychiatric treatment. Salaries for counselors working in inpatient psychiatric treatment settings are likely to exceed those of counselors working in residential addictions treatment settings.

42. RESIDENTIAL COUNSELOR IN LONG-TERM PSYCHIATRIC CARE

There are psychiatric centers that offer long-term treatment; they are different from the standard, traditional hospitals addressed previously. For example, there are many long-term treatment centers for adolescents and adults that operate in every state. Long term can mean anywhere from three months to one year depending on insurance coverage and the ability of the family to pay.

Degree Required

Some residential psychiatric centers continue to hire baccalaureate-level "counselors." However, due to licensure and the evolving field, a master's degree is definitely advantageous. Social workers with an MSW degree continue to hold an advantage over master's-level counselors, though this is likely to change as counselors are now licensed in all 50 U.S. states, Washington, DC, Puerto Rico, and Guam.

Issues to Understand

Residential treatment in psychiatric settings revolves around addictions, major mental disorders (bipolar disorder, major depression, etc.), and behavioral concerns (suicide attempt, aggressive child or adolescent, etc.). Unlike acute psychiatric hospitals, counseling is likely to be emphasized, though the model is group counseling over individual counseling. Still, counseling and medication will both be important for patients undergoing treatment. Many adults in long-term care are there voluntarily, though a good deal of adolescents have been committed by their parents or adjudicated by their state of residence.

Residential treatment runs on "milieu" treatment, meaning everything at the treatment center is part of therapy: group sessions, individual check-ins, playing basketball with the patients, having a cup of coffee with patients, eating lunch with them, and so on. Counselors in residential settings must become skilled in setting flexible though clear boundaries in order to promote the therapeutic encounter. Milieu treatment has many challenges, especially in that it can be difficult to move from a more social encounter of playing soccer with clients to group therapy, where the counselor may have to confront the client on denial of an addiction.

Best Aspects of the Job

Counselors in residential settings have the advantage of getting to know their clients very well given the nature of 24-hour care. As relationships may be deeper, this might be more rewarding for residential counselors than for counselors in outpatient settings. As a former residential counselor, this was the most rewarding part of the job for me and for most of my fellow residential counselors.

Challenging Aspects of the Job

There are many challenges to residential-based counseling. Milieu treatment means that you see clients after group therapy, and maintaining therapeutic versus "social" relationship can be challenging. Patients may also see the counselors more as "authority" enforcing rules than therapists promoting healing. Another challenge is that many residential settings will likely pay less than outpatient clinics. Residential counseling can be emotionally and physically demanding due to the lack of separation between therapeutic time and social time.

Occupational Outlook and Salary

The Bureau of Labor Statistics has compiled salary and occupational outlook for counselors in residential addictions treatment and in residential settings treating patients with developmental disabilities (DD). For counselors in residential addictions treatment, the median salary is $31,300 and in residential settings treating patients with DD, the salary is $29,950. These are two of the lowest counselor salaries. Occupational outlook has to be gleaned from general mental health and addictions growth rate and these are 24% and 21%, respectively. It is also my experience that many counselors begin their career in residential treatment and then move to outpatient settings.

43. COUNSELOR IN OUTPATIENT CHEMICAL DEPENDENCY CLINICS

Counseling in outpatient addictions clinics is very different from that in inpatient chemical dependency units. Unlike milieu treatment, outpatient treatment involves more clear boundaries, as clients are not residing at the setting.

Degree Required

The field of addictions has evolved considerably in the past 20 years. Originally, addictions counseling was a bachelor's-level profession or below (associate degree and no degree), and there was a preference for hiring former addicts who had been in successful recovery for three to five years or more. Currently, the profession has moved toward master's degrees, and being a recovering addict is no longer required (it is interesting that in addictions treatment, having been an addict was advantageous.) Some counseling programs even offer a master's degree in addictions counseling. Hazelton, a well-known treatment facility in Minnesota, now offers master's degrees in addictions counseling.

Issues to Understand

Addictions counseling has come a long way since the days when ex-addicts, many of whom had no degree, provided counseling. Though many former addicts continue to work in the field, a former addiction is no longer required. The current focus is on advanced degrees and training. Addictions treatment is still closely affiliated with famous 12-step models such as Alcoholics Anonymous (AA), though secular approaches are becoming increasingly popular, especially cognitive approaches. Still, the language of AA, NA, and similar spiritual approaches permeates the field, as many addicts in treatment will be involved with AA and NA.

Best Aspects of the Job

The best part of being an addictions counselor is assisting people to regain sobriety and rebuild their lives. As addiction is so ubiquitous in society, clients with addictions are very resistant to treatment. Counselors who can help addicted clients get sober and retain sobriety are likely to feel a strong sense of professional fulfillment.

Challenging Aspects of the Job

Addictions counseling is a very demanding work (Miller & Rollnick, 2002). The recidivism rate for addictions hovers above 50%, and most clients will relapse one to two times after long-term treatment (Miller & Rollnick, 2002). This means addictions counselors will see many of their former clients recycled through their treatment programs.

Addictions counseling also tends to pay less compared with standard mental health counseling, though directors of addictions clinics make considerably more money than line staff. Clients in addictions treatment also tend to have other mental health issues. Because of these dual-diagnoses issues, addictions counselors need to work with mental health counselors, psychologists, and social workers who treat general mental health concerns.

Occupational Outlook and Salary

The occupational outlook for addictions counselors is very good and likely to remain so given the insidious nature of addictions and the prevalence of legal and illegal drugs (Miller & Rollnick, 2002). The Bureau of Labor Statistics (2010–2011) estimates a growth rate of 21% and a median salary of $37,030.

44. COUNSELOR IN INPATIENT RESIDENTIAL ADDICTIONS TREATMENT

Many counselors work in inpatient addictions treatment. There are traditional, 28-day residential units and additional residential treatment where clients may stay for acute periods of time that can vary from few days to two weeks.

Degree Required

It depends. There are still many addictions counselors working in inpatient treatment who hold only a bachelor's degree. However, for counselors hoping to move up to a clinical supervisor's position, master's degree (and licensure and certification) is very likely to be required.

Issues to Understand

Working in inpatient addictions settings can be very challenging on many levels. First, as with other types of residential treatment, setting clear boundaries is essential for both patients and staff. Because manipulation is a key dynamic of addicts in treatment, counselors will need to be firm in setting limits with the residents. Because addictions are often "comorbid" with other mental disorders (e.g., depression, anxiety, and post-traumatic stress disorder), counselors will need to be able to recognize co-occurring disorders.

Counselors will also need to be ready to manage therapy groups and the treatment of choice in residential addictions settings. A big part of group treatment will involve counselors confronting the patients on minimizing their addictions and assisting the patients in accepting responsibility, whether it is legal, moral, or familial. Denial is a key dynamic among addicted populations, and counselors should expect the patients in this setting to be resistant to admitting the harm their drug of choice (or "drugs" of choice) has caused to them, their families, friends, and coworkers.

Best Aspects of the Job

Many counselors who choose to work in inpatient addictions treatment are themselves recovering addicts, though not all counselors are in this category. Counselors who choose to work in residential addictions treatment enjoy the challenge in addressing and confronting addictive behaviors in a direct fashion. It is also accurate to mention that jobs in residential addictions treatment frequently come open due to the degree of difficulty in working with this population. Therefore, while many counselors working in this setting have been there long term, many beginning counselors also start their careers in residential addictions treatment, get experience, licensed, certified, and then move to an outpatient setting.

Challenging Aspects of the Job

Counseling in an inpatient residential addiction setting offers many challenges. Once again, as with other inpatient units, the treatment is milieu therapy. Basically, the counselor is "on" throughout the entire eight-hour shift, with few moments of separation from the patients. Counselors must always be aware of the patient's issues during each encounter, whether in group sessions or playing cards with the residents. Due to the degree of closeness in residential treatment, counselors must be ready to mediate arguments between patients, as conflict between patients (and between patients and staff) is common.

Finally, many residential treatment programs do not pay their staff well. Good salaries are typically a function of experience and licensure, with higher wages paid to directors and assistant directors.

Occupational Outlook and Salary

The Bureau of Labor Statistics (BOLS, 2010–2011) reports the growth rate of addictions counselors to be 21%, which is very positive for counselors seeking jobs in this field. The BOLS reports a median salary of $31,300 for in-patient addictions counseling, which is several thousand less than out-patient addictions treatment, which was reported by BOLS (2010–2011) to be $37,030. The reader can draw the conclusion that residential addictions treatment may be a good place to gain experience before either moving up in the setting or transferring to an outpatient clinic.

45. COUNSELOR FOR DEVELOPMENTALLY DISABLED

Counseling clients with developmental disabilities is a common job for a segment of the counseling profession. Working with developmentally disabled (DD) clients will be very different from counseling clients with mental illnesses.

Degree Required

Once again, many counselors will hold bachelor's degrees, though to have upward mobility in this segment of the counseling field, a master's degree is required. (For licensure purposes, a master's degree will be required in all 50 U.S. states, Washington, DC, and Puerto Rico.)

Issues to Understand

Counseling clients with DD is very different from counseling other segments of the population. Due to the nature of DD, a 30-year-old client will present as being far less mature than a 30-year-old person with depression. Counseling DD populations will require an ability to make concepts understandable to clients without seeming to insult them. Though DD clients are socially and intellectually deficient, they are people and their feelings can be as sensitive as anyone else's. Also, DD clients will need a lot of assistance in managing conflicts with fellow DD clients (as many live in supportive communal housing), in addressing issues with their families, and in understanding appropriate behavior in social settings. Many counselors will work in rehabilitation agencies or supportive work environments as a "job counselor" or a "life skills counselor or coach."

Like counselors of adults or adolescents with chronic mental illnesses, much of the counselors' work will involve addressing issues with family members. Counselors must be aware, however, that DD adult clients retain adult rights and can refuse the presence of their families in treatment rooms, prohibit their families' reading of their counseling file, and so on. Some family members may have gone to court and been granted "guardianship" over the DD client, however, and may be empowered to make treatment decisions along with the counselor.

Best Aspects of the Job

Counselors must enjoy the challenge of working with DD clients. Counselors must also be ready to advocate for their clients as much pejorative language still permeates all communities ("retard," "idiot," etc.). Many counselors working with DD clients simply enjoy the challenge of assisting one of the most vulnerable populations in society.

Challenging Aspects of the Job

Pay for counselors working with DD clients will likely be low. Counselors must also be prepared to address and mediate conflicts between DD clients and their family members who may have strong feelings of attachment with their family member. Naturally, families will be very concerned about the welfare of their DD relative. However, because DD clients will have adult rights (in most cases) and can choose to live their lives in the manner they see fit, conflicts will arise. Family members may even blame the counselor for the decisions the clients have themselves made. Counselors must also be prepared to address workplace issues with the clients, residential conflicts and concerns, and legal issues as some DD clients may have committed felonies.

Occupational Outlook and Salary

Most counselors (at least, counselors with master's degrees) working with DD clients likely work as rehabilitation counselors (though there are exceptions to this). For rehabilitation counselors (who work with a wide range of disabilities), the Bureau of Labor Statistics (BOLS) reports the occupational growth as 19% with a median salary of $30,930, which is on the low side for the field. For counselors working in residential treatment with DD clients, the median salary is $29,950. Now, it is likely that the BOLS has grouped counselors with BA/BS degrees with those with MS/MA. Counselors with master's degrees will certainly earn more in salary.

46. REHABILITATION COUNSELOR

Rehabilitation counselors work with a wide variety of clients with disabilities such as mobility restrictions, deafness/hard-of-hearing, chronically mentally ill, and many more.

Degree Required

Master's degree in rehabilitation counseling.

Issues to Understand

Rehabilitation counselors serve clients with a wide range of issues. They are expected to help disabled clients manage stressors in the workplace, schools, and universities, and assist clients in managing mental illnesses, addressing addictions, and many other issues. Training of rehabilitation counselors is separate from training of mental health counselors, school counselors, and so on. Readers interested in the field of rehabilitation counseling must be flexible and understanding in order to assist needy disabled populations. Rehabilitation counselors must also serve as advocates for their clients, particularly in educational institutions and in the workplace. Because the federal Section 504 of the Rehabilitation Code and the Americans with Disabilities Act mandate accommodations for the disabled and address discriminatory practices, rehabilitation counselors will occasionally be presented with violations of their clients rights.

Best Aspects of the Job

Rehabilitation counselors enjoy counseling disabled clients and assisting them in addressing the same types of mental health issues of other populations (e.g., addictions, depression, and anxiety). Rehabilitation counselors must also assist their clients in dealing with and managing their disability (hearing loss, sight loss, mobility restrictions, etc.) and be advocates for the disabled. Many rehabilitation counselors have a personal reason for going into the field, such as their own disability or a disabled family member, and a strong conviction to help vulnerable people.

Challenging Aspects of the Job

Helping disabled clients manage their disability and addressing other mental health issues, workplace issues, and such can be very stressful work. Rehabilitation counselors, though prominent in the counseling field, often receive less pay compared with other counseling professionals. Rehabilitation counselors should also have a good support system in order to manage the challenges of their job.

Occupational Outlook and Salary

The Bureau of Labor Statistics reports the growth rate of rehabilitation counselors at a positive 19%. This is a very good outlook though the median salary is $30,930, which is somewhat on the lower end of the pay scale for counselors. Achieving licensure and certification would be a way to move up in salary.

47. COUNSELOR FOR THE HOMELESS

Though a smaller part of the counseling field, many counselors work with homeless populations. Unfortunately, the homeless population appears to be growing (U.S. Conference of Mayors, 2007). Counselors working with the homeless may work in agencies, halfway houses, homeless shelters, and religious institutions (synagogues, churches, mosques, etc.).

Degree Required

Counselors with BA/BS degree work with the homeless, though once again, a master's degree in counseling is optimal (and required for state licensure).

Issues to Understand

Anyone who has worked with the homeless understands that there are numerous issues to negotiate: life on the street, mental illness, health issues, addictions, legal issues, and so on. It is likely that most homeless clients will also have at least one documented mental disorder (if not more) and struggle with multiple addictions. Many homeless clients also suffer from post-trauma as the result of experience on the battlefield, sexual assault, industrial accident, and so on (U.S. Conference of Mayors, 2007).

Counseling the homeless can also be a frustrating experience in that most homeless clients often drop out of therapy unexpectedly. Homeless clients also are a heterogeneous population. Homeless people residing in a shelter will differ from those living in a cardboard box in an alley or under a bridge. Many, if not most, homeless clients will be undernourished and in poor health for a variety of reasons, including exposure to the elements and addictions (U.S. Conference of Mayors, 2007).

Best Aspects of the Job

Because the job can seem so overwhelming, counselors working with the homeless must simply love the challenge of providing services for this most marginal of populations. Counselors will need to be good advocates for the homeless and be well versed in the addictions profession. Many counselors working with the homeless will work out of religious establishments and may offer shelter as well.

Challenging Aspects of the Job

The challenges, many of which are outlined in the section "Issues to Understand" above, are enormous. Salaries for counselors in this segment of the field are low. Counselors will also need to be prepared to manage the criticisms from larger society, much of whom will blame the homeless themselves for being homeless. Additional frustrations are that there are few shelters for this population, and food banks and religious institutions that serve food to the homeless are constantly overwhelmed and underresourced. Many communities will also be unsupportive of the counselor's work, as homeless people present as dirty, foul mouthed, and all too frequently panhandlers for money. To work with the homeless, you must simply see it as a "calling," much as Mother Theresa saw hers in Calcutta.

Occupational Outlook and Salary

Occupational outlook and salary are difficult to glean as the Bureau of Labor Statistics did not report statistics for counselors working with this population. My own experience in working with homeless people is that such positions pay very poorly. Many homeless shelters solicit volunteers to provide counseling (usually graduate students on internships, or recent graduates seeking additional hours for licensure).

9 Counseling in Private Practice

Making a switch from investment banker to counselor was viewed by many as going in the "wrong direction." To me, trading stocks and bonds was just not a very meaningful contribution to the planet. So, I chose to enter a counseling program at the University of Vermont. I knew upon entering that I was most likely going to pursue private practice since I was interested in the autonomy it offered, plus having spent my 20s in banking and finance, I was confident in my business acumen. What I did not predict was the path that befell me.

For the first 10 years postdegree, I created interesting mélanges of professional positions to accompany my small but growing private practice. I ran a statewide drug- and alcohol-prevention program, was an adjunct faculty member at the University of Vermont and area colleges, supervised graduate interns while seeing clients at the university counseling center, and presented a number of local and national workshops. This multifaceted career lifestyle suited me. It had the "craziness" of the New York Stock Exchange floor, appealing to my appetite for busy, dynamic, and engaging experiences.

Working part-time as a salaried university employee allowed for some aspect of my income to be consistent given the inconsistent financial ebb and flow of private practice. Furthermore, my university position provided health benefits and a built-in networking opportunity for colleagues to refer clients to my private practice.

A decade later, however, I was ready to concentrate on private practice. The challenges of private practice are numerous, ranging from cash flow challenges to managed care nightmares to being your own back-up coverage for clients in crisis. Agency work has several advantages, particularly collegial support. To prevent therapeutic isolation, it is imperative to find a solid group of practitioners as partners. My first venture into part-time practice was with another newly minted counselor. Although it was a good beginning for the most part, we both lacked the experience and the grounding of seasoned clinicians. My next practice was in a group of 12, social workers, counselors, and psychologists. I was the youngest both in age and in experience, and I learned a tremendous amount from this cohort of excellent psychotherapists. Some 10 years after that, I formed a practice with three colleagues with whom I had done peer supervision for years and this has turned out to be an excellent blend of clinical skills, use of theory in the practice, collegial support, and regular supervision. Most importantly, we all enjoy one another, making the workplace an exciting and supportive and enjoyable environment.

My clinical focus is on adolescents and families (young adults age 15 to 25), and this practically ensures that each hour is different from the next. I relish the opportunity to help young men and women successfully negotiate the path toward adulthood while partnering with parents in order to better address the needs of their children. Getting the pieces to align in private practice took far more time and effort than I would have imagined. Perhaps the most significant challenge for many of my peers and I is grappling with managed care. Most insurance companies are reimbursing counselors at the level of the 1990s. Many insurance companies have actually lowered their reimbursement rates due to market forces, while expenses such as office rent, technology, billing services, health and liability insurance, and utility expenses increase. These challenges have driven many private practice counselors to move to a fee-for-service system requiring clients to pay large fees out of pocket. Some counselors have left private practice altogether. Our practice continues to accept all insurance plans offered in Vermont as we realize the financial strain on families. Billing insurance, though challenging, provides us the ability to work with a wide variety of clients. I would be a less informed and less skilled counselor if I had not worked with some of the homeless, immigrants, and other marginalized members of my community.

I still augment my clinical work with lots of professional developmental activities. I have served as Chair of the Vermont Board of Allied Mental Health Practitioners, President of the Vermont Counseling Association, Treasurer of the American Association of State Counseling Boards, Director of the National Board for Certified Counselors, and Secretary of the Center for Credentialing and Education. These activities have allowed me to feel connected both to the practice and to the policy aspects of my profession and given me opportunities to shape the future of our field.

I imagine that in the next 15 to 20 years of professional activity, I will pursue more public speaking, sit on other professional boards, mentor new and experienced counselors, teach graduate counseling classes, and continue the clinical work that I enjoy immensely. Personally, this profession of counseling has been so wide in scope and so multifaceted that I believe that any student who catches the "counseling bug" is likely to be satiated personally and professionally well into their future.

48. COUNSELOR IN PRIVATE PRACTICE (SOLO)

Counselors working in private practice have expanded in the era of counselor licensure. Now that all 50 U.S. states, Washington, DC, and Puerto Rico have enacted counselor licensure, private practice has become a viable option for licensed counselors. There are many things to understand about private practice and how different it is from working in a school, agency, or hospital. For any counselor contemplating opening a private practice, Walsh and Dasenbrook's *The Complete Guide to Private Practice* is handy. Walsh and Dasenbrook also write a regular column on private practice in *Counseling Today*, the monthly magazine of the American Counseling Association.

Degree Required

Master's degree. Some counselors in private practice will also hold a doctoral degree (PhD or EdD). A license is also required in order to bill insurance.

Issues to Understand

Counseling in a private practice means you are essentially a small business owner. Like all business owners, you have to think about profit versus overhead. Profit comes in the way of individual, couples, family, and group counseling, as well as mediation services, professional coaching, and consultation. Overhead is represented by paying rent, utilities, equipment, Internet bills, paying to retain legal services, professional liability insurance, and so on. Unlike counseling in a school, agency, college, or hospital, you are responsible for all aspects of your operation. You will need to advertise, seek employee assistance program with corporations, and offer training in order to generate new business. Many counselors whom I have known have a regular job and use private practice to supplement their income, though some counselors operate a private practice as their sole income source.

Two major concerns of private practice lie in professional isolation (especially in a solo practice) and liability. In an agency or school, a counselor has numerous colleagues to consult with when challenging cases present themselves. In addition, a regular job at an agency means a regular paycheck, insurance benefits, and more protection from liability. Private practice means you have fewer colleagues to consult with, and in some cases, you will need to pay for consultation. You will also need to pay to retain the services of a lawyer, as well as having an attorney draw up papers to separate your practice from your personal property; otherwise, a lawsuit could wipe you out.

Best Aspects of the Job

The main draw to private practice is the ability to be your own boss. Being in private practice means that you can practice self-determination without a supervisor looking over your shoulder telling you what clients to take. Many other counselors also enjoy the ability to set their own schedule and to focus on areas of specialization. In agencies and schools, counselors must often take whatever client walks through the door. Though private practice might mean the same thing, private practitioners do have the ability to screen clients whom they find are not appropriate to their practice.

Challenging Aspects of the Job

You are responsible for everything. This means paying rent, maintaining equipment, being liable for everything in your practice, having to purchase your own health insurance, and making an individual retirement account. Consultation can be an issue, especially if you are in a solo practice.

Occupational Outlook and Salary

There will be wide variation in the earnings of private practitioners. Very successful private practitioners can make anywhere from $55,000 to $80,000 depending on how well known they are, diversity of services offered, advertising and word-of-mouth referrals, and their own skill level. Most private practitioners in a solo practice are likely to earn less than $50,000. In terms of occupational outlook, it is also likely that most counselors in private practice likely use their private practice to supplement their income from a regular job in a college, school, or agency. Finally, no counselor should undertake a private practice until she or he is licensed and has several years experience in the field. Experience at a school, agency, or college also provides necessary contacts for referral resources.

49. COUNSELOR IN PRIVATE PRACTICE (WITH ASSOCIATES)

Counseling in private practice with associates may likely be more viable than a solo practice. Working with associates (or partners) means that you are not professionally isolated and you have others to share the rent, utilities, assessment materials, and liability and have in-house referral resources.

Degree Required

Master's degree is the minimum. Some private practitioners will hold doctoral degrees. A license will also be required in order to bill insurance.

Issues to Understand

You will have partners to assist in bringing in clients and sharing expenses and liability. However, what if you do not get along with one or more of these partners? Also, if one partner gets sued, all partners could be dragged into the lawsuit as well. It is very important that you interview and carefully screen anyone you are considering taking on as a partner as the relationships in the practice are paramount. Another issue revolves around productivity. Some counselors will simply be more successful than others in generating clients, and this can generate hard feelings, especially as clients are the lifeblood of any private practice.

Best Aspects of the Job

Working in a private practice with people you like and respect is clearly a big draw for counselors. Private practice means you and your partners are responsible for operations, upkeep, and profit margins. A private practice should comprise several counselors, many of whom have different strengths and specialty areas, so as to maximize the range of clientele they can bring in the door.

Challenging Aspects of the Job

You and your partners are responsible for everything that happens, no matter how positive (profitability and a good name) or negative (lawsuit and bad press). In private practice, you need to be able to advertise, develop referral resources (with a psychiatrist), understand tax issues, retain an attorney, and address conflicts in the practice. You will also not have the safety net that an agency, school, or hospital offers, that is, your paycheck depends on your and your partners' ability to generate clients, and you will need to purchase your own insurance and individual retirement plan (unless your spouse or partner has these through their work).

Occupational Outlook and Salary

As previously mentioned, most counselors in private practice are using the practice as part-time employment to supplement their job in a school, agency, college, or hospital. Salaries will depend on what area of the country you live in and how much business you generate. Though some groups of counselors in private practice earn good money (say, $45,000 and above), most will need a second job to make the practice viable. In addition, no counselor should contemplate going into private practice until she or he is licensed and has several years of experience.

50. COUNSELOR IN EMPLOYEE ASSISTANCE PROGRAM

In today's counseling work force, a number of counseling professionals work in Employee Assistance Programs (EAPs), either in large corporations or as private practitioners who contract with businesses and industries. EAPs have become common and popular in some segments of society, especially in large corporations. EAP also holds some advantages over traditional practice in that it offers steady income for private practitioners or for counselors who work for a corporation EAP.

Degree Required

The master's degree is most common. A doctorate is not required although some EAP counselors will have one. License is required or, in some cases, a new graduate of a counseling program is hired and supervised by a licensed counselor, social worker, or psychologist.

Issues to Understand

While EAPs represent a good option for many counselors, they may also be somewhat limited. For example, you may believe the client needs more than say six to eight sessions to deal with their issue, the EAP contract is likely to be somewhat rigid where extended services are required. Counselors working in EAPs, or who provide EAP services through a contractual arrangement, may feel the terms of arrangement are not favorable to them. For example, many EAP contracts will pay the counselor less than she or he could charge non-EAP clients. While the EAP contract provides steady income, successful private practitioners may feel they are losing out on more profitable work.

Some EAPs are run in-house in large corporations, which means the counselor is an employee of that corporation. This may work very well, but counselors working in such private corporations will need to be vigilant to ensure that the confidentiality of the EAP employees is protected. Counselors in in-house EAP may also have to work to make inroads with employees who are reluctant to believe that counseling services will remain private and not shared with management.

Best Aspects of the Job

EAPs, whether contractual or in-house, offer steady work for counselors. For in-house EAPs, this also means a reliable paycheck, health benefits, and a retirement package. For EAP counselors in private practice, the steady income can be a big relief to private practitioners struggling to get established in a mental health profession crowded by private practitioners (counselors, social workers, psychologists, marriage and family therapists, psychiatrists, etc.).

Challenging Aspects of the Job

While EAPs have their advantages, they also have drawbacks. It has been noted that they will likely pay less per session than regular private pay clients. EAPs also can be somewhat rigid with regard to the types of services the counselor can offer. In-house EAP may also have some particular challenges. For example, what is the EAP's reputation among the corporation employees? Do the employees trust the counselors in the EAP to maintain privacy? Are there corporate executives who pressure the EAP staff for sensitive information? These are questions the counselors will need to grapple with if they are working in in-house EAPs.

Occupational Outlook and Salary

It is very difficult to estimate the occupational outlook for counselors working in in-house EAPs. Given that most U.S. citizens work for small businesses, few counselors are likely to find full-time employment in EAPs. Contracts for most counselors working with EAPs will be contracts for services. EAPs can definitely help private practitioners supplement their income. Regarding salary, counselors working full-time with EAPs will likely earn somewhere in the range for mental health counselors reported in the Bureau of Labor Statistics (median, $36,810).

10 Counseling in Corre(Institutions and the Legal Arena

Spotlight: Counseling in Correctional Settings
Correctional Counselor Spotlight: Leigh Falls Holman, PhD, LPCS, RPTS, NCC
Process Addictions Committee of the International Association of Addictions and Offender Counselors, Assistant Professor, Argosy University, Executive Director, First Lotus, Dallas, TX

Although now an assistant professor of counselor education and executive director of a group practice, a large part of my clinical experience was gained while working with individuals who were involved with the correctional system. Work in correctional settings may occur at different levels in the system. I have worked with probated adjudicated youth and adults, youth in juvenile detention facilities who were held at level-4 boot camp (day treatment) and level-5 boot camp (residential), and an adult prison setting. There appears to be a growing trend toward government funding moving from mental health settings to correctional settings, which indicates that counseling with adjudicated individuals will likely be a growing field for counselors.

Most counselors working with adjudicated populations are expected to work from a cognitive behavioral theoretical (CBT) perspective. Frequently, the programs involve a therapeutic-level system that rewards desired behaviors with more freedom or

leges, as well as increased responsibility for the client. This
n serve as a challenge if the counselor does not work out of that
paradigm. For instance, I work from the relational psychodynamic
theoretical perspective, but because I was trained using Edward
Teyber's interpersonal process in psychotherapy, I am able to integrate relational processing with CBT interventions. Based on my
experience, I believe it is possible to utilize the nomenclature of
CBT for the purposes of treatment planning and documentation of
services, even if the counselor conceptualizes the client dynamics
from a different theoretical orientation.

There are unique legal and ethical issues that counselors working with adjudicated populations need to be aware of regarding
informed consent, confidentiality, boundaries, assessment, and professional competency. First, professional competency in working
with offender populations frequently includes the need to obtain
specialized training and supervision. For instance, when I began
working with juvenile and adult sex offenders, I had to go through 40
hours of didactic training specific to working with these populations
and obtain 1,000 hours of experience under the supervision of a registered sex offender treatment provider before I could perform this
work independently. I also actively read literature published by the
Association for Treatment of Sexual Abusers and the International
Association of Addiction and Offender Counselors, among others. I
also attended conferences that were specific to the populations with
whom I worked and built networks of professionals that I consulted
with regarding legal, ethical, and treatment-related issues.

Because clients are generally court mandated, many believe
that they do not have a choice regarding consent to treatment. As a
treatment strategy, I always present treatment as the client's choice
even when they do not initially see it that way. It is, in fact, their
choice to participate in treatment or not, each choice bringing its
own consequences, but the choice belongs to the client. By empow-
ering the client to choose, he/she is also choosing to take responsibility for engaging in and progressing through the treatment program.
Informed consent for mandated clients also often includes more
limitations on confidentiality than for an average client because
of the need to share information with the facility and probation/
parole officers, and/or the potential for being subpoenaed to testify.
Additionally, it is important to remember that even if the correctional setting or judicial system is paying for the treatment, the individual who is receiving treatment is your client, not the system.

When obtaining informed consent, it is important that the client understand fully what treatment consists of; so I spend a good deal of time going through informed consent line by line, facilitating a discussion with the client that includes different realistic scenarios of how each area of the assessment, treatment, and limit to confidentiality may impact the client. Even when I worked with civilly committed sex offenders, they had the choice not to participate in treatment, which we would document with their signature on a form stating such each month. Many counselors entering the field do not realize that in certain settings, limits to confidentiality may include items beyond what they learn about in school. As long as the informed consent clearly outlines the limits and the client agrees to them, it is ethical and legal to limit confidentiality by informing other interested parties (the court, probation/parole, etc.) of the client's diagnosis, assessment, treatment goals, progress, and so forth.

Spending the time necessary to ensure my clients were truly signing an *informed* consent was invaluable in establishing and maintaining trust. When clients made choices resulting in negative consequences, they were more likely to accept the consequences as resulting from their choices, rather than placing responsibility on me or someone else for betraying their trust. This facilitated an ongoing therapeutic relationship even when there were potential relationship ruptures during the treatment process.

Clear therapeutic boundaries, which are important in all counseling relationships, are an absolute imperative when working in forensic settings. Adjudicated individuals frequently have personality disorders or are adept at interpersonal maneuvering that contributed to their criminal behaviors, and they will utilize the same interpersonal tactics to manipulate you as a counselor. Therefore, the ability to define and maintain clear therapeutic boundaries while also building a therapeutic rapport with the client is often a balancing act that is a constant challenge. It is important to build a therapeutic relationship on trust, respect, genuineness, accurate empathy, and unconditional positive regard, but it is also important to remember that you are dealing with individuals who frequently have serious mental health issues that may result in skewed perceptions and manipulative behavior. This balancing act is one of the reasons that interdisciplinary treatment teams and multiple counselors for individual, group, family, and so on are important, as well as ongoing case consultation and supervision, to help you identify when a client is using your therapeutic relationship to engage in these maladaptive interpersonal maneuvers so that they may be addressed in a therapeutic manner. When that happens—and in these settings, it will—I have found that it is best to use it as a therapeutic opportunity. It is a manifestation of the targeted treatment behavior and therefore a "here-and-now" opportunity to address in vivo the behavior in the context of a respectful genuine trusting therapeutic relationship.

Sociocultural diversity is also frequently an issue that must be addressed, given that most counselors are White, well-educated females and most clients are minority, poorly educated, and male. As a counselor in this system, it is important to continually be aware of potential bias that you may bring into counseling offenders from often very different backgrounds than your own. By being open to feedback from clients regarding my potential biases and facilitating genuine conversations about the power differentials inherent in issues of race, ethnicity, religion, gender, socioeconomic status, and so on, I was able to build sound, respectful relationships with the boys and men who were my clients. It also helped me grow immensely as a counselor, counselor educator, and human being.

One of the biggest challenges in working with offenders is the high level of stress and burnout that results. You are generally working in systems (corrections, detention centers, etc.) that are designed in such a way that it works against the therapeutic work you are attempting to engage in as a counselor. Although not always, frequently front-line staff (correctional officers, probation/parole officers, etc.) often do not have the training or supervision to deal with the clients in a therapeutic manner and thus often engage in activities that work at odds with therapeutic goals. Even the lawyers and judges can frustrate your counseling efforts in ways that are beyond your control. Additionally, the clients often have long-standing interpersonal problems, addictions, and other untreated mental health issues that make progress difficult to sustain. Therefore, it is crucial that a counselor in correction settings maintain a wellness plan to mediate against becoming an impaired professional due to burnout.

51. COUNSELOR IN COUNTY JAILS

Some counselors are now employed to provide services to inmates in county jails. While more counselors would likely find employment in state prisons or in juvenile detention centers, counselors employed to work in county correction seems more commonplace.

Degree Required

Master's degree in counseling. Many correctional institutions will also prefer experience and credentialing in addictions counseling.

Issues to Understand

As a counselor educator who has supervised many counseling interns in correctional settings and a former clinical director who supervised counselors working in corrections, I find that one critical issue to understand is that many corrections professionals will see mental health work as ancillary to corrections work. Counselors are also likely to view inmates in a very different light than are guards and general correctional staff. While counselors will often view inmates as "clients," they will be viewed as inmates serving a sentence by other jail personnel. Counselors will need to be diligent to dialogue with other jail staff regarding mental health issues of inmates. The correctional system in the United States was set up to be more punitive than rehabilitative, and counselors represent a recent change to this type of philosophy. Counselors will also need to work very hard to gain the trust of the inmates who may view them as authority figures as opposed to therapeutic professionals.

Best Aspects of the Job

The opportunity to assist inmates in breaking the cycle of addiction and recidivism is perhaps the best part of the job. Counselors working in correctional settings must also be people who relish the opportunity to create understanding in an institution not noted for discernment.

Challenging Aspects of the Job

As one might expect, counseling in a county jail carries with it many challenges. For example, inmates have all been charged, and some convicted and sentenced for crimes. Many of the inmates will be in the jail as a transition to prison and may not be amenable to counseling. Others will be serving shorter periods of time (usually less than six months) and may be more interested in counseling. Some inmates have little family to visit and others may have been abandoned by their families due to shame. Any counselor who has worked in correctional settings is likely to say that drug use is rampant. This all adds up to the counselor needing to work to create trust so that inmates will feel like talking to counselors.

Occupational Outlook and Salary

Though the Bureau of Labor Statistics did not cite figures for counselors in correctional facilities, my own sense is that more counselors are being hired to work in county jails to assess inmates' mental functioning and provide various types of counseling. Furthermore, most counselors do not want to work in corrections settings, and this means that counselors interested in this population will likely have a good opportunity to get hired. Acquiring experience and credentialing in addictions counseling is a good idea for counselors interested in a career in corrections. Regarding salary, my experience is that county jails often pay higher than average wages in order to attract counselors.

52. COUNSELOR IN PRISONS

More counselors are being hired to work in state and federal prisons. Though the work will be similar to counseling in a county jail, inmates in prisons will be serving longer sentences.

Degree Required

Master's degree in counseling is required. Experience and credentialing in addictions counseling are advantageous.

Issues to Understand

Similar to counseling in a county jail, counselors working in prisons must combat the "correctional" mentality (emphasis mine) of some prison staff who view inmates as subhuman and persons in need of punishment more than anything else. Counselors working in prisons will have to work hard to establish trust with the inmates who may fear that counselors will simply be "spies" of the administration. Addictions will be commonplace in prisons and counselors must be versed in addictions treatment. Sexual abuse is also common in prisons, and counselors will need to work with victims and prison staff to help reduce sexual assault.

Best Aspects of the Job

Prisons provide counselors the opportunity to make a difference in the lives of inmates, many of whom have led very troubled lives. Counselors also can serve as a bridge between the inmates and their families and prepare inmates for the day they are released back into society. Many prisons will provide counselors the opportunity to do individual, group, and addictions counseling, as well as counseling on addictions, post-traumatic stress disorder, depression, and major mental illness. In fact, over 50% of prisoners may have a documented mental illness (Eckholm, 2006).

Challenging Aspects of the Job

Are you prepared to work in a correctional setting harboring violent offenders, including pedophiles? Do you have the confidence to mediate disputes between inmates and between inmates and staff? How good are you at detecting dishonesty and minimization? These are all common issues you will need to address should you choose to work in this counseling field. The counselors who survive and thrive in prisons are the ones who feel challenged at meeting these demands and are not fearful of encountering them. Basically, you will need to be assertive without being punitive.

Occupational Outlook and Salary

Occupational outlook, though not addressed by the Bureau of Labor Statistics, seems to be improving for counselors desiring to work in prisons. The American Counseling Association even has a division devoted to counselors working in prisons. My own experience is that most counselors are uncomfortable working in prisons, so those interested will have a good chance to be hired. Experience in addictions counseling is helpful as is experience with trauma. Salaries in state and federal prisons will likely exceed those in most public mental health facilities.

53. COUNSELOR IN JUVENILE DETENTION FACILITIES

Counseling in juvenile detention facilities has been more common than that in jails and prisons. Juvenile detention is often the setting of last resort before an adolescent is sent to prison.

Degree Required

Master's degree in counseling.

Issues to Understand

Juveniles placed in detention will, like adult inmates, often be mistrustful of counselors and other mental health professionals and view them as authority figures. Counselors must establish their primary role as therapeutic staff as opposed to general correctional staff. Juvenile detention will require counselors to work in groups, as well as individually. Some family work will be required as most juveniles will be released either to their families or to foster care. As in jails and prisons, counselors will have to combat the perception that adolescents placed in juvenile detention are "bad" kids. Many of the adolescents in detention will be survivors of sexual abuse, neglect, and addictions. This does not excuse their choices and actions, but it does provide an understanding of the complex issues faced by many adolescents.

Best Aspects of the Job

Providing adolescents the chance to turn their lives around before moving them to prisons is the best part of this position. Many adolescents will also be isolated, lonely, and depressed and may be relieved that counseling staff are there to provide a listening ear.

Challenging Aspects of the Job

Working with ungrateful youth can be very challenging for counselors (most of whom are very idealistic). Like older prison populations, many adolescents in juvenile detention have become cynical and are suspicious at attempts to provide "help." It is also fair to state that a good percentage of residents in juvenile detention have been sexually, physically, and verbally abused. Post-trauma will be common, and bullying is likely to be a common issue in juvenile detention. Counselors will also need to address unsympathetic staff who see counselors as ancillary or "unnecessary" staff. Community members may view the counselor's roles in a negative manner preferring to view adolescents in juvenile detention as "bad" kids needing punishment.

Occupational Outlook and Salary

There are few statistics available on job openings, though counselors interested in working with adolescents in juvenile detention can find jobs, provided they are willing to relocate. With the movement of charging adolescents as adults, juvenile detention may receive less funding, which means less counseling positions. Some residential psychiatric treatment centers may also serve as ad hoc detention centers. Salaries may be roughly similar to those in general mental health clinics.

54. FORENSIC COUNSELOR

In the past, forensic work was exclusively the domain of psychiatrists and clinical psychologists with regard to the mental health professions. In recent years, however, counselors have made some inroads in the forensic field. Many counselors now work in correctional settings, generally state prisons, county jails, and psychiatric detention centers. Now that all 50 U.S. states and major territories license counselors, it is likely that more counselors will gravitate to forensic roles.

Degree Required

A master's degree in counseling or a related field is required; most likely, a master's degree in clinical mental health counseling. Counselors interested in this line of work should also check with the National Board for Forensic Counselors, who offer a certification in this area.

Issues to Understand

There is still much growth to be made before this becomes a major specialty in the counseling field. While counselors certainly are working with inmate populations, the major assessment work is likely to be carried out by a clinical psychologist. However, as this counseling field matures, counselors will likely take over simpler areas of assessment and be supervised by psychologists.

Best Aspects of the Job

Counselors interested in forensic work should understand that it is not quite as breathtaking as Jodie Foster's character in *Silence of the Lambs* (fortunately!).

You will also be working with sex offenders, violent inmates, and other adjudicated populations who will not want your intervention. Counselors interested in this type of work will need to be resilient in the face of unremorseful offenders and must understand that "success" may mean you are protecting vulnerable third parties (e.g., children).

Challenging Aspects of the Job

As mentioned previously, counselors working in this area will often work with inmates and other persons charged with violent crimes. You will need to develop a "thick" skin so that you are not intimidated by violent offenders and, at the same time, remain open to the possibility that some inmates will indeed be willing to change their behavior. You will also be working alongside corrections staff, such as guards, prison administrators, and probation officers, many of whom may have become cynical about their jobs and the population they work with.

Occupational Outlook and Salary

Like many segments of the counseling field, hard figures are difficult to come by. However, I have noticed more counselors who are employed by prisons and juvenile detention centers. It is also realistic to state that most counselors and social workers do not want to work in this area and thus jobs may become more available over time. The American Counseling Association has a divisional affiliate organization (Association for Addictions and Offender Counselors) devoted to this particular specialty area, and they publish professional journals. Regarding salary, my limited experience in talking with counselors working in this field is that the pay is comparable to that of mental health counselors, so a median salary around $35,000 is not far off.

55. COUNSELOR AS DIVORCE MEDIATOR

Counselors have long provided services related to counseling. A recent popular service that many counselors, or many professionals trained in counseling, offer is mediation. Currently, there are few graduate programs in mediation, so mediators come from many fields such as law, social work, business, criminal justice, and, of course, counseling.

Degree Required

Master's degree in a counseling field is optimal.

Issues to Understand

Mediation is similar to counseling, though distinctly different from therapeutic work. Now, many counselors, especially those who work with couples, often provide "informal" mediation as part of their counseling work. Divorce mediators are a separate branch of mediation work who assist divorcing couples (or domestic partners) dissolving their relationship. Mediators can assist ex-partners from lengthy court battles and help make transition from couple to ex-couples a little smoother. The role as divorce mediator, however, is not therapeutic. So the mediator would need to make a referral should one or both parties need counseling.

Challenging Aspects of the Job

Divorce mediators assist ex-couples in the separation process of their relationship. This fact means that mediators must be "grounded" professionals able to manage conflict without taking that conflict on in a personal manner. As a counselor who has provided mediation services to couples who were breaking up, I find that it is very natural for both members to try to elicit the mediator to side with them over the ex-partner. Mediators must be vigilant to recognize and refrain from any behavior that would seem to align them with one party over another. Of course, the mediator can do a fantastic job of even-handedness and still the perception by one party could be that the mediator favored the other party. Because people involved in divorce mediation are often hurting from the break up, such sentiments are commonplace.

Best Aspects of the Job

The best part of the job likely is the satisfaction that you helped a couple from a more acrimonious breakup. Because children may also be involved, establishing a working relationship between the ex-partners is crucial. After all, with children, ex-spouses and partners may need to remain in contact for several years. Many divorce mediators I have met through my own work take divorce mediation work as very challenging and this provides a sense of professional pride.

Challenging Aspects of the Job

Anyone working with couples in the process of breaking up has, by nature, a difficult and, often, stressful job. Like counseling in the corrections field, this work is not for all counselors. Divorce mediators will need to clearly and firmly establish the "ground rules" for mediation sessions so as to limit the verbal "sniping" that is all too common in such situations. Furthermore, the mediator must be able to understand when the ex-couple needs a break from mediation sessions. While teaching in a counseling program in Australia, I recall a divorce mediator (also a counselor) express that a mediator is part counselor, part teacher, part rabbi (or priest or other spiritual leader), and part referee. The facility to utilize these roles may go a long way in determining how successful the mediator is in assisting the couple end their relationship with dignity and lessen the infighting.

Occupational Outlook and Salary

The Bureau of Labor Statistics lists no statistics for divorce mediators. Occupational outlook will vary widely depending on the geographic location. Salaries will also depend on the type of agency (and how well funded it is) and the experience of the divorce mediator.

56. COUNSELOR AS THERAPEUTIC MEDIATOR

Mediation has quickly become a broad field (Barsky, 2004). Mediators provide many services distinct from counseling (such as divorce mediation just previously highlighted), though counselors are also now being trained to provide "therapeutic" mediation. Therapeutic mediation occurs with a couple in the context of relationship counseling. While many counselors provide this informally, therapeutic mediation has become a formal part of the training many counselors now receive in their graduate program or as certification training.

Degree Required

Master's degree in one of the counseling fields.

Issues to Understand

Therapeutic mediation is natural for any counselor who works with couples or families (Barsky, 2004). Most counselors, although holding a master's degree in the field and a license, are likely not ready to provide therapeutic mediation without additional training (Barsky, 2004). Therapeutic mediation is a type of mediation work that combines mediation with counseling work. It involves role plays to teach couples how to recognize conflict at early stages and then how to negotiate their way through conflict. Mediation basically means both parties agree to give something in order to get something. This willingness to compromise seems very difficult for many couples.

Best Aspects of the Job

Therapeutic mediation provides couples in conflict the opportunity to address conflict in the context of counseling. Therapeutic mediation also means the couple gets to continue to work with the counselor with whom they already have an existing relationship (provided that counselor has been trained in therapeutic mediation).

Challenging Aspects of the Job

As with many other types of mediation work, therapeutic mediation means the counselor is in the middle of the couple's conflict.

Counselors providing therapeutic mediation must develop the ability to make conflict work as a catalyst for the counseling relationship (Barsky, 2004). Conflict must then be viewed as a tool by the counselor and eventually by the couple if compromise and change are to occur. (If the couple can be coached to accept conflict as a tool, this may well prove an important ingredient in their relationship.)

Occupational Outlook and Salary

It is likely that virtually all counselors providing therapeutic mediation and working in outpatient settings (clinics, private practice, etc.) provide mediation services as part of their job. Therefore, occupational outlook is probably comparable to the Bureau of Labor Statistics projections on mental health counselors or marriage and family counselors/therapists (at 25% growth [which is very good]) and the salary is likely to be comparable as well (median income around $35,000 depending on years of experience).

57. COUNSELOR AS PROBATION WORKER

Counselors have worked as probation workers for some time. Though probation workers are likely to come from fields such as criminal justice and social work, counselors are also employed in this field.

Degree Required

Many professionals with baccalaureate degrees work in probation and parole. A master's degree in one of the counseling fields (clinical mental health counseling, school counseling, etc.) is optimal for future promotion.

Issues to Understand

As with many occupations in this section of the book, the job of probation worker is very different from that of a counselor. While both counselors and probation workers will spend much of their time listening and problem solving, the probation worker's focus is more geared to legalities and less on therapy. Probation workers will spend their time with offenders who have either been paroled or been convicted of a felony but not given jail or prison time. Because many issues, violent or otherwise, involve drugs or alcohol, a counseling background could be an advantage. Still, a probation department will be staffed with corrections and criminal justice professionals who are likely to have a philosophy different from that of counselors.

Best Aspects of the Job

Years ago, I worked with a probation officer who had a number of sex offenders on his caseload. "I tell myself my job is about protecting kids" he exclaimed, "else I might not be motivated to work in this field." I suspect that many probation officers will reframe their job in a manner similar to my former colleague. I also have known many juvenile probation officers who saw their job as trying to help wayward youth before they wound up in a prison. Other probation workers are likely to cite the challenges of working with convicted felons, protecting society, or something similar.

Challenging Aspects of the Job

Like all the careers in this section of the book, there will be many challenges to deal with. First, probation workers work directly with adolescents and adults who have gotten into legal trouble and are on a "short leash" with the legal system. Veteran probation workers are likely to instruct beginning probation workers to develop a strong sense of skepticism regarding the excuses and stories clients on their caseload provide for their difficulties. However, effective probation workers must, at the same time, remain open to encouraging and promoting positive change. The reality of course is that many people on probation will reoffend and return to a correctional environment. It is very difficult to see a client make significant gains (finish degree, get a job, create healthy relationship, etc.) and then watch them reoffend and return to prison. Recidivism is going to be very common, so counselors interested in this type of career will need to be very resilient or else they will not last long in this field.

Occupational Outlook and Salary

The occupational outlook is very good for probation officers, with the Bureau of Labor Statistics (BOLS, 2010–2011) predicting 19% growth rate over the next 7 to 10 years. The BOLS reports the median salary for probation workers at $45,910, so the salary is competitive.

58. COUNSELOR IN THE RESTORATIVE JUSTICE FIELD

Restorative justice has become very popular in many communities in the United States. Restorative justice is similar to mediation, though with the intent of an offender making verbal, financial, and moral restitution to the person or persons he or she has hurt.

Degree Required

Master's degree in one of the counseling fields.

Issues to Understand

Restorative justice is a very common and popular option in which offenders meet victims to apologize and take responsibility for the suffering they have caused. A therapeutic background would seem to be an advantage, as the mediator, advocate, or someone with such titles needs to be able to move conversation through emotionally difficult stages. Restorative justice professionals will work with the court system, juvenile department, parole and probation, corrections system, social services, and religious institutions. The linchpin in this type of work is to facilitate responsibility on the part of the offender (be it financial, emotional, etc.) and a sense of justice on the part of the victim.

Best Aspects of the Job

A popular variation in the restorative justice field is the Victim Offender Reconciliation Program (VORP), a national program providing restorative justice work at the community level. I have known several VORP workers and most stated their occupational satisfaction came from providing a forum for the offender and victim to meet. (Note that both parties must agree to the meeting, and the VORP worker must believe the offender is ready to take responsibility and that the victim, or victims, is ready to meet the offender.) In an ideal meeting, the offender will take ownership of her or his offense, and the victim will feel some sense of justice having taken place.

Challenging Aspects of the Job

There are likely to be variations on responsibility and justice. Many offenders will take only partial responsibility for their actions, and victims may express they do not feel a sense of justice. Anger, frustration, and occasional outright hostility will sometimes be expressed by the victims. In some cases, the restorative justice professional will become a natural target for both victims and offenders to vent their anger upon. Counselors interested in this type of career will need to be able to set clear boundaries, the ability to assess whether a victim–offender meeting is a good idea, and prepare both offender and victim for the meeting. Restorative justice workers will also need to be able to explain to their friends, colleagues, and neighbors why restorative justice is a viable option, given that the correctional mentality usually involves punishment. Naturally, many offenders will reoffend and this can be challenging for the restorative justice professional.

Occupational Outlook and Salary

The Bureau of Labor Statistics does not yet compile statistics for restorative justice specialists. Most likely the job would pay less than parole and probation specialists, due to the relative newness of the field. Occupational outlook is also difficult to assess at this point.

59. COUNSELOR AS PROBATION OFFICER

Similar to a parole officer, the probation officer works with offenders who have been convicted of a crime, including those who have been released from jail or prison. The probation officer differs from the parole officer in that parole officers usually work with inmates who will/may be discharged from a correctional setting, whereas probation officers work entirely with former inmates and others who have been convicted, served their time in prison or made restitution, and continue to be under a "probationary" period.

Degree Required

BA/BS. Master's degree in counseling or a related field is preferred.

Issues to Understand

Once again, for professionals who have been trained in counseling or a related field, working in corrections or a justice field is a very different environment. The role of a probation officer may include referrals for counseling and assessment, but the focus of the probation officer is to ensure that the offender follows the conditions of her or his parole. Probation officers are likely to have a large caseload (40–60 persons is a rough estimate) and short meetings with each person (say 15–20 minutes) plus follow-up with employers, family members, the employment office, and so forth will be required.

Best Aspects of the Job

It is likely that many probation officers cite protecting the public as one of the high points of their job. Others may include assisting former inmates in finding viable alternatives to crime. Naturally, one concrete aspect in reducing recidivism is viable employment, including education and training. An understanding of this and the ability to network with potential employers is very important. Probation officers will need to hold their clients accountable for actions and inactions related to the conditions of their probation.

Challenging Aspects of the Job

Many of the offenders on parole are likely to reoffend and wind up back in prison. This very fact can make many probation officers cynical and wonder if they are making a difference. Many people on parole will also lie to probation officers because they are violating parole conditions (common violations include theft, alcohol and drug use despite having sobriety as a parole condition, contacting former victims, not looking for employment, and carrying a weapon). Probation officers will need to develop a strong sense of resilience in the face of recidivism. Resilience can also be aided by joining professional organizations, a strong support network, and hobbies and recreational pursuits.

60. GANG-PREVENTION COUNSELOR

A gang-prevention counselor is another example of a counseling/criminal justice hybrid job. As gangs have become ubiquitous in U.S. cities, efforts to reduce gang activity and gang violence have intensified. Gang-prevention counselors are likely to work with the police, schools, neighborhood block clubs, churches and religious institutions, and human services organizations.

Degree Required

BA/BS. A master's degree in counseling or a related field is optimal for occupational mobility.

Issues to Understand

Though counseling programs train graduate students to become counselors, many related jobs such as gang-prevention counseling will require a different, though related, set of skills. Good communication skills, active listening, empathy, and a nonjudgmental attitude are all attributes the gang-prevention counselors employ. Instead of psychotherapy, however, the focus will be on working to reduce gang involvement and activity. Counselors interested in this field need to develop a good sense of why adolescent males join gangs (sense of belonging, strong social connections, mentoring, etc.) and understand the societal forces that increase gang activity (poverty, run-down neighborhoods, racism, unemployment, lack of hope for the future, etc.). Gang-prevention counselors will need to take a broad approach to addressing gang activity by outreach activities to schools, churches and other religious institutions, neighborhood organizations, social clubs (YWCA, YMCA, etc.), PTA organizations, and to gang members themselves.

Best Aspects of the Job

Probably, one of the best aspects of the job is a sense that you are helping to reduce gang violence in some small way. Counselors who can entice a gang member or potential gang member to seek education (college, community college, vocational/technical school, etc.) are likely to have the most luck. Many churches and social and educational organizations are also likely to be supportive of your work.

Challenging Aspects of the Job

Readers of this book should certainly be aware by now that there are no easy counseling jobs. Working to assist people in changing their lives has never been easy; otherwise, recidivism would not be such a problem. Gang-prevention counselors are likely to discover that gangs are popular because they provide adolescent males with many vital connections that are otherwise missing from their lives: as mentioned, sense of belonging, identity, purpose, social connections, and so on. Of course, gangs pervert these otherwise positive attributes and use them to construct a life of violence that results in serious injury, incarceration, and likely a violent, untimely death. A frustration that many gang-prevention counselors grapple with is the fact that gang members and potential gang members do not see education and legitimate careers as viable in their communities and their personal lives. In fact, these are significant factors why gangs exist. Counselors working with gangs are also going to experience the heartbreak of losing many of their clients to a violent death on the street, and it will take significant resilience to remain active in this field. Still, many people choose to work in gang reduction due to the very fact they have witnessed friends, teammates from athletic programs, and relative who lost their lives due to gang violence.

Occupational Outlook and Salary

The Bureau of Labor Statistics does not report statistics for gang-prevention counselors. This field likely is part of law enforcement, and salaries will probably vary widely depending on municipal budgets. Occupational outlook is also difficult to assess.

61. COUNSELOR AS VICTIM'S RIGHTS ADVOCATE

Victim's rights advocates are often employed by law enforcement programs (e.g., sheriff's department, city police, and state department) as opposed to mental health clinics. Like most of the counseling-oriented careers in this section of the book, these counselors will work closely with law enforcement and corrections, which certainly is a different culture compared with traditional mental health work.

Degree Required

BA/BS degree. Master's degree in counseling or a related field may be required in many regions and will offer more occupational mobility.

Issues to Understand

A victim's advocate job will involve some active listening and basic counseling, though the focus will be less on mental health and more on a justice perspective. A recent student of mine went into a victim's rights position, and her job included counseling victims and their families, as well as providing advocacy work for them with police forces, the court parole hearings, and so on. So, for many professionals going into this line of work, mental health training could be very beneficial, as many victims or their family members will be traumatized. Victim's rights workers who can calm and reassure victims and facilitate victims in the justice process can be very effective.

Best Aspects of the Job

My former student and some of her colleagues expressed that supporting and advocating for victims, many of whom are forgotten in the legal process, is the most fulfilling part of their job. Victims often face hostility from neighbors, the press, and a legal system focused more on punishing the offender while giving less attention to the victims. In many cases, when the offender has been convicted and sentenced (or not convicted in many cases), the victims still have to bear emotional scars from the offense. Victim's advocates then step in to help address these residual needs.

Challenging Aspects of the Job

No matter how well victim's advocates do their job, many victims will continue to experience significant trauma and will feel that a lack of justice has been done. Even when offenders have been punished and incarcerated, the victim may feel that the punishment did not match the offense. The family members of murdered victims, for example, are unlikely to feel that justice has been served. Rape victims may feel similar, and victims of white-collar crime, such as embezzlement, where people have lost their life savings, their jobs, homes, and so on, may continue to be embittered.

Occupational Outlook and Salary

There are no reported figures from the Bureau of Labor Statistics, so salary and occupational outlook are difficult to determine.

11 Counseling in the Military

Spotlight: Counseling Military Veterans and Their Families
Military Counseling Spotlight: David L. Fenell, PhD, Professor of
Counselor Education, University of Colorado at Colorado Springs; and
Colonel (retired), U.S. Army Medical Service Corps Reserve

The global war on terrorism is in its tenth year. During those 10 years, well over one million service members have been deployed to Afghanistan, Iraq, and surrounding Middle Eastern countries to interdict terrorist operations and prevent a recurrence of the tragedy of September 11, 2001. Many of these service members have been deployed two, three, or even four or more times since the beginning of the war. Many have participated in or witnessed violence, death, injury, and destruction that most civilians cannot comprehend. The impact of combat changes all who participate in it and affects some more intensely than others. Reports suggest that up to 30% of the returning combat veterans need some level of counseling support to help integrate and assimilate their combat experiences. Moreover, all the veterans deployed to the combat zone leave family members behind, including wives, children, parents, and siblings, who may also be in need of counseling services for the problems that develop during the separations. The need for professional counseling services is great.

Counselors who serve military personnel and their families require a unique skill set to augment their traditional counseling expertise. First, counselors should be familiar with the military culture. They must be able to communicate that they value the mission of the client, to defeat the enemy by means of force and violence. Not all therapists agree with the politics of the war; however, to effectively support returning veterans and their families, the counselor must be able to employ multicultural counseling skills that permit the service provider to set his or her values aside while identifying strengths in the veterans they counsel and building upon those strengths. Well-qualified military-friendly civilian counselors are in high demand. Some military personnel are judgmental about help seeking and attach the stigma of weakness to those in their unit who seek mental health treatment. Stigma is especially strong in front-line combat units, especially those in the Marine Corps and Army. Because of the stigma associated with mental health treatment, many returning warriors fail to obtain needed services or, on a positive note, seek services in the civilian community where confidentiality can be ensured. Civilian therapists need strategies to publicize their availability, specialties, and skills.

I have been an ardent supporter of the military and the role the armed forces play in supporting and defending the Constitution of the United States against all enemies, both foreign and domestic. My father was an Air Force pilot in World War II and the Korean and Vietnam Wars. My son is currently an infantry officer serving as a major in the Marine Corps. He has had two deployments to Iraq. Our daughter served four years as a surface warfare officer in the Navy. My wife's father served in World War II and the Korean and Vietnam Wars as an army officer, and my wife's mother was an Army nurse in World War II. Thus, it was natural that I would follow in this tradition and enter the military. I served during the Vietnam era, becoming an army behavioral sciences officer in 1988, after receiving my PhD. I have served combat tours in both Afghanistan and Iraq. Much of my recent work as a counselor educator has been in preparing civilian therapists to serve our military families as they respond to the challenges of multiple combat deployments and family separations.

Over the years, many graduates of counseling programs have asked how they can become uniformed behavioral sciences officers in one of the military services. My answer is always a disappointment to them and to me. At the present time, the only graduate degrees accepted by the Department of Defense for commissioned, active duty mental health service providers are the doctorate in clinical or counseling psychology or the master's of social work. Of course, psychiatrists and psychiatric nurses provide uniformed mental health services as well.

However, there are other ways for professional counselors to serve our military population. I have already described the crucial role of the private practitioner in providing services to veterans and families who seek a confidential therapeutic relationship that is not known to their fellow warriors. This allows the clients to avoid the stigma associated with receiving mental health services and being identified as weak.

Another way counselors can serve the military is to be hired by one of the contracting companies such as MHN Government Services. MHN Services places qualified counselors around the globe in consultant roles in support of returning service members and their families. Moreover, all military installations have education offices that provide career and academic counseling for veterans and their families. Professional counselors with a specialty in career counseling may qualify for these positions. School counselors who work in districts near military installations provide invaluable services to military children and their parents. Finally, the Department of the Army and the Department of Veterans Affairs recently opened career tracks and therapy positions for professional counselors. There are two areas of increasing need in the Department of Veterans Affairs. The first area is rehabilitation counseling for returning service members who have been wounded in combat. The second area of growth is addictions counseling, which is to provide services to returning veterans with substance abuse problems. More positions should be available in these agencies and announced during the next year.

Our military personnel have served the nation honorably in combat for the last 10 years and in all our nation's previous conflicts. Some of these veterans and their family members require counseling assistance when the service member returns from combat. There is no better feeling for a professional counselor than to be able to serve our nation by serving our veterans and their family members in responding to the challenges that have emerged during the combat deployment. The need for mental health services for the military population will continue to grow in the future as disturbing memories of battle emerge unexpectedly and as the demand for Department of Veterans Affairs services increases as the military begins a drawdown of personnel in response to the nation's economic problems. Whether treating active duty military personnel or those who have left the service, professional counselors are skilled metal health service providers and are well equipped to respond to the counseling needs of military clients both today and in the future.

62. COUNSELOR FOR THE MILITARY

Due to recent governmental action, especially counselors being approved to work in Veterans Affairs (VA) hospitals and recently being approved to bill TRICARE (the military's version of Medicare) without the formerly required physician referral, the U.S. military is a market just beginning to open for counselors.

Career opportunities for counselors interested in serving military personnel has improved, but options still are somewhat restricted. The armed forces commission only doctorate-level psychologists and professionals holding a master's degree in social work. But there are other ways for professional counselors to serve the military. Private health care contractors such as MHN Services place qualified counselors around the globe in consultant roles in support of returning service members and their families. Moreover, all military bases have education offices that provide career and academic counseling for veterans and their families. Recently, the Department of the Army and the Department of Veterans Affairs, opened career tracks for professional counselors. There are two areas of particular need in the VA. The first area is in rehabilitation counseling for returning service members wounded in combat. The second area of growth is in addictions counseling, providing services to returning veterans with substance abuse problems. Additional positions should be available in the VA, Army, and with private contractors in the future. In addition, some private, nonprofit independent agencies, sometimes called "Veterans Counseling Center," also hire licensed counselors for mental health and addictions work.

Degree Required

A master's degree in clinical mental health counseling, rehabilitation counseling, addictions counseling, or another related degree. Additional training and certification in trauma counseling is highly recommended due to the large number of traumatized battlefield veterans.

Issues to Understand

The military and veterans administrations are large bureaucracies with multiple branches and likely to be more rigid than most settings where counselors are employed. The primary focus of the military is the stated goal of protecting the country from threats from within and beyond the borders. Counselors having served in the military, who have military family members, or who grew up as children of a military parent or parents are often good candidates to counsel military personnel or returning veterans. It is likely fair to state that soldiers are more likely to trust counselors who have served in the armed forces.

Best Aspects of the Job

For some counselors, the opportunity to support and assist the men and women who serve in the armed forces would be a common answer. Given the U.S. involvement in the dual wars in Iraq and Afghanistan, this also means providing treatment to soldiers suffering from complex post-traumatic stress disorders as a result of the battlefield or in medical units that treat severely injured soldiers, counseling veterans struggling with addictions, or, just as importantly, counseling the family members of military service members serving in a war zone.

Challenging Aspects of the Job

Counseling in a governmental contractor such as MHN will present many challenges. One issue is whose needs come first: the soldier, contractor, or that of the military? How does seeking counseling impact a soldier's career? What if a client discloses being sexually harassed by an officer or supervisor in a leadership position; will the contractor or the military take that accusation seriously? Will an accusation of sexual harassment actually impair the accuser's career? The military and some governmental contractors have long held very prejudicial views against gay and lesbian soldiers (who have always served in the military, albeit in a closeted manner). While it is no longer a court-martial offense and "don't ask, don't tell" has been done away with, homophobic traditional sentiments continue to run strong in the military.

Occupational Outlook and Salary

Teasing out exact figures from the Bureau of Labor Statistics for counseling military personnel is difficult. Soliciting information from contractors upfront is a critical need for counselors looking to work with active duty personnel.

One additional bit of information is worth noting. As previously mentioned, counselors are currently barred from serving as "active duty" mental health professionals in the armed forces. This may not always be the case as licensed counselors, who were once barred from working in VA hospitals, are now being recruited to work in them. Counselors interested in repealing the current restriction against active duty counselors in the military should join the American Counseling Association and help lobby the military. Counselors should also be activists and pressure their congressional representatives (e.g., members of the U.S. Senate and House of Representatives) to change this. Remember, things *do* change, but often slowly and only with persistent work.

63. COUNSELOR FOR VETERANS AFFAIRS HOSPITALS

As previously mentioned, the newest segment of society now hiring counselors is the Veterans Affairs. It was only in 2007 that counselors were approved to work in VA hospitals, and only in 2010 that advertising to hire counselors began. Counselors and social workers share the same pay grade.

Degree Required

Master's degree in clinical mental health counseling from a CACREP accredited program.

Best Aspects of the Job

Though I have no data to go on, given the newness of this occupational area, I would expect that counselors serving in VA hospitals would cite many of the same reasons as their close colleagues counseling in the armed services, such as the opportunity to assist men and women who have been injured in service to their country.

Challenging Aspects of the Job

Any member of the military or family member who has visited a VA hospital will likely express a variety of opinions on the standard of care in VA centers. Some VA hospitals are well funded and well maintained, while others are marginally funded and the standard of care is something less. A few years back, an unflattering video of care at Walter Reed Hospital made the rounds of TV news and the Internet. It is fair to say that some VA hospitals do a very good job in treating the needs of veterans and some do not.

Any nonmedical professional serving in a medical center is prone to face some degree of competition from their medical colleagues. I have known psychologists and social workers serving in hospitals who have complained their work and opinions are taken less seriously than that of physicians, nurses, and other medical personnel. This is likely to be an issue in VA hospitals as well.

Occupational Outlook and Salary

The occupational outlook for counselors has gone from no outlook to promising.

Counseling in Health Care Organizations

My interest in mental health counseling started in high school when I was struck by how a schoolmate could transition from a beautiful, young, vivacious track star to someone requiring mandatory hospitalization due to being in an uncontrollable state of mania with delusional beliefs. I was perplexed and filled with questions such as: How could this be? How did this happen? On my quest for understanding I applied to volunteer on the psychiatric ward of the local hospital. There I spent afternoons playing cards and going for walks with the patients. Sometimes, if they felt comfortable, they would share stories from their lives. Wanting to learn more I enrolled in a Bachelors of Arts in Psychology Program and also started volunteering for a local call center for people in distress.

The combination of volunteer work and education fed my interest to enter the field of psychology. After graduation with a bachelor's degree in psychology, I was hired as a crisis worker in a hospital. My fellow crisis workers had varied educational backgrounds ranging from nursing to social work to peer support workers. Crisis work was a fascinating job, involving working shifts and being on-call through the night. I worked closely with the emergency department of the hospital where the main objective was to provide prompt and compassionate care to individuals with mental health concerns. My job was to interview and assess the patient and develop a plan of action to address individual needs. This plan would then be presented to the emergency room physician who would oversee the patient's care. The work could be very challenging depending on the particular needs of the patients. A crisis worker could be called to the cardiac unit to assess a patient presenting with a heart attack, who might actually be experiencing a panic attack. I might be called to interview a patient in restraints or a young teenager under the influence of drugs, or to assess the suicide risk of someone engaged in self-injurious behaviors. My experience as a crisis worker taught me a lot about acute and chronic mental illness, professional limitations, individual strengths, and a population of people that I was interested in serving.

To further my education and skill level, I began to explore master's-level programs. Because I enjoyed crisis work, I looked for programs that had a strong clinical focus. Niagara University in Lewiston, New York, offered everything that I needed. It was a short drive over the Canada–United States border, and the program was rigorous and demanding, but flexible enough that I was able to continue to work while attending graduate school.

Being comfortable in a health care setting I completed my internship at St. Joseph's Healthcare, Hamilton, Ontario, and upon graduation, I was hired as a counselor. The role of a counselor in a health care setting is multifaceted. In this arena, a counselor is a diagnostician, a therapist, a consultant, and an educator. One of the main jobs for a counselor in a health care setting is as a psychometrist. At this time, a psychometrist is ideally registered with the College of Psychologists as a psychological associate. To become "registered" (the equivalent of "licensed" in the United States), a master's-level clinician would need 4 years of post-master's work experience, to be supervised by registered member of the College of Psychologists, and to write (pass) the Examination for Professional Practice in Psychology and the Jurisprudence and Ethics Exam. The final step is to pass the College of Psychologists Oral Exam.

Currently, membership for master's-level clinicians within the College of Psychologists is being questioned and challenged.

Fortunately, in 2007, a new door started to open for master's-level clinicians in Ontario when the Minister of Health and Long-Term Care passed Bill 171 (Healthsystem Improvements Act, 2007) regulating the profession of psychotherapy. The new college is called the "College of Psychotherapists and Registered Mental Health Therapists of Ontario." It will include professionals with a degree in mental health counseling and will oversee the scope of practice of psychotherapy, which includes assessment and treatment of cognitive, emotional, or behavioral disturbances through the use of psychotherapy.

Of note, while the members of the College of Psychotherapists and Registered Mental Health Therapists will be permitted to perform psychotherapy, they will not be able to diagnose mental disorders. Thus, counseling will likely remain the counselor's primary role. Counselors involved in assessments in a health care setting will likely be exposed to one of the most common assessment tools, the Structured Clinical Interview for *Diagnostic and Statistical Manual of Mental Disorders, Fourth Edition (DSM-IV)* Disorders (SCID). The SCID is a semistructured clinical interview that assesses the major *DSM-IV* (American Psychiatric Association, 1994) disorders. It can take from one to four hours to administer depending on the complexity of the patient's symptoms. The SCID can be administered by a counselor or similar mental health professional. After the completion of the SCID, a diagnostic report is generated; however, the counselor's report must be cosigned by a psychologist or psychiatrist.

Health care settings can offer a wide variety of treatment programs. One of the most popular forms of psychotherapy is cognitive behavioral therapy (CBT). CBT is an empirically validated form of psychotherapy based on the belief that one's thoughts, feelings, and behaviors are interconnected. Individuals seeking treatment are taught skills and strategies to manage their symptoms. The treatment is designed to be short term and focused on the "here and now." CBT provides the patients with a new way of understanding their problem so that they can move toward making changes to modify their distorted thoughts and problematic behaviors. For approximately 10 years, I have utilized CBT on patients with combined diagnoses of a mood disorder (unipolar and bipolar disorders) and anxiety disorders (e.g., panic disorder, social anxiety disorder, obsessive-compulsive disorder, post-traumatic stress disorder, specific phobias, and generalized anxiety disorder). To practice CBT, counselors have completed experiential courses and have had a significant amount of supervised training. McMaster University's Clinical Behavioural Sciences Program and the TAPE Program, in affiliation with the Continuing Education Division, St. Michael's College, University of Toronto, are popular training programs for CBT in Ontario. In the United States, intensive CBT training is offered through the National Association of Cognitive Behavioral Therapists, the Beck Institute for Cognitive Therapy, and the Albert Ellis Institute, among others.

In a health care setting, counselors typically work in a team of multidisciplinary professionals. They are often in the role of consultants as they dispense information to others about services available in the community. The counselor in a health care setting will find themselves on a team of psychologists, psychiatrists, social workers, occupational therapists, undergraduate students, and graduate students. The richness of the team promotes understanding of the multifaceted needs of the patient. Further, as counselors in a mental health setting, they will share in educating the students by providing individual supervision by reviewing audio-taped recordings of treatment sessions. In addition, students may co-lead their therapy groups or may sit in on an individual treatment session.

The role of a counselor in a health care setting can be multifaceted and demanding; however, it can be a very rewarding career. The combination of assessment, treatment, consultation, and teaching roles functions to promote one's personal and professional growth. Over the years that I have been practicing, I remain awestruck by the devastating effects of mental illness. But through experience with patients grappling with mental illness, I have had the privilege to observe the power of human strength to overcome such adversity. The satisfaction of improving people's lives through a combination of counseling, assessment, and teaching can make mental health counseling a long and satisfying career.

64. COUNSELOR IN HOSPITALS

Counselors have only recently begun working in hospitals in significant numbers. Previously, the hospital was an environment reserved for psychiatrists, clinical psychologists, and social workers. In recent years, counselors have gained a foothold in hospitals in many states. Naturally, psychiatric hospitals have hired counselors, as have hospitals with a psychiatric ward. Some hospitals have hired counselors for emergency departments or as professionals to go out on trauma calls. Just a few years ago, counselors were approved to work in Veterans Affairs (VA) hospitals and are now being hired into the VA at a rate equivalent to that of social workers.

Degree Required

Master's degree, most likely in clinical mental health counseling, rehabilitation counseling, or addictions counseling. Also, counselors who also hold credentials as registered nurses, paramedics, or EMTs, or have previous medical training will have an advantage.

Issues to Understand

Hospitals still tend to prefer psychologists and social workers to counselors, though counselors are making inroads. One limitation remains that prevents counselors from achieving more success in this vocational arena, and that limitation is the issue of Medicare. Counselors cannot bill Medicare at present, and this is a limitation regarding hospital employment. On the positive side, Medicare is the last big hurdle for counselors to achieve, and the profession is likely to be granted Medicare privileges in the near future. Still, many counselors are employed in hospitals across the United States and Canada. With VA hospitals now open to licensed counselors, the counseling profession will likely realize more hospital employment in the future.

Best Aspects of the Job

One of the best aspects of working in a hospital is that the standard of care tends to be higher than that of most outpatient facilities. Of course, many hospitals also will offer mental health services for outpatients, or for "partial hospitalization" as it is sometimes called. Hospital jobs pay competitive salaries and offer direct access to a wide range of mental and physical health professionals such as psychiatrists, surgeons, nurses, and occupational and physical therapists.

Challenging Aspects of the Job

I have supervised a lot of graduate students placed in hospital settings and have friends and colleagues who work in hospitals. These students, friends, and colleagues who are counselors, psychologists, and social workers sometimes complain they are not taken as seriously as physicians, nurses, and other medical professionals. Though frustrating, this situation probably should not be a surprise to mental health professionals as hospitals specialize in medical care and medical care implies medications, surgery, physical exams, and so on. Still, there are many advantages to hospital work; quick access to in-house referral is one of the most advantageous.

Occupational Outlook and Salary

Though the Bureau of Labor Statistics does not classify counselors in hospital employment, it is my experience that while this is an emerging field for the counseling profession, jobs are still few. Counselors who hold credentials in nursing or another medical profession will have a big advantage over counselors without such a background. Salaries are likely to range from $35,000 to $52,000 (estimated), depending on the type of hospital and years of experience.

65. COUNSELOR IN HEALTH CLINICS

Another very recent occupational opening for counselors is in outpatient medical clinics. Like the hospital "market" above, employment opportunity for counselors in medical clinics will need more time to mature before counselors are hired into clinics in large numbers. Still, what I have seen across the United States, and to some extent in the Canadian province of Ontario, leaves me optimistic for the future.

Degree Required

Master's degree, most likely in clinical mental health counseling, addictions counseling, or rehabilitation counseling. Like hospitals, clinics will also prefer counselors who also hold credentials in nursing or another medical field.

Issues to Understand

Understand that this is an emerging field for counselors, and if you are just headed to a graduate program in counseling, you might expect it will take another decade before this becomes a strong market for counselors. (Again, it is much stronger for counselors who also are nurses, physician assistants, etc.)

Best Aspects of the Job

One of my former students who has been counseling in a clinic since her graduate internship says that direct access to medical referrals (from doctors and nurses and to doctors and nurses) is what she most appreciates. Another student who counsels in a clinic cites that the acknowledgment that mental health and physical health are intertwined is what she most appreciates. Then there is the reality that many clients in counseling were referred to a counselor by their primary care physician or nurse.

Challenging Aspects of the Job

Like all work settings, there are challenges in this job. As health care clinics are primarily medical in nature, medical issues will take precedence over mental health issues. Practically every psychologist, social worker, counselor, and graduate intern I have known has mentioned this to me. Some counselors (and social workers) have told me that physicians have a tendency to refer to clients being seen separately by counselors as "my patient" even after a referral has been made. Thus, ownership of responsibility and issues that drive treatment can be challenging for counselors working in health clinics.

Occupational Outlook and Salary

Again, this is a relatively new movement, and the Bureau of Labor Statistics provides no figures. My best estimate is that it will be several years before health clinics become a viable market for counselors. Once again, for counselors who have been nurses, physician assistants, paramedics, and so forth, health clinics may be a viable option right now. Salary range could be anywhere from $35,000 to $50,000 (this estimate is very loose).

13 Counseling in Crisis Intervention and Emergency Management

Author's Note: Some of the following counseling "jobs" are actually more like different counseling roles. However, because counselors are now beginning to assume emergency roles, some of the following could in fact be full- or part-time careers in the future. One counseling program, the mental health counseling graduate program at the Boston University School of Medicine, trains counselors to work in emergency departments with victims of trauma. I recently completed a certificate course in trauma counseling at the University at Buffalo. A colleague of mine, who lives in Australia, actually is employed by the police force to debrief survivors of industrial disasters. Therefore, I will posit many of the counseling occupations profiled in this section as jobs.

In addition, I have recently begun to see advertisements for "emergency team clinicians" (mostly counselors and social workers), "crisis support counselors," and similar titles. Most of these crisis-trauma type jobs require a master's degree and a license in counseling or social work. It is likely that such positions will become more common in the mental health profession in the same manner as they have in the medical profession, and graduate school training programs will eventually reflect such changes in the marketplace.

Spotlight: Trauma Counseling
Trauma Counseling Spotlight: Gregory K. Moffatt, PhD, LPC,
Counseling and Human Services, Point University, West Point, GA

I knew when I was an undergraduate at a small liberal arts school in Tennessee that I wanted to be a counselor, but it was not until I was in graduate school that I decided to focus on trauma counseling. During my master's residency and internship, I worked with children, adults, and groups, and about every form of counseling you can think of. What stood out most to me was the incredible impact that early childhood experiences had on even my oldest clients. People in their 50s and 60s would cry as they told me about things that happened in their childhoods. I realized that if I wanted to make a difference, I needed to get to these people at the point of their traumas rather than trying to deal with 30 or 40 years of decision making based on flawed thinking and traumatic experience.

I finished my master's degree and pursued the PhD to improve my expertise in my field. I earned my license in Georgia in 1990, and during those early years, I specifically sought out clients who had trauma experiences. I focused my continuing education in this area and read everything I could get my hands on. Over the last quarter century, I have invested my energies as a college professor, a clinician, public speaker, and advocate for children. I pursued and achieved my national board certification in post-traumatic stress, specializing in child physical and sexual abuse.

Working with traumatized children has led me into a variety of environments. It has led me into the medical field as I studied and learned how trauma affects a child's physical, social, cognitive, and emotional development. It has led me into the courtroom as an advocate, expert witness, and supporter of children who have come through my practice. I have worked extensively with social workers, foster care, and in the prison system. My work has also led me into the publishing world as I have written dozens of articles, a regular newspaper column for the past 18 years, and numerous books.

It took a long time but in my private practice, I now have the luxury of deciding what clients I will work with and what clients I will not. Early in my practice, I had to take anyone who came through the door that I was ethically capable of treating, but as I have grown professionally, I now have achieved a level of practice where I do not have to scramble for clients. In fact, I refer about three-fourths of all inquiries made to my office. My financial life is sustained through client fees, speaker's fees, and a variety of other sources of income including my books and consulting work.

Trauma takes many forms. I have worked with child victims of all natures of crime: victims of assault, rape, automobile accidents, severe weather, devastating abuse, neglect, and domestic violence situations. I worked with many victims of the 9–11 tragedy, war, and genocide. I have worked with patients in two dozen countries on four continents.

Early on, I learned that what is traumatizing for one person is not necessarily traumatizing for another. I have worked with many children who have experienced traumatic loss of parents through sudden, tragic death, but who dealt with it quite well. And as hard as it is to imagine, other children I have worked with have experienced sexual molestation and yet did not even realize it. They were too young to recognize what was happening to them, and the intrusiveness of the perpetrator was limited enough that it did not create any traumatic effects.

Yet at other times, I have worked with children who were literally traumatized by relatively minor life interruptions. My job is to assess the level of trauma, if any, and to help the children who are traumatized to master the effects of these events.

Learning never stops. Even though I am often the keynote speaker at conferences and I am invited to speak, write, and present more often than I can accept, I am always a student. I learn from the children in my practice, from my students, and from the stack of books that never runs dry beside my desk. As long as I am always a student, I will always be at the cutting edge of my field and I can be most helpful to my clients.

66. COUNSELOR IN THE AFTERMATH OF NATURAL AND MAJOR DISASTERS

For decades, agencies such as the Federal Emergency Management Administration (FEMA) have coordinated professionals and volunteers to assist survivors of earthquakes, hurricanes, and floods, as well as terrorist attacks, such as that on the World Trade Centers on 9–11. Counselors are one of the latest professions to have assisted in such times, and though few seem to be employed by FEMA or other federal and state organizations, it is conceivable that counseling and debriefing survivors of natural disasters will be a common occupation for counselors in the near future. Now, many counselors indeed counsel survivors of natural disasters, though likely it is several months or perhaps even years since the disaster.

Degree Required

Master's degree in one of the counseling fields. In addition, you may wish to earn an advanced certificate in trauma counseling, critical incident stress management (CISM) offered by the American Red Cross (ARC), or other such certificates.

Issues to Understand

Once again, this is a field that is emerging and is not yet an occupation within the counseling profession. However, counselors are doing this type of work mostly as a part of private practice. Counselors who were previously police officers and first responders (fire fighters, paramedics, etc.), as well as former military personnel and others, may be natural professionals when they retrain as counselors. Counselors who may be interested in this field but do not have the background listed above should speak with their faculty advisor and see about professional training such as those listed under the "Degree Required" section.

Best Aspects of the Job

I have had friends, family members, and students who have served as first responders to trauma and disaster. In every case, all expressed that responding to trauma was a challenge they enjoyed. A couple even explained it as part of their risk-taking personality. My guess is that most professionals would not want to work with people in the immediate aftermath of trauma. It probably takes a person who can reframe trauma as "a challenge," otherwise the counselor may not be able to manage the stress and shock of the situation (Tunnecliffe, 2007).

Challenging Aspects of the Job

Are you able to manage mass hysteria and shock? In the aftermath of major traumas such as 9–11 and hurricane Katrina, could you envision yourself being one of the professionals responding to people in dire need? If you have any hesitation, this may not be a good field for you. But if you have experience in dealing with trauma and find you feel challenged by it, then perhaps this emerging field is viable for you.

Occupational Outlook and Salary

As this field is still emerging, salary and occupational outlook are difficult to gauge. It is likely to take several years before counselors are employed in large numbers providing frontline assistance to survivors of major disasters. The ARC is one of the best contacts as they offer CISM training (the ARC requires counselors to be licensed or certified to participate in CISM training). Counselors serving in the armed forces are also likely candidates to work in the aftermath of disasters.

67. COUNSELOR IN THE AFTERMATH OF A TRAGEDY (SCHOOL SHOOTINGS, SUICIDE, ETC.)

Many counselors already provide regular intervention when a school shooting or a suicide occurs. In most cases, the counselor may be employed at a school, college, agency, or hospital, or be in private practice. However, as counselors in the future may specialize and advertise themselves as having a specialty area in trauma counseling or other related areas, I have listed this as an emerging field within counseling. (Clearly, as evidenced by the title of this book, counseling is a very broad field.)

Degree Required

Master's degree in one of the counseling fields. It is recommended to seek additional training in areas such as trauma counseling, critical incident stress management, or other related areas. Police officers, fire fighters, paramedics, nurses, and so forth who have retrained as counselors will also have an advantage in this area.

Issues to Understand

Unfortunately, many counselors will be required to use their skills in the aftermath of a tragedy. School shootings such as those at Columbine, CO; Jonesboro, AR; Paducah, KY; and the air force base in San Antonio have necessitated the expansion of the field. Suicide intervention and postsuicide work have always been a part of the mental health field. Readers interested in counseling as a profession will need to become facile in addressing suicidal thoughts and intention and in debriefing students, friends, and family members after a loved one has committed suicide.

While all counselors will have to address suicidal issues, most counselors will not feel comfortable debriefing large groups of people after a suicide or a major trauma such as a school shooting. Incidentally, as I write this section of the book, a school suicide just occurred in the community in which I live. Furthermore, in January 2011, a disgruntled person shot and killed several people in Arizona, critically wounding Congresswoman Gabrielle Giffords. Unfortunately, counselors will need to be trained and facile in debriefing and then counseling victims of traumatic crimes such as shooting sprees, wars, torture, and the like.

Best Aspects of the Job

Best aspects of the job may well be the satisfaction of addressing significant community, school, and family tragedies. Some trauma will be more complex than others; for example, a school shooting that kills several students and staff will be more challenging than a single suicide, though both will be difficult.

Challenging Aspects of the Job

Once again, counselors working in this field will have their professional lives devoted to trauma, suffering, and grief. Counselors and others professionals who work with major tragedies and suicides will frequently cite that survivors may initially be "numb" and that more work may be necessary several days after the traumatic event. Working with survivors may also trigger anger among many of them, as you are asking them to address what many would still like to deny (understandably so). Finally, trauma work can be emotionally draining, and counselors working in this field will need strong support systems of family, friends, social organizations (religious, social, recreational, etc.), and perhaps support groups themselves.

Occupational Outlook and Salary

As this is an emerging field, it is difficult to estimate salary and occupational demand. It is likely that many mental health counselors, school counselors, and the like will provide many services for victims of tragedies. However, many counselors in private practice are likely to advertise themselves as being able to provide services to survivors of trauma.

68. COUNSELOR IN DOMESTIC VIOLENCE SHELTERS

Counselors have for some length of time been providing mental health services to women and children escaping violent homes. Some counselors will have a special "calling" to provide this important and challenging work.

Degree Required

Master's degree in one of the counseling fields. Previous experience in the field of an internship in a domestic violence shelter is highly recommended.

Issues to Understand

Domestic violence is an insidious and pervasive problem in the United States. It has been estimated that roughly 40% of couples in counseling have a history of domestic violence (Gladding, 2009). My own experience as a counselor is that this figure may be low, as roughly two-thirds of the women I have counseled report being in or having gotten out of a violent home. This means that even counselors who work in schools, mental health clinics, private practice, governmental agencies, and such need a solid understanding of the issues victims (both women and children) of domestic violence face.

One of the most difficult issues for any counselor working in a shelter, or anywhere else for that matter, is women who choose to return to a violent relationship. It is estimated that women are likely to return to violent relationships for reasons such as finances, family, religion, community, and a belief that "he's changed" or that "he only does this because he loves me." It is very painful for a counselor to watch a woman who has left a violent relationship to continue a career, education, and healthier relationships relapse and return to the one of violence.

Best Aspects of the Job

Counselors in domestic violence shelters are dedicated to providing women and children a safe space to heal and sort out the issues involved in ending a violent relationship. Counselors working in shelters also have the perspective to work across the mental health and social services system to help work for a more just and equitable society where crimes against women and children are not tolerated.

Challenging Aspects of the Job

No counselor, social worker, psychologist, religious leader, or anyone else should kid themselves that domestic violence is not a serious problem. There has been far more recognition of the reality of violence against women and children in the past two decades, but domestic violence remains a serious crime. There is no easy answer to the problem, because, while laws get tougher, many perpetrators go unprosecuted, many women refuse to press charges against the abuser and also return to the abuser, and educational, social and religious institutions often turn a blind eye to the reality of domestic violence. Counselors working in domestic violence shelters are performing a valuable, though vastly underappreciated, and near-impossible task.

While domestic shelters have certainly increased in many communities, small, rural ones do not have such a service. Many suburban and urban shelters also do not have adequate services for women and children.

Occupational Outlook and Salary

Because counselors working in domestic violence shelters come from many fields and because shelters often fall under the umbrella of "social services agencies," salary and occupational outlook are difficult to discern. Due to the degree of difficulty, counseling jobs in shelters are likely to open and close with regularity. Salaries, in my experience, tend to be on the lower end of the scale. Thus, many counselors spend part of their career in domestic violence shelters before transitioning on to work in addictions, community mental health, or private practice.

69. COUNSELOR FOR VICTIMS OF SEXUAL ASSAULTS

Similar to domestic violence, sexual abuse, particularly against women and children, is a pervasive crime. Counselors who work in shelters, schools, agencies, and colleges will need to be prepared to counsel victims of sexual assault.

Degree Required

Master's degree in one of the counseling fields.

Issues to Understand

Counselors working with victims of sexual assault will actually work in many different agencies. One of the more recent venues for sexual assault victims is Centers Against Rape and Domestic Violence (CARDVA). Thus, sexual assault victims may be housed together with women and children fleeing domestic violence. Of course, sexual assault often is part of domestic violence.

Counselors working with victims of sexual assault also face the reality of educating the general public on matters of rape and intended

rape. Many people in society will effectively blame the victim, questioning what she wore, where she was, how much she drank, and the like. Regardless of any of the issues and circumstances, no one should be raped. Communities also tend to see sexual assault as an outside problem. What I mean is that the general perception is that rapists are perpetrators lurking in the bushes in darkness waiting to pounce on their victims. The reality is that roughly 90% of sexual assault victims know their attacker. Perpetrators live down the hall in a college dormitory, meet the victim at a beer bash, are coworkers, fellow parishioners, or, most egregiously, family members (Tjaden & Thomas, 2000). Yet, in my experience, college administrators and civic leaders will often point to the need to have more lighting on their campus or in their city, a solution that might address 10% of sexual assaults at best.

Best Aspects of the Job

Like counseling victims of domestic violence, counseling victims of sexual assault is an opportunity to help victims heal from the aftermath of personal violation. Many victims will experience a feeling of shame that they could not protect themselves (Tjaden & Thomas, 2000). Counselors working with sexual assault victims will by necessity become active in their community to help address the problem and the realities of sexual assault.

Challenging Aspects of the Job

It is likely that a prejudice against sexual assault victims has always existed: Statements like "She asked for it," "It only happens to bad girls," "Why was she walking in that neighborhood anyway?," "If she didn't want to have sex why was she in his room?," "She could have fought harder," "Well, it's partly her fault for wearing such provocative clothes!," "I'll bet she was drunk, wasn't she?" are just some of the insensitive and inane comments I have heard expressed by people in the aftermath of a sexual assault. Counselors must understand they are combating a community mindset that wants to believe the victim was at fault. Sadly, many victims will have internalized these types of beliefs as well.

Many law enforcement professionals and religious, civic, and community leaders will be supportive of your work. However, many people will not be sympathetic to your work and will blame the victims. Prosecuting a sexual assault case can also be very traumatizing for the victim, as she will be forced to relive the trauma over and over, especially if the case goes to court. Victims of sexual assault will often develop post-traumatic stress disorder and self-medicate with alcohol and other drugs and will resist the counselor's efforts to help them heal.

Occupational Outlook and Salary

Most counselors working with survivors of sexual assault will work in schools, agencies, and private practice as opposed to CARDVA. Thus, readers interested in counseling sexual assault victims usually will work in community mental health agencies and university counseling centers. Demand for mental health counselors is expected to have 24% growth, a very high figure. Median salary for mental health counselors is $36,810.

70. CRISIS LINE COUNSELOR

An increasing number of counselors are staffing crisis lines to provide immediate mental health services to people contemplating suicide, victims of violence, and people who are lonely who feel a need to reach for support.

Degree Required

Master's degree in a counseling field.

Issues to Understand

Many communities, especially in urban areas, have created crisis lines to address people in crisis. Traditionally, these lines have been staffed by volunteers, and while this continues to be the case to some extent, many professional counselors are being hired to provide the service. Some private companies have also begun to contract out this service.

Counseling on the crisis line naturally differs from traditional counseling in that the caller and the counselor are not present in the same setting, and the caller usually has had no previous contact with the counselor. The counselor's job on the crisis line is to establish a relationship, provide temporary assistance, assess the degree of risk, and provide a plan for when the call is over. Then, another counselor or other mental health professional will take over to provide more acute care. Many counselors may find the lack of face-to-face contact challenging, as well as the reality that every call can be stressful. Counselors who thrive in this environment are likely to be people who enjoy the challenge of addressing immediate needs.

Best Aspects of the Job

Knowing that you have prevented a suicide attempt or simply provided comfort to someone who is lonely can be very fulfilling. In addition,

I know some counselors who work in trauma teams, taking calls for crisis, and then going out with a partner to meet the person in crisis. In some cases, one counselor staffs the phone and a separate counselor (or tandem of counselors) goes out to meet the caller.

Challenging Aspects of the Job

Readers interested in this type of work must be able to manage the stress of counseling unknown callers in crisis. Many counselors will not be comfortable with this type of work and will prefer traditional face-to-face work. Another factor in staffing a crisis line is that there will be periods of inactivity punctuated by very intense therapeutic conversations with people who may be suicidal or have just been assaulted. Yet, for resilient counselors who enjoy providing services to those in extreme need, this could be meaningful work.

Occupational Outlook and Salary

Once again, as this segment of the field is evolving and expanding, there are no reliable statistics to report. In addition, I have known many counselors in private practice who worked part time for an organization that provided after-hours calls or 24-hour crisis services. Therefore, many people providing this service may be part-time employees. There are also organizations that hire counselors to work as full-time trauma counselors, and they may take crisis calls and then go out to deal with the crisis.

71. COUNSELOR FOR INDIVIDUALS WHO ARE TEMPORARILY HOMELESS

This section is slightly different from the next chapter on spiritual-based counseling. Many individuals and families are referred to as being in *transitional housing*. This means they are living in supportive housing until they are able to find permanent housing.

Degree Required

Many such jobs require a BA/BS degree. For career mobility, a master's degree in one of the counseling fields is optimal particularly with regard to moving into a managerial role.

Issues to Understand

The homeless are one of the most visible, yet from my perspective, ignored populations in society. They are present in virtually every community in the country, yet society would prefer to ignore them. Homeless people also are not monolithic culture. If readers were to ask people to describe the homeless, those questioned likely would describe a population of homeless who are mentally ill and struggling with multiple addictions, and who sleep under bridges, in abandoned care, and in crack houses. This would describe a large percentage of the homeless, but would not include individuals and families in shelters, those in government housing after a natural disaster like hurricane Katrina, and a small subgroup of people who live at their worksite. (I became aware of this latter group of people while working with a human services agency in Oregon. They would sleep somewhere in the building, use the showers or bathroom to clean up, and eat in the break room.) Basically, there are different classes of homeless people, some of whom actually hold jobs. One of the best representations of the various categories of homeless can be found in novelist John Grisham's work *The Street Lawyer* (Grisham, 1998).

The homeless are a subculture that few people in our society have sympathy for; their feeling, in my experience, is that the homeless are people who "have no ambition." It has been estimated, however, that as many as 30% have a major mental illness (U.S. Conference of Mayors, 2007) and many have lost their homes through the recent recession. Counselors who work with the homeless face numerous challenges, both with the homeless population themselves and with society's callous view toward them. I will say more on this topic under the section "Challenging Aspects of the Job."

Best Aspects of the Job

As counselors who spent part of their career working with the homeless, many of my colleagues express that their sense of fulfillment comes from the knowledge that they are serving one of society's more vulnerable populations.

Challenging Aspects of the Job

The challenges are legion, to coin a phrase. It is likely that half the homeless population struggle with mental illness and/or multiple addictions. Then there is the reality that while many politicians, business leaders, and others will complain about the homeless, few are willing either to hire a homeless person or to pay taxes to create more transitional housing. Clearly, a large part of the problem lies in the reality that our society has not funded space for the long-term mentally ill, as this is the most challenging segment of the homeless population. Domestic violence, extreme poverty, recession, and a lack of affordable housing are some of the causes for homeless families (National Center on Family Homelessness,

2010). Families also are among the faster growing segment of the homeless population, something few seem to be aware of.

Occupational Outlook and Salary

Occupational outlook is difficult to estimate. It is likely that most counselors, social workers, and caseworkers who counsel the homeless will
work in nonprofit human service agencies where they serve a number
of other functions. This was my experience at the agency in Oregon.
Nevertheless, I would estimate occupational outlook to be "good."
Salaries will fluctuate widely, depending on whether the caseworker or
"counselor" has a bachelor's or master's degree. For full-time work, readers could expect a salary range running from, say, $28,000 to $45,000
per year depending on bachelor's or master's degree, years of experience,
and agency funding.

14 Spiritual-Based Counseling

Spotlight: Pastoral Counseling
Pastoral Counseling Spotlight: Anthony Terndrup, PhD, MA, LPC, LMFT, Fellow, American Association of Pastoral Counselors, Pastoral Counseling Center of the Mid-Willamette Valley, Corvallis, OR

Pastoral counseling is a professional discipline for specialists who integrate counseling theory and pastoral theology (i.e., the science of the care of souls) in their clinical practice in order to relieve human suffering and to promote human flourishing. Accordingly, the vocational formation of pastoral counselors includes academic preparation in both theoretical and theological fields of study.

The American Association of Pastoral Counselors (AAPC) is the first professional organization in the United States to certify pastoral counselors. Two pathways lead to AAPC certification in pastoral counseling. Traditionally, an ordained minister with a graduate degree in theology would complete a second graduate degree in counseling or an approved clinical training program. Otherwise, a licensed mental health professional with a graduate degree in counseling will complete a second graduate degree in theology or an equivalent pastoral core curriculum.

The nontraditional pathway led me to AAPC certification in pastoral counseling. After completing my master's degree in counseling at California State University, Bakersfield, in 1989 and my doctorate in counseling at Oregon State University in 1998, I returned to graduate school once more to complete my master's degree in pastoral ministry at the University of Portland, Oregon, in 2009. In the words of a layperson, I am an AAPC-certified pastoral counselor (i.e., fellow), as well as a state-licensed professional counselor and licensed marriage and family therapist.

For 15 years, I have practiced at a pastoral counseling center with a mission to provide community mental health services to low-income and uninsured individuals, couples, and families based on their need for care rather than their ability to pay. Financial contributions from over a dozen religious congregations subsidize the fees for our clients that are discounted on the basis of their economic necessity. Four years ago, I was promoted to serve as the executive director for the nonprofit corporation.

In my role of executive director, I dedicated two days each week to my administrative tasks. These duties include establishing and maintaining relationships with board members and faith communities, raising funds and writing grants, monitoring budgets and finances, and managing human resources. As a pastoral counselor, I devoted the rest of the days in each week to my clinical responsibilities. These activities include counselor training and supervision, as well as pastoral counseling and psychotherapy.

Our pastoral counseling center offers an approved clinical training program for clergy following the traditional pathway to AAPC certification, as introduced above. On Thursday afternoons, our interdisciplinary team of licensed mental health professionals and certified pastoral counselors meets with our cohort of trainees for a reading seminar and a case conference in order to reflect on the integration of counseling theory and pastoral theology in clinical practice. These dynamic gatherings of our intentional community are the best moments of my week and embody the collective spirit and shared wisdom of our professional discipline and ecumenical ministry.

For me and for many of my colleagues, pastoral counseling is not only a career but also a calling. In other words, it is a religious vocation that calls each and all of us to enter into compassionate solidarity with human suffering in order to share a vision of hope and healing with other travelers on the journey to emotional wellness and spiritual wholeness. My vocational identity and

experience sustain me with a profound sense of meaning, fulfillment, and gratitude. Accordingly, I deeply appreciate and keenly
anticipate the opportunity to further serve my community as a pastoral counselor.

72. COUNSELOR IN PASTORAL COUNSELING CENTERS

Counseling in a pastoral counseling center is a natural fit for counselors
who also have an active spiritual or religious practice or who have an
interest in spiritual issues. Many counselors working in pastoral settings
are also ministers, rabbis, priests, and so on, though this is not a requirement for most pastoral counseling centers.

Degree Required

Master's degree in counseling or pastoral counseling.

Issues to Understand

As a counselor who worked in two pastoral counseling centers, I say that
there is often a lot of misunderstanding about what services the pastoral counseling centers provide. Pastoral counseling centers are often
accredited by the American Association of Pastoral Counselors (AAPC),
an organization with high clinical standards. Many counselors in AAPC-
accredited centers will hold doctoral degrees, or dual master's degrees
in counseling and theology. AAPC-accredited pastoral counseling center
staffs tend to be very well educated, and the counselors who are affiliated
with religious organizations tend to be affiliated with main-line liturgical
Protestant churches, with some Catholics and a few Jews.

Another factor for readers to be aware of is that AAPC-accredited
pastoral counseling centers have historically been influenced by the
psychodynamic approaches (post-Freudian movement). The more contemporary theoretical approaches such as cognitive behavioral therapy,
solution-focused therapy, and Gestalt have made inroads though psychodynamic approaches likely continue to dominant.

Pastoral counseling centers also will, by their nature, be aligned to
religious and spiritual traditions. Agnostic and atheistic counselors might
likely find some of the issues they deal with to be a challenge given
that many religious clients will come for counseling expecting to be
able to address spiritual and religious issues. Though many nonspiritual

counselors will certainly be able to assist clients explore their spiritual development, such work could be challenging for some agnostic and atheist counselors.

Best Aspects of the Job

For many counselors working in pastoral settings, the best part of their job may lie in the freedom to help clients explore spiritual themes and issues of life's purpose. Pastoral centers are natural settings for counselors interested in the intersection of psychotherapy and spirituality. As previously noted, many clerical professionals will take extra training in counseling (or social work, psychology, and marriage and family therapy) and work in a pastoral center.

Challenging Aspects of the Job

Though a natural setting for many counselors, pastoral counseling is certainly not for everyone. AAPC ethics mandate nondiscrimination on the basis of religion (or the lack of religion), but pastoral counseling centers will by and large be staffed by religious counselors. Many pastoral counseling centers are located in churches that lend them free or low-cost space, so the offices are often marginal with regard to comforts. (One office I used was previously a Sunday-school classroom with furniture from the late 1960s.) For counselors practicing from a cognitive-behavioral therapy, Gestalt, Narrative, or Existential framework, the psychodynamic approach, with its focus on long-term therapy, neo-Freudian terms, a focus on the unconscious, and so forth, can be very challenging. Pastoral counseling centers are becoming more open to other theoretical approaches, though this is happening very slowly.

Occupational Outlook and Salary

The Bureau of Labor Statistics does not compile statistics on pastoral counseling, and my experience is there are only few pastoral counseling settings. There are many "Christian" counseling centers separate from pastoral centers; however, these may or may not be staffed by professionally trained counselors, so I have chosen not to include them in this category. So, pastoral counseling centers are relatively few with regard to other outpatient centers. This means there will be few counseling positions available, though I teach in a program with a woman who counsels in a pastoral counseling center and they frequently hire staff, as counselors tend to move on every three to four years. Salaries are likely to be on the lower end of the pay scale as pastoral centers are private entities that must search for various revenue streams. The United Way, local Council of Churches, federal grants, donations, and fee for service are common ways pastoral counseling centers generate money. Many pastoral centers do indeed bill insurance but this can be limited due to the nature of the counseling work (spiritual, marital, etc.), much of which is not billable.

73. COUNSELOR IN CHURCHES, SYNAGOGUES, OR OTHER RELIGIOUS INSTITUTIONS

In addition to pastoral counseling centers, counselors may also work in religious institutions. Counselors providing counseling services in churches, synagogues, mosques, and the like may also be clerics of that particular religious institution, or counselors who are members of the institution where they work. Unlike pastoral counseling centers, counseling offices that are part of a particular religious institution are likely to be unaffiliated with the American Association of Pastoral Counselors. It is also likely that such counseling offices will be more inherently religious and may require the counseling staff to adhere to a particular religious doctrine.

Degree Required

Because religious institutions can claim that their service is "religion based," counselors may or may not have graduate degrees in counseling. I would encourage readers (and future counselors) not to accept jobs in religiously affiliated institutions unless they are professionally trained counselors (or social workers, psychologists, etc.).

Issues to Understand

As mentioned previously, counseling as part of a church or synagogue may require an adherence to that particular religious creed. If you are a member of that particular church, this may not present an insurmountable challenge. If you do not share the religion of the religious institution, you will not be hired, and even if you are hired, the job may be untenable due to value conflicts.

Counselors working as part of a religious institution may also be expected to use a religious text to guide sessions. The *Bible, Torah* or *Tenach, Koran, Tibetan Book of the Dead,* or another religious text may be given more credence than one from Freud, Rogers, Perls, Ellis, and so on. Basically, you would need to share the religion of the institution; if not, this type of counseling position would likely not be healthy for you.

Best Aspects of the Job

The best part of the job would likely be the ability to merge religious faith and counseling practice. Religious faith may play the dominant role, as religious institutions are about religious matters, though religious institutions can vary greatly.

Challenging Aspects of the Job

As previously noted, counseling is likely to be religion based. Another issue is that multiple relationships with clients will simply be a reality. The counselor will see clients for counseling, often regarding very sensitive issues (such as marital infidelity), and then see them at service or on a church/synagogue committee. This mixing of roles can be uncomfortable for both counselors and clients.

Occupational Outlook and Salary

The Bureau of Labor Statistics reports no statistics for counselors working in religious institutions. It is likely that larger religious institutions are the types who hire these counselors. Salaries are likely to be low as churches and other religious houses of worship must pay the religious staff and support staff, pay for building upkeep, and so forth. The counselor may also be a cleric who also has counseling training, and as such she or he may be expected to assume additional roles in religious education.

74. BEREAVEMENT COUNSELOR

Related to counseling in a pastoral center or in a religious institution is the field of bereavement counseling. Bereavement counselors may work in hospice centers, religious institutions, or clinics, or do private practice.

Degree Required

Generally, a master's degree in counseling or a related field (social work, theology, etc.) is required. Some agencies, especially those that do not bill insurance, may hire bachelor's-level counselors or social workers.

Issues to Understand

Bereavement counseling will involve a lot of work with bereaved spouses, children, partners, parents, in-laws, and anyone else in grief.

Bereavement counselors must develop a comfort zone in assisting people work through the grieving process. Counselors providing bereavement support will utilize individual and group counseling modalities (and in some cases, couples and family counseling). Other common issues to address are depression, anxiety, anger at the person (or people) who has died, and unexpressed emotions (surviving loved ones who never expressed "love" to the decedent, or loved ones who were hurt or abused by the decedent and are now unable to hold that person accountable).

Counselors providing bereavement work must have done their own personal work on death anxiety and grief as their entire jobs will revolve around loss and separation. Counselors providing grief counseling need to establish a strong support network to help them manage the stress inherent in the work. Another challenge for many bereavement counselors is that many agencies provide counseling only to the family of a terminally ill patient and not to the patients themselves. This irony can be very frustrating for counselors in this field.

Challenging Aspects of the Job

Challenging aspects of the job are many: stress, counseling people in the throes of grief, working with angry clients, and the issues of poor pay. Bereavement counselors are frequently employed by hospice agencies, where pay will be better for those with master's degrees and licensure. Naturally, bereavement counselors must be skilled in helping loved ones address grief, loss, depression, and related issues. Every client the counselors see will be dealing with grief issues, making it imperative for the bereavement counselors to have done extensive work on their own grief issues.

Occupational Outlook and Salary

Occupational outlook is difficult to assess. The Bureau of Labor Statistics does not separate bereavement counselors from general mental health counselors. Most bereavement counselors are likely employed by hospice services, though pastoral counseling centers may also offer grief counseling and counselors in private practice may also provide grief services. Occupational outlook is likely less than for general practice areas (mental health counseling, rehabilitation counseling, school counseling, etc.). Salaries for master's-level counselors are likely somewhere within the range of mental health counselors (mid-$30,000 or so).

75. COUNSELOR FOR THE HOMELESS IN SPIRITUALITY-BASED CENTERS

For some counselors, providing mental and support services to the homeless is a rewarding challenge. All major cities have large populations of homeless people, with the majority living on streets and some in transitional housing.

Degree Required

Bachelor's degree is the minimum, but a master's degree counseling or a related profession is preferred.

Issues to Understand

Homeless people are among the most vulnerable in any society. They are susceptible to random acts of violence (sometimes by the police) and disease, have little access to health or mental health care, are exposed to the elements (cold, rain, snow, etc.), and often are the enmity of society leaders.

Many homeless people also suffer from mental illness. Whether this is due to being mentally ill and winding up on the street or due to being on the street and the stress and elements precipitating a psychosis is debatable. The homeless may also be reluctant to receive mental health care, as many of them have a history of being institutionalized and harbor unpleasant memories of their treatment. A good example of the homeless and mental illness can be seen in the recent film *The Soloist*, where Robert Downey Jr., playing a journalist, befriends Jamie Foxx, a mentally ill homeless man who also is a musical genius. The film illustrates that many homeless people have multiple *Diagnostic and Statistical Manual of Mental Disorders, Fourth Edition-Text Revision*, Axis I diagnoses, and most of the mentally ill in the film do not want any additional contact with the mental health profession.

Best Aspects of the Job

Anyone who works with the homeless is likely to be underappreciated by general society, the mental health profession, religious institutions, politicians, and so on. Counselors serving this population will find themselves providing more in the way of social and survival needs than psychotherapy. Many counselors working with the homeless will be employed by religious institutions (Salvation Army, for example) or be partially funded by them. I recall a nun telling me the life was very hard, lonely, and underappreciated. "You just have to be called to this work," she told me.

The same could potentially be said of counselors (or anyone else) who work with the homeless.

Challenging Aspects of the Job

The challenges are legion, to borrow a phrase. The needs of the homeless are overwhelming: not enough housing, not enough food, inadequate medical and mental health care, poor diet, and reliance on alcohol and other chemical substances as a means of self-medication. Though the homeless are difficult to track due to their mobility, it has been estimated that more than 50% suffer from chronic mental illness (Nicholas, 2008). In many instances, counselors will be trying to provide counseling services to an audience who does not want their help and who are suspicious of the mental health profession (Nicholas, 2008).

Women with dependent children are one of the fastest growing populations of homeless (National Coalition for the Homeless, 2011). Because of the vulnerability of children, women with children will typically be given first priority at transitional housing, though many will also wind up living in abandoned buildings, tents, and vehicles.

In short, counseling the homeless is likely to seem overwhelming for counselors on a daily basis and will at times be downright heartbreaking. Counselors interested in serving this population need to establish a strong support group and be able to network with religious institutions, community leaders, the police, and local politicians.

Occupational Outlook and Salary

Though there are no statistics to back it up, my experience is that jobs are available in this area simply because of low pay and the fact that few counselors or social workers will want to work with the homeless due to the multitude of issues and needs involved. Salaries are likely to be low (high $20,000 to mid $30,000).

76. HOSPICE COUNSELOR

Hospice counseling is closely related to bereavement counseling profiled earlier in this section. There will be some differentiation between the two types, as many counselors will provide bereavement services, hospice provides specific bereavement services.

Degree Required

Bachelor's degree is the minimum, but a master's degree in counseling is preferred.

Issues to Understand

You will be dealing with people in various stages of grievance. Many clients, family, and close friends of the terminally ill patient or the decedent, may also be angry and project that anger on the counselor who may be viewed as a "safe" target. Other issues than can emerge are family members who have been hurt by the terminally ill or decedent and who have been unable to express their anger with this person. Sometimes, a loved one is the "other woman" or man, and the family wants nothing to do with this person in grief.

Best Aspects of the Job

In hospice work, you simply must enjoy the challenge of providing a therapeutic outlet for people in grief. Hospice centers have become far more common, respected, and better funded in the past 20 years. In addition to counseling services, they provide art therapy, music therapy, and a number of means of artistic expression to make the terminally ill's last days or weeks more comfortable. Counselors working in hospice will network with a variety of professionals such as doctors and nurses, religious leaders, and politicians.

Challenging Aspects of the Job

Once again, hospice work means dealing with people in grief, anger, or denial. This can be draining for counselors serving this population, and, even more than other types of counseling, hospice counselors need a good support system. Other challenges are that while hospice centers offer valuable services to the family members, many hospice centers do not offer counseling to the terminally ill patient. I have met numerous hospice counselors critique the irony of this situation. (Hospice centers vary with their regulations.)

Occupational Outlook and Salary

Hospice centers have become quite commonplace in most mid-size to large communities. Jobs are available, though readers interested in this area of counseling would be wise to serve an internship in a hospice center during their graduate program. No statistics are available from the Bureau of Labor Statistics, though my experience has been that master's-level staff make "reasonably" good salaries (say, $35,000–$45,000 per year). Bachelor's-level counselors would earn considerably less salary.

15 Creative Arts Counseling

Spotlight: Creative Arts Counseling
Dance/Movement Therapist Spotlight: Christina Devereaux, PhD, LCAT, LMHC, BC-DMT, NCC, Dance/Movement Therapy and Counseling, Antioch University New England, Keene, NH; Department of Creative Arts Therapy, Pratt Institute, Brooklyn, NY

At a young age, I enthusiastically participated in creative dance classes and quickly learned about the expressive and connective qualities of dance. Through high school, I formalized my dance training in ballet and various styles of modern dance along with my academic learning. It seemed as if I was always involved in some form of movement or dance as I continued to learn and grow. Innately, I sensed the value and importance of the body–mind integration and its impact on my own well-being. I pursued college studies with a fascination in psychology and minored in dance, continuing to keep the two curiosities connected, not knowing that as a profession, I could utilize them both simultaneously. After being introduced to the profession of dance/movement therapy through an intensive workshop focusing on family work, I immediately explored pursing graduate studies.

I completed my master's degree in dance/movement therapy from the University of California, Los Angeles, in 1998. I learned through my training about the importance of all of the creative art therapies (dance/movement therapy, art therapy, music therapy, poetry therapy, drama therapy, and psychodrama therapy) as alternative ways to assist clients in expressing feeling states and gaining deeper clarity about life. Also, I learned how much training each discipline encounters to learn both verbal and nonverbal approaches to psychological assessment and intervention. I did an extensive internship working with children with various psychiatric diagnoses and learned how to build a therapeutic relationship and intervene through not only traditional verbal counseling approaches but also through nonverbal techniques. It was especially useful for clients who had very limited language skills or those who struggled in articulating their feelings verbally. Following my graduation, I immediately began working in various mental health settings including inpatient psychiatry, residential treatment, domestic violence centers, public and nonpublic schools, and day treatment facilities. The significant portion of my work, regardless of the population, was to develop a therapeutic alliance that was safe and nonjudgmental to give way to enhanced expressive experience. This was done through individual sessions or in group formats. Over the many years of clinical practice with a variety of presented challenges, it was acutely important to me that my own movement of life needed to remain active to continue my capacity stay embodied with my clients.

Dance/movement therapists (DMTs) see movement as a metaphor for how we think, feel, behave, and relate. They also learn to articulate the movement process through extensive training in systematic movement analysis tools such as the Laban movement analysis, the Kestenberg movement profile, and others. However, one of the realities of the profession is the lack of understanding about the work. Some people may misunderstand that the profession is only for dancers who need counseling or that one must know how to or like to dance in order for the discipline to be effective. Another incorrect assumption is that DMTs provide instructive classes actually "teaching" their clients dance moves or dance steps. Again, this is a real misinterpretation. Instead, a dance/movement therapy session can include both structured and unstructured experiences as a method for intervention. Each intervention, as is in a verbal therapy session, is tailored to the need levels of the client.

DMTs need to be versed in verbal and written presentation skills and stay attuned to current trends in therapeutic practice to accurately communicate with other mental health professionals the goals and treatment planning of their clients. Throughout the profession at large, DMTs are also becoming more versed in research that is providing more expansive empirical evidence for the validity of the work; however, this continues to be a strong need that is highlighted in the profession.

I consider myself a lifelong student, deepening my own knowledge and continually expanding and refreshing my skill set. I decided after many years of clinical practice that I would pursue a doctoral degree in clinical psychology in order to develop my clinical techniques and enhance my education to provide a pathway to teach at the graduate level. Currently, I teach dance/movement therapy in graduate programs and training institutions nationally and internationally, highlighting to my students the importance of the integration between the mind and the body in therapeutic interventions. I offer presentations at national conferences such as American Dance Therapy Association, American Counseling Association, and American Mental Health Counselors Association. Students who pursue graduate study in dance/movement therapy are required to have a background in dance because it is important for one to have expansive movement range to be accessible to a range of affects, movement qualities, and client presentations.

I have found that a career in which one can use dance and movement as a therapeutic tool to assist others in enhancing social connections, building body awareness and healthy boundaries, expressing and channeling underlying feelings, and gaining deeper clarity about various challenges is personally and professionally rewarding.

77. COUNSELOR AS ART THERAPIST

In the United States, some counseling programs provide training in art therapy, and occasionally offer a certificate in art therapy. In addition, there are a small number of graduate degree programs in art therapy.

Degree Required

Optimal is an MS/MA in art therapy, or master's in a counseling field with a credential (e.g., graduate certificate) in art therapy.

Issues to Understand

Many counselors and art therapists will use drawing as a means to enhance the therapeutic encounter (Kottman, 2003). Though numbers are difficult to come by, my sense is that most counselors using art therapy were trained in counseling, as opposed to art therapy programs, due to the greater numbers of counseling programs. There is no doubt that a program specializing in art therapy would provide greater depth of training in that area than, say, a mental health counseling program with a course in art therapy. Still, many counselors receive training in art therapy and use it as a part of their practice. Far fewer will advertise themselves as an "art therapist."

Best Aspects of the Job

Art therapy is a very creative method of building therapeutic attachment and a means of personal catharsis for clients of all ages (Kottman, 2003). Drawing provides clients a creative means of expressing anger, depression, abuse, marital strife, mental illness, and numerous other issues. Though art therapy is probably considered an approach to use when counseling children and adolescents, it can be tailored for clients of all ages. I have known addictions counselors, career counselors, and certainly couples counselors who use art therapy. One art therapist I know used it in her work with torture victims by asking her clients to draw themselves before the trauma, as they currently are, and where they would like to be when they have successfully addressed the trauma. I have used art with career clients, requesting they draw the career they have, then the one they want (using as much detail as possible, including surroundings, colleagues, and region of the country). Drawing, as opposed to talk therapy, may also be less threatening as the process provides the client the opportunity to choose how deep they wish to go into the issue.

Challenging Aspects of the Job

The most challenging part of being an art therapist may lie in the fact that some people may not take you as seriously as a more conventional counselor (rehabilitation counselor, school counselor, etc.). Art therapists will likely need to be good advocates for themselves and their profession. The American Art Therapy Association (www.arttherapy.org) is a good professional organization, as is the Association for Creativity in Counseling (www.creativecounselor.org).

Occupational Outlook and Salary

The Bureau of Labor Statistics does not compile statistics on art therapy. But there are many art therapists in the United States and many counselors who have incorporated art therapy into their practice. I would suggest readers interested in this field contact an art therapist through e-mail, phone, or an informational interview and get a sense of the job picture, salary, and so on. Also, many states do not license art therapists as a separate profession. Many art therapists likely hold a license in a counseling field. A few states, such as New York, license "creative arts therapists," and art therapy is one of those creative arts fields.

78. COUNSELOR AS DANCE THERAPIST

One of the creative art therapies is dance therapy. Dance therapists have been practicing for several decades in inpatient settings, outpatient clinics, and private practice. The American Dance Therapy Association is the primary professional organization promoting the profession.

Degree Required

Master's degree in dance therapy is optimal

Issues to Understand

Dance therapists work with a wide variety of clients, including those in the autism spectrum (Asperger's syndrome included), people with developmental disabilities and chronic mental illnesses, school-age clients, and the elderly. Dance therapists will typically complete a two- to three-year degree with an intensive internship. Some programs in dance therapy also gear their programs in such a way that their students are eligible for licensure as counselors due to the infrequency that states have licensed dance therapists.

Challenging Aspects of the Job

First, there are very few graduate dance therapy programs in the United States. I formerly taught at an institution that offers one: Antioch University New England. Most states do not yet license dance therapists, meaning that graduate programs will need to structure their programs in such a manner that graduates can be licensed as counselors. (Readers interested in dance therapy should inquire about licensure when looking at graduate programs.) It is also fair to state that while dance therapy is a legitimate profession, some people are likely to view it with skepticism. I myself have run into this skepticism when people ask about the field of dance therapy.

Occupational Outlook and Salary

The Bureau of Labor Statistics has not provided figures for the profession. I do know through my dance therapy colleagues that many of their graduates are hired into jobs at the salary level of counselors ($36,810 is the mean salary for mental health counselors). Occupational demand is very difficult to discern. But, like most creative therapy art fields, they may be most viable if the practitioners can be credentialed as, say, licensed mental health counselors.

79. COUNSELOR AS MUSIC THERAPIST

Like other creative art therapy fields, music therapy has begun to emerge as a profession separate from counseling. Also, like other creative art therapies, there are some realistic difficulties the profession has to encounter, in particular, the lack of licensure in most states.

Degree Required

Master's in music therapy, or a master's in counseling with an emphasis in music therapy, or a master's in a counseling field and an additional certificate in music therapy.

Issues to Understand

There is little doubt that music can be healing, particularly when used by qualified professionals in an intentional manner. Music therapists use the art form of music in a similar fashion that art therapists use art (drawing, painting, sculpture, etc.) and dance therapists use movement (through assessments such as Laban Movement Profile, Kestenberg Movement Profile, and particular movements). Music therapy requires a great deal of training and practice in order to utilize it as a healing art. Many counselors, social workers, and psychologists do indeed incorporate music in their practice (as I have done), but that does not mean they are "music therapists."

Music therapy is often used with mute populations; people with autism, Asperger's syndrome, developmental disabilities, and chronic mental illnesses, and clients recovering from trauma, etc. Music, like dance and art, provides the therapeutic means to reach clients otherwise unsuitable to conventional talk therapy.

Best Aspects of the Job

The best aspects of being a music therapist may lie in providing a therapeutic outlet for many clients who have not fully benefitted from traditional therapy. Music therapy can also serve as an additive treatment approach to traditional therapy and in particular may be very helpful for clients less comfortable with talk therapy or who are nonverbal.

Challenging Aspects of the Job

Again, creative art therapists are not as established in the mental health field as are counselors, social workers, psychologists, and so on. Music therapists will need to advocate and educate the general public about their qualifications and effectiveness. Furthermore, music therapists will need to educate their fellow mental health colleagues about their field. Until very recently, what I knew about music therapy came from an interview with singer Sheryl Crow, a former music therapist.

Occupation Outlook and Salary

Once again, I have very little to offer readers in this area. If you were to pull up a search engine, type in the word "music therapists" and hit return, you will likely turn up such professionals in urban areas. It would be prudent to contact such professionals and ask for career guidance regarding salary and future job prospects.

80. COUNSELOR AS DRAMA THERAPIST

Drama therapy has been around for a long period of time. The field was established by Jacob Moreno, who began using psychodrama with patients in psychiatric hospitals. Currently, many counselors and other professionals do utilize drama in their practice, though few would likely refer to themselves as "drama therapists."

Degree Required

Master's degree in drama therapy, or a master's degree in a counseling field and a certificate in drama therapy.

Issues to Understand

Like many of the creative art therapists, many, if not most, drama therapists hold degrees in a general counseling field (e.g., mental health counseling and pastoral counseling) and then specialize by earning a credential in drama therapy or something similar. Many counselors use drama in their practice. Techniques such as role play, empty chair technique, and family sculpting are very common in the therapeutic field. So, while many counselors and other mental health professionals incorporate drama into their practice, there are few actual "drama therapists" in the United States.

Readers interested in drama therapy should understand they could go into the few drama counseling programs or earn a conventional counseling degree (rehabilitation counseling, mental health counseling, etc.) and then receive additional training either in a graduate class or a postgraduate credential. Professional organizations promoting the field include the American Dramatic Therapy Association and the Association for Creativity in Counseling (www.creativecounselor.org).

Best Aspects of the Job

As with the other creative arts fields, drama therapy offers a creative approach to addressing the various and sundry issues clients struggle with. In my own practice, I have used role plays extensively as I have discovered that practice seems to increase my client's opportunity for success. Psychiatric centers have long incorporated drama into their therapeutic milieu, as patients have portrayed their psychiatrists, nurses, and other staff, each other, their own illness, and so on.

Challenging Aspects of the Job

The reality is that many counselors will use drama in their approach, although few will advertise themselves as drama therapists. Readers interested in this part of the creative arts field should carefully examine graduate programs to ensure they could receive some training in this part of the field. There are also very few drama therapy graduate programs in the United States.

Occupational Outlook and Salary

The Bureau of Labor Statistics does not compile statistics on drama therapists. My best guess is that most drama therapists simply incorporate it as part of their practice. It is highly recommended that readers get formal training in drama therapy (in courses, workshops, certificate programs, supervision, etc.) if not through a drama therapy program. The most likely scenario is that a drama therapist also holds a credential in counseling (e.g., Licensed Mental Health Counselor) or another related profession and offers drama as simply one of his or her skills.

81. COUNSELOR AS ANIMAL-ASSISTED THERAPIST

Animal-assisted therapy is a more recent approach in the mental health field. Most animal-assisted therapists are counselors and social workers with additional training. I was unable to uncover any graduate programs in animal-assisted therapy. However, I am unaware of professional training offered in animal-assisted therapy.

Degree Required

Master's degree in a counseling field with a certificate in animal-assisted therapy or additional training and supervision.

Issues to Understand

Animal-assisted therapy has become widespread throughout the United States. I am aware of many therapeutic horse riding programs, and counselors and other clinicians using dogs. Animal-assisted therapy has been used to assist treatment for people with autism and other developmental disabilities, elderly shut-ins in nursing facilities, trauma victims, adolescents in residential psychiatric programs, and many other populations. Thus, animal-assisted therapy is a viable approach for counselors and other clinicians.

Best Aspects of the Job

I asked a colleague who provides animal-assisted therapy what she regarded as the best part of her work and she replied that it was seeing clients open up to animals in ways they could not in regular therapy. Working with therapy animals, whether horses or dogs (the most commonly used animals), offers clients the opportunity for a healthy attachment with the animal. Counselors using this approach can then begin to generalize this attachment toward appropriate people in the client's life.

Challenging Aspects of the Job

There has not been much research on the efficacy of animals in therapy. Most positive reports come from counselors using animal-assisted therapy or from clients themselves. This is important, but the field will need more research support in the future. This may be the most challenging part of animal-assisted therapy. Readers interested in this therapeutic approach will likely need to get practical training on their practicum or internship as I am not aware of any graduate programs in animal-assisted therapy. I do know agencies, especially residential settings for adolescents, that utilize animal-assisted therapy. A graduate student could potentially receive graduate training and supervision at such an agency.

Occupational Outlook and Salary

Again, I could find no statistics regarding occupational outlook or salary. But my experience is that many counselors and other therapists in private practice also offer animal-assisted therapy.

Spotlight: Play Therapist
Play Therapist Spotlight: Tony C. Lai, MA, LPC, Registered Play Therapist—Supervisor, Mental Health Specialist II, Yamhill County Health and Human Services, Family and Youth Programs, McMinnville, OR

Play therapy is a structured, theory-based approach, which builds on the normal communicative and learning processes of children. The curative powers inherent in play are used in many ways. Play therapists strategically utilize play therapy to help children express what is troubling them when they do not have the verbal language to express their thoughts and feelings. In play therapy, toys are like the child's words and play is the child's language. Through play, counselors may help children learn more adaptive behaviors when there are emotional or social skill deficits. The positive relationship that develops between therapist and child during play therapy sessions provides a corrective emotional experience necessary for healing. Play therapy may also be used to promote cognitive development and provide insight about and resolution of inner conflicts or dysfunctional thinking in the child.

Initially developed at the turn of the 20th century, play therapy today refers to a large number of treatment methods, all applying the therapeutic benefits of play. Play therapy differs from regular play in that the therapist helps children to address and resolve their own problems. Play therapy builds on the natural way that children learn about themselves and their relationships in the world around them. Through play therapy, children learn to communicate with others, express feelings, modify behavior, develop problem-solving skills, and learn a variety of ways of relating to others. Play provides a safe psychological distance from their problems and allows expression of thoughts and feelings appropriate to their development.

The Association for Play Therapy (APT), a national professional society in the United States, defines play therapy as "the systematic use of a theoretical model to establish an interpersonal process wherein trained play therapists use the therapeutic powers of play to help clients prevent or resolve psychosocial difficulties and achieve optimal growth and development." Although everyone benefits, play therapy is especially appropriate for children aged 3 through 12 years. Teenagers and adults have also benefited from play techniques and recreational processes. To that end, use of play therapy with adults within mental health, agency, and other health care contexts is increasing. In recent years, play therapy interventions have also been applied to infants and toddlers.

Play therapy allows trained mental health practitioners who are specialized in play therapy to assess and understand children's play. Further, play therapy is utilized to help children cope with difficult emotions and find solutions to problems. By confronting problems in the clinical play therapy setting, children find healthier solutions. Play therapy allows children to change the way they think about, feel toward, and resolve their concerns. Even the most troubling problems can be confronted in play therapy and lasting resolutions can be discovered, rehearsed, mastered, and adapted into lifelong strategies.

Families play an important role in children's healing processes. The play therapist will make some decisions about how and when to involve some or all members of the family in the play therapy. At a minimum, the therapist will want to communicate regularly with the child's caretakers to develop a plan for resolving problems as they are identified and to monitor the progress of the treatment. Other options might include involving (1) the parents or caretakers directly in the treatment in what is called filial play therapy and (2) the whole family in family play therapy. Whatever the level that family members choose to be involved, they are an essential part of the child's healing.

Each play therapy session varies in length, but usually it lasts about 30 to 50 minutes. Sessions are usually held weekly. Research suggests that it takes an average of 20 play therapy sessions to resolve the problems of the typical child referred for treatment. Of course, some children may improve much faster, but more serious or ongoing problems may take longer to resolve.

The practice of play therapy requires extensive specialized education, training, and experience. A play therapist is a licensed (or certified) mental health professional who has earned a master's or doctoral degree in a mental health field with considerable general clinical experience and supervision. With advanced, specialized training, experience, and supervision, mental health professionals may also earn the registered play therapist or registered play therapist-supervisor credentials conferred by APT. Therapists must satisfy the following criteria in order to earn these credentials:

- *License/certification*: Must hold current and active individual state license (or certification) to engage in either independent or supervised clinical mental health practice.
- *Education*: Must have earned a master's or higher mental health degree from an institution of higher education and completed APT-designated core graduate coursework, that is, ethics, child development, theories of personality, principles of psychotherapy, and child/adolescent psychopathology.
- *Clinical experience*: Must have completed at least 2 years and 2,000 hours of supervised clinical experience, not more than 1,000 hours of which may be pre-master's degree.
- *Play therapy training*: Must have completed at least 150 hours of play therapy–specific instruction, not more than 50 hours of which may be noncontact hours, from an institution of higher education or APT-approved provider of graduate-level continuing education.
- *Play therapy supervision*: Must have completed at least 500 hours of supervised play therapy experience that included at least 50 hours of play therapy supervision. For registered play therapist-supervisor, candidates must have completed an additional 500 hours of play therapy experience, which must be verified but need not be supervised by a licensed mental health professional. If a therapist receives supervised play therapy

experience from a registered play therapist-supervisor, he or she would only need to document 334 hours of supervised play therapy experience. When calculating play therapy supervision, the therapist only need to document 34 hours of play therapy supervision if he or she receives play therapy supervision from a registered play therapist-supervisor.

■ *Supervisor training*: If interested in becoming a registered play therapist-supervisor, the therapist must be a state-approved supervisor or have earned at least 24 hours of supervisor training that is not included in the 150 hours of play therapy training.

82. COUNSELOR AS PLAY THERAPIST

Counselors have been providing therapy to a wide range of ages. Children are one of the most important populations the counselors work with. But because children often lack the vocabulary and emotional awareness required of traditional talk therapy, play therapy and its variations have become popular. Counselors in settings such as schools, agencies, and hospitals provide play therapy to children recovering from maladies like abuse and neglect. Play therapy is also utilized with children having difficulty establishing peer relations.

Degree Required

Master's degree in a counseling field and some additional training and supervision in play therapy. However, a certificate in play therapy is optimal.

Issues to Understand

Play therapy is a creative though very serious approach to treating children suffering from a variety of adjustment issues (Kottman, 2001). Play therapy has variations such as client-centered play therapy, Adlerian-based play therapy, cognitive behavioral play therapy, integrative play therapy, and many others. All play therapy involves setting up a child-centered play therapy room, complete with therapeutic "toys" available from a variety of retailers (Kottman, 2001). Some common play therapy toys are sandboxes, dinosaurs, puppets, clay or Play-Doh for sculpting, crayons and coloring books, and drums.

Play therapy involves the use of interactive play to build therapeutic attachment with children and then to utilize the toys in a manner that addresses their emotional and psychological treatment needs. Counselors will need to be patient and active in order to move the sessions so that they address the issues that brought the child into therapy. Play therapy certainly involves play, but it is not the same as playing, as there is a specific therapeutic objective behind play therapy. For example, many children in play therapy will have been subjected to major trauma such as sexual abuse and thus therapeutic play is very serious.

Best Aspects of the Job

Play therapists are counseling professionals who enjoy providing therapeutic services to children and younger adolescents in a manner consistent with their developmental stage. Play therapy also is a very creative means of therapeutic expression and has numerous variations and uses. Play therapy also requires the counselors to be actively involved in cooperative activities, as well as simply pulling back and using general behavioral observation. Play therapy could also be utilized with developmentally disabled clients, and those with autism.

Challenging Aspects of the Job

Like all the creative art approaches to therapy, play therapy has had to advocate for recognition in the mental health field. Play therapy, however, may have had more success than some of the other variations in the creative arts field, as it seems to be quite popular. Play therapists will still need to be ready to explain to parents, school administrators, medical professionals, and others why they are a valuable resource.

Occupational Outlook and Salary

Like all the creative therapeutic arts, discerning the job outlook and salary is challenging as statistics are difficult to come by. My experience is that play therapists are among the most common of the creative art approaches and likely the most numerous. There are few if any degree programs in play therapy, though some counseling programs may offer an emphasis in this area. A notable example of this is the University of North Texas, which probably is the most well known in the country. I would estimate a salary roughly similar to that of mental health counselors (mean salary of $36,810). Also, some school counselors at the elementary and middle school level may also be trained and using play therapy in public schools, and their salary would approximate that of school counselors (mean salary of $57,800).

16 International Counseling Careers

Spotlight: International Counseling
Counseling in Australia Spotlight: Dr. Randolph Bowers, Adjunct Senior Lecturer, School of Humanities, Faculty of Arts and Sciences, University of New England, Australia; Consultant Counseling Psychotherapist and Educator; Founding Editor, *Counselling, Psychotherapy & Health* (www.cphjournal.com); www.randolphbowers.com

Counseling and psychotherapy is viewed by many in Australia as one field of practice. The discipline's first tertiary programs were developed during the mid to late 1990s. The first national peak body was voted into existence by members of my team back in late 1998 at an inaugural conference at the University of New England in New South Wales. Soon after the Psychotherapy and Counselling Federation of Australia was founded, issues of conscience arising in the manner in which PACFA was created inspired other members of the profession to found a national competing organization called the Australian Counselling Association. These two peak bodies have come to represent the bulk of practitioners in Australia. They have attempted to work together recently to create one national umbrella administrative body called the Australian Register of Counsellors and Psychotherapists, which would list members of both still-independent bodies and speak with one voice to certain national issues.

In Australia, my sense is that we have a close relationship with Asia Pacific nations, partly due to the fact that my prior university had me teaching and managing a program in Hong Kong that eventually inspired the creation of associations and other professional infrastructure in that region. But we also look overseas for many relationships of professional support, and have close ties with New Zealand, the United States, Canada, the United Kingdom, Ireland, and other nations. Generally, in my experience, the Australian professional community tends to be more internationally linked and concerned about global issues, and more culturally aware of the international community, perhaps in part due to our geographic isolation and our smaller size—we need to reach out and form alliances in solidarity for many reasons.

As a practitioner, my story goes back to Canada. My undergraduate degree was in religious studies and philosophy. Later, I gained a master's of education counseling degree from Acadia University in Nova Scotia during the 1990s. Issues of meaning and purpose, spirituality, culture and human growth, and healing have inspired my career. My desire to train counselors led me to Australia under a PhD teaching and research scholarship. After graduation, the university hired me as faculty, and in 2006, I was honored to be sponsored by Aboriginal elders from the region and became a citizen of Australia.

Having taught and managed counseling programs in universities for some time now, my overall concerns for the profession relate to what I see as the narrow cultural views of the Western academe that come to play in the theory and practice of undergraduate and graduate training in our field. Alongside this issue are the industry and governmental issues that inform practice and, in many ways, limit practice to dependency on funding arrangements. The lobby effort is ongoing to have counseling psychotherapy recognized by social support systems like national Medicare schemes, but the impact of not having these and other third-party payment systems in place sets the field back and causes a lack of appropriate access to affordable care for members of society.

These are the related issues that set counseling psychotherapy within an era of postmodern critique. Cultural, global, and technological revolutions are asking the field to rearticulate the whole nature of theory and practice along emerging themes of post-person-centered practice that speaks to more expansive concerns of environment, ecology, family, and community within a transformed landscape of meaning. Perhaps my vision for the field is futuristic, but nonetheless, it is also very contemporary. Concerning for me are the many gatekeepers that tend to prevent the new generations from presenting new theory and practice models, including university academics, editors, and publishers. At the same time, I wish to encourage students from year 1 onward to generate a complexity of awareness within a divergent skill-set that allows them to develop an integrative philosophy of practice at the beginning of training rather than at the end—and this perhaps is the one defining characteristic of my approach that challenges many of the dominant models of the field that rely on teaching the Western cannon first while asking questions last.

83. COUNSELOR IN FOREIGN COUNTRIES

The counseling (commonly spelled "counselling" overseas) profession has only recently become an international profession. Currently, counseling is a small, though growing movement, seemingly strongest in Western countries, though it is gradually spreading beyond them (Stockton, Garbelman, Kaladow, & Terry, 2008). There remains some confusion regarding how a counselor differs from a psychologist. Still, the counseling profession is gradually gaining an international foothold. The International Association for Counselling (IAC) is a relatively new organization formed for the purposes of promoting the international counseling profession. The National Board for Certified Counselors (NBCC) also promotes the international counseling profession.

Degree Required

Master's degree in a counseling field.

Issues to Understand

Understand that many people overseas will confuse a counselor with a psychologist. You will need to be an ambassador for the profession by educating clients and government officials about the profession of counseling. Professional organizations are crucial for support, and should you land a counseling position in another country, you need to join that country's national counseling association. In some cases, you might need to start that organization! You would also need to work with the American Counseling Association (ACA), IAC, and the NBCC, as these professional counseling organizations are crucial to the growth and development of the international counseling profession.

Best Aspects of the Job

It might be the fact that you are an active part of expanding the profession into corners of the globe where counseling has not existed, or at least where it is new. Many people are likely excited about the prospect of relocating and working in a foreign country. It is also likely that in 10 to 15 years, many more counselors will have the opportunity to work in a foreign country due the evolving global nature of work. As the global economy expands, counseling and every other profession expands with it.

Challenging Aspects of the Job

How prepared are you for variations in culture, religion, social class, government, marriage, education, and so on? It is likely that a person locating from the United States to, say, England will experience less cultural shock than a U.S. citizen who moves to Egypt. You will also confront laws that can challenge your sense of equity. Though it is true to state that women in the United States continue to face challenges in equity pay, sexual harassment, sexual assault, and so forth, in many non-Western countries the problem is magnified. Some societies provide no legal protection against domestic abuse and sexual harassment, and, in a few settings, a rape victim will be the party that gets punished.

Other challenges include radical poverty on a scale most Westerners cannot comprehend. Counselors in many societies will also need to maintain more flexible boundaries than would be practiced in the United States or Canada. For example, while teaching as a professor of counselor education in Australia, I listened to a talk by an addictions counselor. The man, a white Australian, lived and worked in the vast Australian outback. He stated that if he did not go on kangaroo hunts and participate in some cultural events, he would not be trusted by the Aboriginal tribe he worked with. Again, prepare to adapt to changes.

Occupational Outlook

Good question! My best estimate is that the counseling profession is very small in most countries, especially in non-Western ones. Your best opportunity may come through knowing someone in that country or through contact with the country's counseling organization. A recent graduate of the mental health counseling program I teach in landed a job in Cairo, Egypt. Her husband, an Egyptian engineer, had contacts in the city. When I was preparing to move to Australia, I contacted the Australian Counselling Association to gather information about the profession. Just recently, the Australian Counselling Association sent out an e-mail for counselors interested in working in the Middle East, so some jobs are out there. Salaries will be difficult to estimate due to wide variations in countries and areas of countries.

84. COUNSELOR AS HUMAN RIGHTS WORKER

Counselors interested in working in a foreign country may wish to expand their repertoire. The United Nations and many international humanitarian organizations such as Amnesty International and the Peace Corps provide services to developing nations. A human rights worker is somewhat akin to a combination of social worker, counselor, and community organizer. Human rights workers work with communities to document human rights abuses and to promote a more just and egalitarian world. Counselors who tend to be idealistic, good listeners, and empathetic are a natural fit for this type of demanding work.

Degree Required

BA/BS degree. Master's degree is preferred.

Issues to Understand

As previously stated, counselors tend to be idealistic, justice-oriented people, much like social workers and the clergy. But idealism will run into harsh reality very quickly in many societies. I saw a program on TV where a former Peace Corps worker was recounting her work in Darfur, amid the aftermath of genocide. Clearly, no one is ever prepared to deal with murder on such a vast scale. Then, as she represented a U.S. government agency, she was not quite trusted by the people she was trying to assist. She also was a woman in a very patriarchal society and an unmarried one at that!

Best Aspects of the Job

My experience in listening to former Peace Corps workers, Amnesty International staff, U.N. staff, and other members of humanitarian organizations is that you simply have to believe you can make a small difference in the world. I have known people of all ages who have joined humanitarian efforts, whether in a formal job or as volunteers, and they tend to be similar in that they are primarily motivated by a benevolent desire.

Challenging Aspects of the Job

The challenges are legion. Human rights workers can expect to confront injustices on a scale they could not imagine. The issues include famine; genocide; crimes against women, including rape and genital mutilation; religious persecution; racial injustice; and many more.

Occupational Outlook and Salary

The Bureau of Labor Statistics does not list Human Rights Worker as an occupation. Therefore, there are no BOLS statistical projections for this type of work. People of course do this type of work through the United Nations and nonprofit organizations. Occupational outlook and salary are difficult to estimate.

85. COUNSELOR EDUCATOR IN FOREIGN COUNTRIES

In the beginning of this section, I made a statement that the international counseling movement is slowly expanding. That expansion has meant a need for professors of counselor education. Though the demand seems small at the present, some young readers perusing this book may find opportunities for themselves should they attain a doctorate in counselor education.

Degree Required

PhD is preferred. Note that some countries will hire professors with a master's degree, but for the sake of the profession and for more employment options, I maintain the need for a doctorate. Furthermore, as the international counseling profession grows stronger, the doctoral degree becomes more important.

Issues to Understand

I have taught overseas, have a brother who has been a professor in several countries, and have worked with colleagues who teach in various international universities. Though academic issues can be very similar, the rules governing higher education can vary significantly across borders. For example, my brother landed a tenure track position in his field.

But, two years later, the government of that country decided that only citizens of that country could hold tenure. Many if not most countries, have university systems that have no concept of tenure and use rolling five- to seven-year contracts. *The Chronicle of Higher Education*, a weekly newsprint and online magazine, has an international section highlighting news in universities across the globe. Also, while the terms "college" and "university" refer to the same types of institutions in the United States, in most other countries, "college" refers to a type of high school.

Best Aspects of the Job

Well, it is exciting to teach abroad. Teaching at a foreign university provides you the opportunity to get to know another culture, visit a land or lands you might otherwise not visit, and interact with people you might not get to meet here in the United States.

Challenging Aspects of the Job

Most foreign institutions will not offer tenure. In developing countries, the infrastructure and facilities of universities can leave much to be desired, as buildings may be decrepit, Internet access unreliable, pay low, and grade inflation a more serious problem than in the United States (it is a problem here also). Counselor education programs may also be expected to have an undergraduate counseling program. In fact, BA/BS degree counseling programs may be as common as master's degree programs. This can create more opportunity but runs counter to the mission of the American Counseling Association and its 19 divisions.

Occupational Outlook and Salary

The demand for counselor education faculty positions in foreign countries likely remains very small. It will grow in the future, but my best guess here is that it will grow slowly. The fastest growth in counselor education programs will likely be in Western countries such as Canada, the United Kingdom, Western European countries, and Australia. Departments of counselor education are located in all continents except Antarctica, so the potential job market is there, though slow growth is my prediction.

86. COUNSELOR IN FOREIGN UNIVERSITIES

In addition to teaching in a foreign university, there will be some opportunity to work in a university counseling center in a foreign institution.

Many universities in Western countries have established counseling centers for their students. Currently, most that I am familiar with prefer psychologists, though I have met some counselors staffing university counseling centers in foreign countries.

Degree Required

Master's degree is the minimum; PhD is preferred. Psychologists are preferred, though some counselors do work in foreign universities. In fact, two of my former students, both of whom hold master's degrees, were hired to work in foreign universities.

Issues to Understand

Should you be hired by a counseling center in a foreign country, I suggest you join the national counseling organization within that country and become familiar with its ethical code as you will likely be held to it. Students and faculty may not understand the distinction between a psychologist and a counselor, and you will need to help them. This is the chance to educate and advocate for your profession. If you happen to work in a non-Western university, you will likely encounter cultural customs that vary significantly from that in a Western country. Parents may have the right to inspect their adult child's counseling record. Homosexuality may be punishable by several years of imprisonment (or worse!), thus putting counselors in a difficult position when the issue arises. Boundary issues and confidentiality may also be much more diffuse, as faculty may have the right to information that would be withheld from them in the United States.

Best Aspects of the Job

Again, despite the challenges, counseling in a foreign university can be exciting! You may feel you are having an adventure and promoting the profession at the same time. In addition, you will be privy to experiences that most counselors in the field may never have the opportunity to experience.

Challenging Aspects of the Job

In many societies, the role of women is far more subservient than in countries like the United States. Gay and lesbian students may have to live far more closeted lives than in a Western country, and some societies more openly discriminate against people of a minority religious group. All these and other social issues will be played out at the university and tensions may run high and even episodically erupt in violence (just as they occasionally do in the United States). Some counselors may be among the first mental health professionals hired to work in a foreign university. While this can be exciting, it also can mean there will be a dearth of resources at your disposal. You may also have a supervisor who is not a trained psychologist, counselor, or social worker.

Occupational Outlook and Salary

As with all occupations in this section, the job outlook and salary are difficult to estimate. My best guess from my travels, work overseas, and contacts is that while the need is great for university counselors, the jobs are scarce. They do exist, however, and counselors interested in this type of work will need to be very thorough to secure such a job. You might see ads for foreign university counselors in *The Chronicle of Higher Education*, higherjobs.net, professional counseling publications in the country of interest (for example, the Australian Counselling Association has a journal and a newsletter and a Web site), and online newspapers in countries of interest, and by word of mouth. Some counselor education professors have contacts overseas and they may be able to assist you.

87. COUNSELOR AS STUDENT AFFAIRS PROFESSIONAL IN FOREIGN UNIVERSITIES

Though university counselors are uncommon at many foreign universities, student affairs professionals are common in every university regardless of location. All "traditional" institutions will need professionals in residence life, dean of students' office, student activities, and so forth. Even virtual institutions need someone to oversee programs, monitor effectiveness, and deal with discipline issues.

Degree Required

Master's degree in counseling or counseling and college student personnel is the minimum. Doctorate in counseling and college student personnel, college student services, adult education, or a related degree is preferred.

Issues to Understand

Just as in all foreign counseling occupations in this section of the text, there may be considerable variation in culture, religion, and rules and norms guiding the institution. Some societies strictly prohibit any social contact between unmarried men and women. (Imagine your responsibilities as dean of students in such an academic setting!) Some societies have strict restrictions on speech, often resulting in frustration for the students. Some countries censor and limit Internet access. In the United States, the practice of *in loco parentis* (Latin for "in the place of the parents") was dismantled in the 1960s. But, in some countries, the university may well act as a bureaucratic parent.

Best Aspects of the Job

Once again, the excitement of living overseas and working in a foreign university is the best aspect.

Challenging Aspects of the Job

How well do you fit with the culture of the institution and the country? Some countries, especially those similar to the United States, will be much less of a stretch. But some societies may impose rigid sex roles, class distinctions, religious issues, and sexual practices. As a student affairs professional, you might be asked to uphold policies you disagree with. Of course all jobs require some compromise, but some jobs will require far more. Would you be able to suspend students for organizing a women's rights march? What about gay and lesbian students who want university recognition in a university and a society that forbid open homosexuality? Imagine working in a society that discriminates against minority religious groups. These are among the types of issues you may encounter in some countries.

Occupational Outlook and Salary

Again, it is difficult to estimate job demand and salary. If you are interested in this type of work, I would suggest you check the job advertisements in *The Chronicle of Higher Education*, higheredjobs.com, professional students affairs organizations overseas (you might start with the American College Personnel Association or the National Association of Student Personnel Administrators and see if they have branches overseas), as well as your own professors. Online newspapers in countries of interest could be another area to check out.

17

Emerging Fields and Professions in Counseling

Spotlight: Adventure-Based Counseling
Adventure-Based Counseling Spotlight: Torey L. Portrie-Bethke, PhD, NCC, Assistant Professor, Antioch University New England, Department of Applied Psychology, Clinical Mental Health Counseling, Keene, NH

Creatively integrating counseling theory, research, and best practices has afforded me the opportunity to constructively engage clients in adventure-based counseling (ABC) activities that foster social, mental, and emotional development. Utilizing ABC as an innovative counseling approach for individuals, families, and groups has increased my enthusiasm as a counselor. While engaging clients in ABC activities, I am able to identify nonverbal cues such as facial expressions and body movements that suggest they are being positively challenged. Clients have also stated that this approach to counseling is a fun and inviting approach to learn about self and others in meaningful ways. As clients enter into the ABC relationship, they begin to break down their resistance toward the counseling process and embrace a more open and positive attitude toward the experiences.

My journey for creating an ABC approach began while I was earning my master's degree in family, marriage, and couples counseling at Idaho State University. The majority of my clients were court ordered and many were resistant to the counseling process. In order to expedite the process, many clients appeared to be communicating simply what they perceived the counselor wanted to hear. In an attempt to provide clients with an alternative counseling experience where they were not already inclined to respond in familiar ways, I began reading ABC literature and explored options for integrating ABC techniques into my counseling sessions. While earning my doctoral degree at Idaho State University with an emphasis in mental health counseling, I had the opportunity to train under Dr. Nicole R. Hill and Dr. Linwood Vereen in facilitating ABC consultation groups for a regional company. Throughout my doctoral experience, Dr. Hill and Dr. Vereen supervised my ABC sessions and copresented at international, national, regional, and state counseling conferences. In addition, they supervised an ABC course that I had developed for master's students.

What compelled me to provide ABC to my clients was witnessing the profound impact this approach had on their motivation toward change. A notable example of how ABC promotes healthy emotional and relational change among clients was demonstrated with a family that I had been counseling for one year who seemed as unhappy in session as they did in all areas of their relationships, and their lives in general. I began to realize that the family longed to experience enjoyment of one another and yet they were stuck in experiencing each other in the same disappointing and unacceptable ways. I discussed with the family an alternative approach to working together in our counseling relationship. The family appeared truly excited to experience ABC so much that they wanted to begin immediately. As an ABC facilitator, I conducted a review of the ABC literature and developed intentional strategies that I felt would be most efficacious and chose to implement these techniques with the family for one year. ABC was reported by the family to be their force of change. While participating in the process, each member began to make personal and relationship changes and began to have fun. Seeing this family genuinely laugh and smile together was truly rewarding. The family's ability to create a working metaphor derived from the ABC experiences and apply this learning to other life experiences had a profound impact on the family's interactions. ABC techniques were the impetus of change for this family. I watched the family develop a pattern of fun, acceptance, and consideration of others that did not exist in prior counseling sessions. This learning generalized to other environments where notable communication and relationship improvements were reported.

I mentioned earlier that ABC has increased my enthusiasm as a counselor. This is because with each counseling session, I develop new ways to access and impact emotional and mental struggles. I have discovered the potential of numerous processing opportunities with the execution of any one simple ABC activity. With ABC training, supervision, and counseling experience, ABC can provide an innovative approach for other counselors to reach challenging clients. One beneficial aspect of ABC techniques is that clients are unprepared for the learning opportunities; therefore, clients are less likely to be resistant since they do not know what to expect. Instead, clients' energy and attention are directed toward interpretation and performance of the ABC activity.

In counseling, I am truly impressed by my clients' willingness to transform and by their ability to do so through the ABC process. Through my professional experience with ABC counseling sessions, I have observed that ABC is therapeutically beneficial for clients. However, I do have two concerns that have the potential to affect the integrity of ABC. First, the term "ABC" may be used by anyone. Any agency, school, or individual may report that they are providing ABC though they may lack the training and credentials. Since other noncounseling professionals are offering ABC without a counseling degree, there are inconsistent research findings purporting the effects of ABC outcome data. A second concern is that it is the ethical responsibility of counselors to research and report findings of ABC that may be duplicated for future research studies. In conducting empirical research with sound methodology on the benefits of ABC, counselors will be able to lead the way for improving the therapeutic benefits for clients.

As a counselor educator, supervisor, and counseling practitioner, I feel a responsibility to our profession to contribute to the ABC research. To begin this process, I have created an ABC course at Antioch University New England, for master's students in mental health counseling. This course will involve each student to personally experience ABC by designing ABC programs for specific client populations in addition to implementing the ABC program with adolescent groups. Throughout the course, the students will receive direct ABC supervision and hands-on experience. To aid in the advancement of ABC knowledge, I am cowriting a book chapter and article on ABC, conducting research on adolescents' experiences with ABC, and collaborating with others to develop ABC best practice methods.

I truly enjoy active collaboration on ABC opportunities, and I look forward to working with others to offer ABC. The greatest reward as a counselor is being included in a client's process. It is a true honor to be given the privilege by clients to join them in their journey of change. My professional goal is to continue building on my knowledge of ABC best practice methods and to integrate my learning with clients perceived needs through the counseling process.

88. GENETICS COUNSELOR

Genetics counseling is one of the newest fields to have emerged in the last two decades. Genetics counseling is a field that blends two different professions: genetics science and counseling. Genetics have become big business in science, industry, and higher education. Because of the mapping of the human genome, some people elect to have a genetic screening to assess markers for diseases such as cancers, multiple sclerosis, Parkinson's disease, and many others.

Degree Required

A master's degree in genetics counseling. There are only a few programs, but they do exist.

Issues to Understand

Genetics counseling is a profession that has emerged outside the general profession of counseling. Having examined the curricula of several genetics counseling programs, the coursework is a blend of science and counseling. Readers interested in this new field will need to be very proficient in science, as they will study biochemistry, genetics, microbiology, and other related courses. Graduate students in genetics counseling will also take courses in counseling and work in internships, most often in research hospitals, where they will meet with patients. Most genetics programs I examined were two-year programs. Graduate programs in genetics counseling look very academically demanding. (I scraped through organic chemistry, and that was tough enough!) Given the curricular requirements, the small number of graduate programs, and the newness of the field, only select people will likely go into the profession.

Best Aspects of the Job

Genetics counseling is an exciting new field blending science and counseling. Professionals in this field are right now building a new profession that is likely to be very important for the future, especially given the way technology has impacted and influenced medicine. My own expectation is for genetics counseling to become a very competitive field in the future. Many hospitals and medical centers will be interested in hiring genetics counselors.

Challenging Aspects of the Job

This is a very new field, and like all new fields, it still must fight for recognition, credentialing, billing rights, name recognition, and many other things new medical and mental health professions have had to fight for. Another challenging factor is that most people have likely never heard of a genetics counselor. Until some 5 years ago, I myself had never heard of one. Graduates of a genetics counseling program are also limited in their workplace options. Currently, they would likely need to be located around a major medical center, as an average hospital or a clinic probably would not be able to hire them at present.

Occupational Outlook and Salary

The Bureau of Labor Statistics mentions Genetics Counseling as a new field but has yet to compile statistics for growth projections.

89. COUNSELOR AS PERSONAL AND CAREER COACHES

In the last several years, the field of personal coaching has multiplied. I am noticing persons advertising themselves as personal coaches, ads for training in "personal coaching," and lately even organizations advertising their certification in personal coaching. No doubt, this is a popular field/occupation/job.

Degree Required

There is no particular degree required for this field. Personal coaches appear to come from numerous fields: counseling, business, education, and so on. But given the nature of personal growth (and that seems to be a big part of personal coaching), my recommendation is that you enroll in a counseling program, as the education and training involved in counselor education is very strong.

Issues to Understand

Personal coaching is a very popular, albeit new, field. The National Board for Certified Counselors now offers a Board Certified Coach credential in conjunction with the Institute for Life Coach Training. Nevertheless, some questions that remain to be answered are as follows: "What are the education and training requirements for the field?" Credentialing for coaches is also very new. "How do personal coaches differ from counselors?" "What types of personal growth activities are personal coaches qualified to do?" "Is there a code of ethics for the personal coaching profession?"

The growth of this field has far outstripped the parameters addressed by the above questions. Many counselors also advertise personal coaching services alongside their regular and traditional counseling duties. Because personal coaching is an unregulated field, personal coaches cannot bill insurance in the way licensed counselors can do. This means personal coaching services will be billed for cash from patrons.

Best Aspects of the Job

I am acquainted with several people who work in the field of personal coaching. Most of these professionals are counselors or other mental health professionals. I would say that freedom to work across various professional boundaries is one of the best aspects of the job. Personal coaching can mentor clients in the fields of education, business, leaders in the nonprofit world, and so on.

Challenging Aspects of the Job

Many people are likely to ask the same thing that I asked when first encountering the term "personal coach": What is a personal coach? Though the field seems very popular, there are questions regarding definition of the term, latitude of the profession, whether in fact personal coaching is a profession or simply an occupation, nature of education and training, and many others.

Occupational Outlook and Salary

The Bureau of Labor Statistics does not report figures for the field of professional coaching. My own experience is that professionals from numerous fields advertise themselves as personal coaches. It is likely that most of these people offer personal coaching alongside other services such as personal and career counseling, mediation, training and development, financial counseling, and so on. People well established in fields such as counseling, business, education, and so forth can likely do very well financially, though personal coaching likely is ancillary and not their primary income.

90. PERSONAL FITNESS COUNSELOR

Personal fitness counselor is also a relatively new occupation. My first experience with the term came about 15 years ago when the college where I worked built a new fitness center. They hired a woman with the title "personal fitness coach." Her background was in fitness training and she had a strong background in strength-and-conditioning coaching. Since then I have noticed that almost every fitness center has professionals with similar titles. Clearly, part of this represents a marketing trend. But there may be issues that go well beyond advertising.

Degree Required

Once again, there is no one degree or credential. BA/BS in a field such an athletic training, exercise and sport science, or something similar is likely a good idea. Now, a bachelor's in one of those areas plus master's in exercise and sport science, or even counseling is probably optimal.

Issues to Understand

In the United States, we live in a society where credentials are of critical importance. Even if we do not know what a particular credential means (licensure, board certified, etc.), we tend to respect someone who holds credentials. The same could certainly be said of personal fitness coaching. But as someone who has been a runner and completed marathons, half-marathons, 10Ks, 5Ks, and triathlons, experience, training, and credentialing are important to me. These likely will be important to others as well, and I'll wager that any "personal fitness counselor" you meet holds some credentials in addition to their experience.

Best Aspects of the Job

Personal fitness counselors are professionals who usually are fit themselves and enjoy training, educating, and "counseling" others interested in getting and staying fit. It is likely that such professionals will work at fitness centers in colleges, private industry, and even hire themselves out for specialized community classes. They are likely to offer private services to people willing to pay for individualized training.

Challenging Aspects of the Job

This particular section of the book involves new and emerging professions (or simply, "occupations") made up from numerous fields. Most significantly, what exactly is a "personal fitness counselor"? People interested in this profession/occupation will need to be able to answer this question in a manner that illustrates their credibility.

Occupational Outlook and Salary

Again, there are no statistics reported for personal fitness counselors. The easiest method of approximating salary for such a position would be to check with someone doing the job at a fitness center. They could provide you a typical range of salary and the job market for this profession.

91. ATHLETIC PERFORMANCE COUNSELOR

Closely related to personal fitness counselors, athletic performance counselors work with clients to address fitness and athletic performance. The difference is that athletic performance counselors will likely work with more serious athletes.

Degree Required

BA/BS in exercise and sport science or a related area. A master's degree in a related area or a master's in a counseling field is probably optimal. Note that some counseling programs now offer a graduate certificate in sports counseling or something similar.

Issues to Understand

This is a relatively new field, though somewhat related to sports psychology. An area of concern is that there are no particular standards for professionals in athletic performance counseling. People interested in an emerging field such as this will need to be athletically inclined, and in fact being a former college or professional athlete is an advantage, as athletes who hire athletic performance counselors are likely to trust former athletes more than nonathletes.

Another issue is that what exactly qualifies someone to be an athletic performance counselor? Is it the experience as an athlete, degrees, experience working with athletes, credentialing, or all of the above? As this is an unregulated occupation, the ability to articulate your qualifications will likely be the crucial part of credibility.

Best Aspects of the Job

Do you enjoy working with serious athletes? (Serious athletes are athletes of all ages who are concerned with maximum performance.) Can you relate to serious athletes and the pressures and issues they grapple with? If the answer is "yes," then this may be a viable occupation for you. Anyone who works in this area or a related field will be someone who enjoys being part of helping athletes achieve some personal milestone. That milestone may involve a college athletic scholarship, helping their team win championships, landing some type of professional contract, or winning or placing highly in competitive sports (marathons, triathlons, cycling races, golfing, etc.).

Challenging Aspects of the Job

Anyone who has followed the sports world is painfully aware of the impact of performance-enhancing drugs (e.g., steroids and human growth hormone) and the permanent mark they have left on the sports world. Clearly, records are being set and broken not by athletic aptitude, but by the aid and assistance of drugs. It is also accurate to state that there are as many unscrupulous athletic trainers, counselors, and promoters as there are athletes. Your challenge is to practice your profession in an ethical manner. Should you work with professional athletes or even serious high school athletes, drugs are a real problem. How will you address the issue of performance-enhancing drugs in a system that encourages peak performance? After all, the reasons athletes risk entire careers by using drugs is that drugs provide an edge in performance.

Occupational Outlook and Salary

There are no statistics provided for this area, though it is likely that few athletic performance counselors (and people in occupations that are equal) will make a sizable salary. However, there is a niche for counselors and other related professionals to work with athletes on performance.

For example, having spent several years in university counseling centers, I have counseled many athletes who were struggling to manage performance anxiety, stress, burnout, pressure from coaches, fans, their families, and so on. It would seem that counselors in private practice could hire out their services as could counselors working in school or agency settings. It is likely that most athletic performance counselors do this work on a part-time basis.

92. ADVENTURE-BASED COUNSELOR/THERAPIST

Adventure-based counseling or adventure-based therapy is a field that has been around for a few decades. It actually grew from the field of therapeutic recreation. For decades, recreation professionals have offered challenge courses and adventure-based outings for adolescents in residential treatment. Eventually, many of the professionals offering adventure-based services began to seek more training in counseling and related professions. Currently, adventure-based counseling has become a viable and popular field with some universities offering degrees and graduate credentials in adventure-based counseling or therapy.

Degree Required

BA/BS in recreational therapy (or related area). Master's degree in adventure-based counseling/therapy or another counseling field is optimal as this provides the option of being licensed.

Issues to Understand

Adventure-based therapy is still dominated by professionals from the recreation field and not the counseling profession. Regardless of this, many counselors and graduate students in counseling programs are interested in getting into this field. Readers interested in this field should examine programs that offer a master's in adventure-based counseling (very few) or ask a professor in the program of interest about the possibility of doing an internship that involves adventure-based counseling. I have supervised several students who selected an internship that provided them the opportunity to get supervised training in adventure-based therapy. Adventure-based therapy can involve therapeutic excursions into the wilderness, mountaineering, camping, overnight cross-country skiing trips that incorporate a therapeutic group model as part of the outing, and challenge courses.

Best Aspects of the Job

The professionals I have spoken to in the adventure-based therapy field have all mentioned the opportunity to blend therapeutic adventure with their love of the outdoors. There is no doubt that merging counseling experience with exotic locations, or at least challenge courses, represents a creative blend of personal therapy. Adventure-based counselors/therapists are not locked into 50-minute sessions in a closed office, but actively engage their clients in hands-on activities designed to break down personal barriers and build trust.

Challenging Aspects of the Job

Some of the challenges this particular field faces are credentialing, the fact many counselors or therapists come from numerous fields, and are entering a job market that is largely still emerging.

Occupational Outlook and Salary

Again, similar to many of the nontraditional counseling occupations, it is very difficult to estimate the job demand and salary. My own estimate from speaking with people in this field is that entry-level jobs do not pay particularly well and are competitive to get. But for counselors and others who are lucky enough to land a job in the adventure-based therapy field and then achieve counselor licensure, there is the opportunity to move up. Some adventure-based counseling/therapy professionals will get a salary of above $50,000 per year. But most will not make this kind of money, or at least, they will not make it without several years in the field. I do recommend a master's degree in counseling due to the ability to be licensed, as it provides additional employment options beyond the adventure field.

93. COUNSELOR FOR GAY, LESBIAN, BISEXUAL, AND TRANSGENDER PEOPLE

Some people in the counseling profession and outside of it might take issue with my listing of gay, lesbian, bisexual, and transgender counseling as an occupation. I list it as such due to the very fact that those people have had such a struggle in being recognized as fully human by many heterosexual societies. Even today, there are laws in our own society dictating who can marry, adopt, and hold certain jobs. Then there is the very real issue of gay, lesbian, bisexual, and transgender people needing to be closeted in order to ensure their safety. The Matthew Shepherd tragedy is the most visible reminder of this, though there are countless others. In many societies, being a person of a different sexual orientation is punishable by death. For all these reasons, and more, this is indeed a specialty area of counseling.

Degree Required

Master's in one of the counseling specialty areas.

Issues to Understand

As I have previously noted, counseling with persons of a different sexual orientation and those who are transgendered is indeed very different. The Association for Lesbian, Gay, Bisexual, and Transgender Issues in Counseling (ALGBTIC) is an organizational affiliate of the American Counseling Association (ACA) promoting scholarship, professional practice, and understanding for gay, lesbian, bisexual, and transgender persons. In many communities, especially in urban and suburban areas, people specialize in this type of counseling. Some nonprofit agencies, such as those calling themselves the Pride Center or a similar name, will offer individual, group, couples, and family counseling for gay, lesbian, bisexual, and transgender people and their families. I expect, however, that many more counselors in private practice or in private agencies will offer such services.

Best Aspects of the Job

Counseling professionals providing services for gay, lesbian, bisexual, and transgender people often cite the opportunity to provide a safe, accepting, and natural environment for this targeted and marginalized group of people. Clients who do not fit into the broader society's version of sexual "norms" can, perhaps for the first time, work with a professional who affirms they are as human as anyone. This is also the opportunity for counselors to advocate for and provide services to people without fear of guilt, shame, blame, or the need to change their basic orientation.

Challenging Aspects of the Job

The challenging aspects to providing counseling services to gay, lesbian, bisexual, and transgender people are numerous. Many communities, especially in rural or conservative regions, will be hostile to even acknowledging people of a sexual difference. Counselors advertising themselves as inclusive and sporting the rainbow flag may find themselves the recipient of threats of violence. Some may have their offices picketed or even damaged. There is always the potential for someone to lash out in violence against the inclusive counselor. Then, there are conservative religious leaders and political commentators who will target these types of counselors. Anyone who decides to specialize in counseling gay, lesbian, bisexual, and transgender clients will need allies and a strong personal foundation. Being active with ACA, American Mental Health Counselors Association, and ALGBTIC are a must, as well as being politically active and organizing other progressive citizens.

Occupational Outlook and Salary

There are no figures for this counseling specialty. But many counselors interested in this specialty area could land a job at a public clinic (likely in a more progressive area) and earn what the Bureau of Labor Statistics (BOLS, 2010–2011) has calculated as the median salary for mental health counselors ($36,810). The BOLS also projects mental health counselors to grow at a rate of 24% over the next 7 to 10 years. But many rural and conservative areas will put political pressure on public and private clinics to not offer, or at least not advertise, services to gay, lesbian, bisexual, and transgender people. Thus, a more realistic option is to work in a community clinic, achieve licensure, make contacts, move into private practice, and advertise your services for this population.

94. FINANCIAL COUNSELOR

Here is another counseling occupation that might likely give many counseling professionals a pause. Now, there are people who advertise themselves as "financial counselors" who have no training in counseling. They are financial planners who counsel people on investment, stocks and bonds, individual retirement accounts, and so on. Then, there is another well-known nonprofit organization called Consumer Credit Counseling, Inc. Again, most of the Consumer Credit Counseling staff likely are not trained counselors but people from business and industry. My intent with proposing this occupation as a counseling (counseling as in therapeutic counseling) is that we are the profession best versed in personal counseling. Given that financial issues can cause such stress and anxiety, there is a viable place for such a counseling specialty.

Degree Required

BA/BS in finance, accounting, or a related field. Master's degree in a counseling specialty area.

Issues to Understand

Readers with a background in business, accounting, and so forth considering a career change are naturals for this new area of the counseling field. I say this because I have had several students with a strong background as Certified Public Accountants, business owners, former corporate executives, and so on. Therefore, a person with the aforementioned background and a master's degree in counseling would appear to be a natural for financial counseling as she or he would have excellent financial knowledge and strong counseling skills. Because financial counselors would work with widows, widowers, people with estate concerns, stocks and bonds, and because these clients may suffer from anxiety, depression, and so on, the personal counseling training and experience could be invaluable. Also, consider that many young and even middle-age people have no idea how to budget and wind up deeply in debt. As a student affairs professional, and then a professor, I have met countless students who got their first credit card and quickly found themselves $2,000 to $3,000 in debt (or more!). There definitely is a niche market here.

Best Aspects of the Job

You would be in a position to provide ethical service to many people who are vulnerable due to death of a loved one or youthful inexperience, or those who have lost their job and been overburdened by a mortgage and dependents. The critical issue here is "ethical practice."

Challenging Aspects of the Job

There are some professions such as genetics counseling that have emerged and are projected to be in demand in the future, though they may be quite small in the present. Then, there are some occupations that emerge due to a need that goes unfulfilled in society. While there are people from the financial world providing financial counseling, there exists a real opportunity for the counseling and financial professions to create a hybrid profession much in the manner that has occurred with genetics counseling (e.g., science field and counseling). In fact, I know of counselors with financial and business backgrounds who provide this very service.

Occupational Outlook and Salary

It is impossible to state occupational outlook and salary details for this counseling-related job. However, there is a need for ethical professionals schooled in finances and personal counseling to provide this service. In a sense, the Consumer Credit Counseling, Inc., organization and financial counselors from the business world have paved a path. Given the severe impact of this severe recession and that financial difficulty brings about such personal anxiety (loss of earning power, loss of home, more divorces, etc.), a need exists.

18 The Counselor in Nontraditional Careers

For several years after finishing my BA in psychology from Michigan State University, I worked as a residential counselor in Oregon group homes for adolescents with mental illness. I completed my MS in counseling psychology in 1989 from Central Washington University. For the next seven years, I worked back in Oregon as a full-time college faculty member in the role of counselor and instructor for individuals in life transitions at a community college.

In 1997, through a position as training coordinator with University of Minnesota, Morris, I was invited to attend the National Service Leadership Institute's six-month training program at the Presidio in San Francisco. Within a year of word-of-mouth referrals, I had sufficient training and facilitation contracts with nonprofit and governmental organizations to leave my university post. Since then, I have been fully self-employed as consultant, trainer, and facilitator. Many consultants serve a niche market, and I am no exception. Just as the Peace Corps trains volunteers to work internationally, the federal government's Corporation for National and Community Service prepares tens of thousands of full-time volunteers and supervisors to serve within the United States. One of my consulting hats is working as one of five AmeriCorps VISTA regional team leaders in the country responsible for leading teams of skilled national service trainer facilitators.

In addition to leading national service teams covering approximately 13 eastern states, I frequently design and lead local, national, and international workshops for varying sizes and types of organizations; facilitate 1- to 3-day staff retreats; offer coaching; and am invited to deliver keynote addresses for statewide and national conferences. In order to stay current with my own professional development and to contribute back to the field, I attend and regularly lead or cofacilitate sessions at international conferences such as the International Association of Facilitators. Many of us in the field are members of organizations such as American Society for Training and Development, Organizational Development Network, and American Business Women's Association, among many others. I have found the investment of time and expense to be invaluable, both for honing my own training and facilitation skills and for the potent networking opportunities inherent in attending these events. Of course, having additional certifications in assessments, coaching, facilitation, and so forth is highly recommended and useful to display on your Web site, LinkedIn account, and the like. With the lightning pace of information and technology in virtually every field of consulting, the consultant without a passion for new learning will rapidly be left in the dust. Beyond paid consulting work (which I contract often on a sliding scale), I enjoy offering several annual pro-bono leadership development workshops in international communities that might not otherwise receive this type of training.

One of the bittersweet realities of independent consulting (as opposed to being on someone else's payroll) is the potential rollercoaster ride of variable income. For example, in 13+ years of self-employed consulting, there have been periods where I earned nary a dollar, but still had expenses to pay. Alternatively, there have been many times when I earned more money in one month than I had previously earned in one year! Furthermore, not everyone has the stomach for the independent consultant's wildly fluctuating work schedule, ranging from sane and sustainable days of preparation and delivery, all the way to a rapid-fire succession of multiple16-hour days working closely with a client on-site.

What is to love about the counselor as consultant's life? At its best, it means being your own boss; determining the scope and focus of your work; how much, when, and with whom to accept work; tremendous opportunities for professional growth and collegial relationships (I sometimes trade consulting and coaching time with my closest colleagues); and did I say freedom to choose? Beyond these logistical perks, there are few things more rewarding than facilitating individual and team transformation. To be an agent of intentional, authentic, and sustainable change; does it get any better than that?

95. COUNSELOR AS HUMAN RESOURCE PROFESSIONAL

The term "human resource professional" is a vague title that can cover a wide range of occupations both in the nonprofit and corporate worlds. It may be arguable that I am duplicating titles by separating it from say, "human resource professional," "human services professional," or something similar. But as this particular title seems broader than most, I have elected to make it a separate category.

Degree Required

BA/BS degree is required; master's degree is preferred.

Issues to Understand

A human resource professional's job responsibilities will likely be very broad. They monitor compliance with agency guidelines and state and federal laws related to labor and antidiscrimination based on disability, gender, veteran status, race, ethnicity, and so on. A human resource professional will not be doing counseling in the usual way as they are not charged with mental health responsibility. But good communication skills, empathy, mediation, and an ability to establish dialogue under difficult circumstances are all valuable traits for this occupation. The human resource professional will likely be the professional charged with addressing sensitive issues such as sexual harassment, job performance correction plans, and sometimes termination of employment.

Best Aspects of the Job

If you are someone who would enjoy working in agencies or corporations and enforcing compliance with state and federal laws, addressing various issues of concern with employees, explaining company salary and benefits, and serving as an ideas person within an agency or corporation, this could be a good occupation for you. There is little doubt that you would have enough work to do, as conflicts in the workplace are common, as are concerns of discrimination (sexual, racial, and otherwise), and many employees will need assistance in improving some aspect of their job performance or behavior. Some employees, sadly, will be fired. You may also assist in hiring new employees for the agency or corporation and may have a role in recruitment.

Challenging Aspects of the Job

Anyone who works an occupation dealing with human behavior will have a challenging and sometimes stressful job. How comfortable are you in addressing a sexual harassment issue with an employee? You may need to be the person who has to fire an employee, and that person may view you as the embodiment of an unjust system and vent her or his anger onto you. Employees and management in the agency or corporation may see you as a necessary evil (for federal, state, and agency or company regulations), but due to your role, you may find yourself an outsider.

Occupational Outlook and Salary

The Bureau of Labor Statistics (BOLS) reports very optimistic figures for human resource professionals. Because there is such a wide range of agencies (public vs. private, for-profit vs. nonprofit, large vs. small agency or corporation, etc.), the occupational outlook and salary range vary greatly. Occupational outlook is reported ranging from 9% growth to 28%, and salary from, say, $38,000 to over $100,000 per year (BOLS, 2010–2011). Realistically, most in this occupation would likely earn between $45,000 and $55,000, given that many corporations and agencies will be small.

96. COUNSELOR AS TRAINER AND FACILITATOR

The late 20th century and early 21st century have seen a proliferation in careers in human resources. One that has become more popular is trainer and facilitator. These professionals may come from the disparate fields of business, organizational development, counseling, social work, management, and many others. Trainers and facilitators work with both corporate and nonprofit organizations to train employees, management, volunteers, other trainers, and so on. While there is no one field for trainers and facilitators, counseling training is a very good background for many interested in this line of work.

Degree Required

BA/BS degree is required; master's degree is preferred. You may need to take specialty training in this field to gain more knowledge and to network.

Issues to Understand

Trainer and facilitator is a growing field, though as a relatively new field, it needs more time before maturation. As mentioned previously, there is no one degree or type of training required for this occupation. However, people who feel challenged by teaching participants in groups, whether they be in the nonprofit or corporate world, may be a good fit.

Trainers and facilitators must develop expertise in communicating concepts to a select audience in short (one to three days), intense trainings (perhaps 12- to 15-hour days, including preparation, training or facilitating, and debriefing). Trainers and facilitators often are self-employed and contract with agencies such as VISTA-AmeriCorps, human services agencies, colleges and universities, large corporations, and state agencies. Professionals in this field would need to enjoy teaching 20 to 40 people and managing and facilitating conflict within organizations as that often emerges in this type of work.

Best Aspects of the Job

My spouse does this type of work, and she reports what she most enjoys are working for herself, training participants, and the challenge of getting her message across to a diverse, and sometimes fractious, group.

Challenging Aspects of the Job

The job may require considerable travel all across the country, or at least through a region of the United States. My wife is often on the road half of most months. This schedule could prove difficult for many people, especially those with young children. Another reality is that it can take several years to get established in the field. Therefore, you may need to supplement your income with part-time work. Then, you will occasionally make two- to three-day presentations to dysfunctional organizations of people who do not want to be at the training and who may try to make your job difficult. So, trainers and facilitators will need to develop resilience and a thick skin. Like anyone who is self-employed, you will need to either purchase your own benefits package or have a spouse or partner who gets them with their jobs.

Occupational Outlook and Salary

The Bureau of Labor Statistics does not list salary and occupational outlook statistics for trainers and facilitators. Through my spouse, I have met a number of trainers and facilitators, most of whom worked part- or full-time. The occupational outlook is very small, though it seems that there is a niche market, especially for a former counselor with deep contacts in schools, colleges, and agencies, or who has worked with VISTA/AmeriCorps, the Peace Corps, or in the corporate world. Salaries vary considerably. Having met numerous trainers and facilitators, I found that all of them had careers prior to beginning work in this field. Realistically, you would need to use a counseling career, whatever specialty area you work in (school counseling, college counseling, student affairs, mental health counselor, etc.) as a springboard into this field.

97. COUNSELOR AS CONSULTANT

Similar to the trainer and facilitator, "consultant" is a term used for a wide array of occupations. I will limit my discussion of this occupation to people I have met through my work as a counselor, student affairs professional, and counselor education professor.

Degree Required

BA/BS degree is required; master's degree is preferred.

Issues to Understand

The world is full of consultants. It is likely that every field from anthropology to zoology (and everything in between!) will have consultants. Most consultants I have met either have transitioned from a full-time job where they parlayed their skills and contacts into self-employment or have a spouse/partner who can supplement their income. The joke I once heard as a young professor was "faculty don't merely retire, they become consultants." This is a bit unfair, but it illustrates that the consultant world is heavily populated. However, it also is worth remembering that many people do have success as consultants.

Best Aspects of the Job

Like many readers, I also have met scores of consultants from a variety of fields. Counselors who transition into consultants may work with P-12 public and private schools, colleges and universities, human services organizations, and nonprofit organizations. Many consultants will likely tell you (as they have told me) they enjoy the freedom of working for themselves, as well as continuing to work in their own field or related fields. Professors who have taught and published in a particular area and school counselors with many years experience, for example, are two types of counseling professionals I have met. The third type is counselors who have worked in human service agencies.

Challenging Aspects of the Job

Like I previously stated, there is no shortage of consultants. That means you would have to market yourself aggressively in order to carve out enough business to make consulting a viable career, or have a regular job and consult only on a part-time basis. The most successful consultants I have met were successful professors, directors of school counseling offices, superintendents, or recognized leaders in others areas of business and industry and the nonprofit world. Basically, nothing breeds success like success.

Occupational Outlook and Salary

This area would be anyone's guess. The Bureau of Labor Statistics does not report any statistics for consultants. My own experience is that many in this occupation have a regular job and consult on a part-time basis. The full-time consultants I met have had successful careers in higher education, human services, business, and industry, and have used their extensive contacts to build their consulting career. You would likely need to do the same.

98. COUNSELOR AS COMMUNITY ACTIVIST

The counseling profession has embraced social justice as a key component of counselor education programs and counseling professionals. Because of training and an emphasis on social justice and antidiscrimination and with exceptional training in communication and attending skills, counselors are well prepared for roles as community activists.

Degree Required

BA/BS degree is required; master's degree is preferred.

Issues to Understand

Community activists (also referred to as "community organizers") are professionals who work with governmental or private nonprofit organizations to assist communities in addressing social, educational, and environmental concerns. While there is no one education program in community activism and no particular experience is required, the most effective community activists are likely to be altruistic, educated, organized, and passionate about their work. They are professionals who will need to be able to work with a wide spectrum of people. This spectrum includes ethnic minorities; religious organizations; gay, lesbian, and transgender people; politicians; and blue and white collar workers. In short, they must be able to engage in dialogue with numerous types of people, even those they find offensive.

Best Aspects of the Job

Perhaps the best part of a community activist's job is the ability to bring together diverse groups to work on issues of common concern. These issues may be crime, addiction, run-down schools, unemployment, discrimination, and so forth.

Challenging Aspects of the Job

It is very difficult to get large numbers of people and organizations to agree on common goals. Community activists must cross political, social, ethnic, cultural, sexual, and religious boundaries as a general part of their work. These boundaries represent the many factions in our society, and getting diverse, often feuding groups of people to meet, is very challenging. Of course, some community activists are very skilled at this. President Barack Obama is himself a former community activist/organizer.

Occupational Outlook and Salary

The Bureau of Labor Statistics does not compile statistics on community activists/organizers. It is likely that community activists work for small, nonprofit organizations and occasionally for state and local governments. The occupational demand is likely to be small, and the salary is unlikely to be very substantial. People interested in this career do it due to strong personal feelings.

99. COUNSELOR AS HUMAN SERVICES CASE WORKER

Human services case work typically is the type of job/career people hold prior to going back for a master's degree in counseling. But I have known case workers who have earned master's degrees in one of the counseling fields who kept their jobs in case management, preferring it to counseling work.

Degree Required

BA/BS degree is required; master's degree is preferred for advancement into management.

Issues to Understand

Many readers of this book are likely to have been case workers, so what I am about to say is "old hat" to you. But for those who have not served as case workers, it is a very demanding occupation. Most case workers I have known will have a very large number of people on their caseload (it is not unusual for some to have over 100 on their caseload!), and keeping track of all these people is near, if not outright, impossible. Some of the most difficult and sensitive case work involves children and families. I have had colleagues (usually with counseling or social work degrees) who cannot keep track of their caseload due to the difficulty in tracking. Many people will move around and not inform their case worker. Some are homeless or living in transitional housing, while others will wind up in jail or prison, alcohol or drug rehabilitation, and so forth. Some clients will get hired (thankfully) and leave the ranks of the unemployed, will finish their GED, will matriculate to community college, and are granted custody over their children.

Best Aspects of the Job

Do you enjoy a challenge? Well, being a case manager certainly is a challenge. Effective case workers I have known are able to transcend the plethora of obstacles and find a way to make a difference in their clients' lives, at least in the lives of some of them.

Challenging Aspects of the Job

I alluded to some of the challenges previously. You will likely have an overflowing caseload due to the large number of people in some type of need and also due to governmental cuts in social services. You will be expected to do the impossible with only meager tools with which to work. Politicians, religious leaders, and community leaders will criticize you for removing a child from an abusive home and chastise you for not preventing a domestic homicide. In short, your occupational life will be lived within a societal contradiction. This explains the huge turnover in case workers.

Occupational Outlook and Salary

Because there are so many different types of case workers, salary can vary considerably. The Bureau of Labor Statistics (BOLS, 2010–2011) lists several types of case workers, with median salaries ranging from the low $20,000 to upper $40,000, depending on the type of agency and the level of education. The occupational outlook is very positive, with a growth rate of 23% over the next several years (BOLS, 2010–2011). Agency managers will have the highest earnings.

100. COUNSELOR AS EXECUTIVE DIRECTOR OF NONPROFIT AGENCIES

Counselors frequently serve as managers and executive directors in non-profit mental health clinics and human service organizations. Although a mental health agency is an example of a human service organization, the distinction I will make between the two is that mental health agencies are only one type of human service agency. Counselors, due to experience and an advanced degree, will often serve as executive directors in nonprofit human service agencies.

Degree Required

Master's degree in one of the counseling fields (most notably, mental health counseling, rehabilitation counseling, and addictions counseling).

Issues to Understand

An executive director is a manager and not a counselor. Your job is to supervise staff and oversee the agency, including budgeting, hiring and firing, contracting, and serving as the public "face" of the agency. Though counseling skills can certainly come in handy, especially when mediating staff disputes and disciplining employees, business skills may become even more important. Counselors who have previous experience as managers in for-profit industry and nonprofit organizations will have an advantage.

Best Aspects of the Job

Do you like the challenge of managing numerous aspects on a daily basis? Counselors who feel energized at the prospect of dealing with employment issues, negotiating with unions (in many states), grant writing, attending numerous in-house and community meetings, and having primary responsibility for the agency are the natural candidates for the role of executive director.

Challenging Aspects of the Job

With regard to the above, responsibility also brings with it additional challenges. Larger paychecks also mean more hours of work per week and the reality that anything that goes wrong (e.g., budget deficits, inappropriate staff behavior, and bad publicity) is your fault. Conversely, anything that goes "right" with the agency will be seen as a "team success." As the executive director, you also will be the lightening rod for disgruntling employees and anyone in the community with an agenda against your agency. You are also the most likely person to be held responsible should the agency be sued. Naturally, larger agencies will offer more responsibility and additional challenges, while the reverse can be said about smaller human service agencies. Being an executive director requires someone with a "thick" skin and the ability to remain calm and focused during turbulent times. Executive directors must also be people who can manage being the target of staff complaints.

Occupational Outlook

The Bureau of Labor Statistics did not publish any statistics on occupational outlook for executive directors of human services organizations. My own experience is that, due to the fact that each agency will have only one executive director, the occupational outlook will be significantly less than, say, line staff. Counselors desiring to become executive directors will need to work their way up to the position, and this means several years at an agency, or several years doing agency work in a similar agency. Executive directors will need a master's degree and say, 7 to 10 years of experience in the human services field. Salaries will depend on the size of the agency and the agency's funding; in large agencies, which are usually better funded, the pay is high.

101. COUNSELOR AS PROGRAM MANAGER IN NONPROFIT AGENCIES

Counselors may also run public and private nonprofit agencies. Examples of the types of social service agencies counselors may run are food banks, domestic violence shelters, employment agencies, energy and weatherization programs, community mediation, and state branch agencies related to family services and child welfare.

Degree Required

BA/BS degree is required; master's degree is preferred and in some cases required.

Issues to Understand

As a manager of an agency, you are responsible for the oversight of all agency programs, functions, policies, procedures, compliance, hiring and firing, and public relations. Managers of large agencies will have the benefit of a larger staff to assist them in the various day-to-day operations and functions of the agency. You may have assistant managers who report to you on the particular areas they supervise. One large agency I spent five summers working for had six different subagencies and five different locations spread over a large geographic area. There were well over 100 case workers and numerous managers and assistant managers. An executive director was the head of the agency, and all managers reported to that person. It was a big job!

Best Aspects of the Job

One of the best aspects is the ability to make a difference in your community. Program or agency managers may run good size organizations, employing numerous people charged with addressing many social ills within the local area. The long-time manager of the large agency that I mentioned previously had worked at the agency for almost 30 years, rising from a graduate intern to case worker, assistant manager, manager, assistant executive director, and finally executive director. During his ascent, he was able to help numerous people and network with key decision makers such as state and local political leaders. My own observation was that he made a *big* difference in the local community in his 30 years.

Challenging Aspects of the Job

"It's your fault!" When you are the boss, whatever happens is your fault. That is why you have the title and large paycheck. When successes happen, it is a "team effort." These are simply the realities of leadership. Furthermore, line staff such as case workers, counselors, and support staff will often be suspicious of your motives simply because you are the boss. If you have risen through the ranks to become a manager or executive director, your old friends may no longer be friends either due to jealously or because of your new role. Can you say "no" to people? Can you manage criticism? How thick is your skin? How will you deal with "hot button" issues such as when one of the case workers is caught having an affair with a client? What about when a staff member embezzles funds? Any issue covered by the local media (including blogs) will focus the attention on you.

Occupational Outlook and Salary

The best answer is "it depends." While the Bureau of Labor Statistics reports no figures for managers of social service agencies, my contacts in human services agencies report job demand as "somewhat low," as there are far more line case worker positions than manager positions. The salary range is wide depending on the type of agency (public or private), size and funding of the agency, and location. Program managers might expect a salary range to run from the mid $30,000 to mid $60,000 depending on the factors mentioned. Some well-funded agencies will pay even higher salaries; however, these are the exceptions.

School and Career Issues

19 Financing Your Education

One of the realities of graduate school is that it costs a *lot* of money. Unfortunately, there are no revenue streams for all students to tap into. This chapter will overview traditional financing for graduate studies such as federal student loans, work study, scholarships, graduate teaching and graduate research assistantships (Graduate Teaching Assistantship [GTA] and Graduate Research Assistantship [GRA]), and work. The reality is that most graduate students will utilize a variety of financing methods to subsidize their graduate education: federal student loans, part-time jobs, support from family, and scholarships. As a former graduate student who spent almost a decade in graduate school, I say, "you finance your education anyway you can."

In the 21st century, graduate students have never had more options for continuing their education. Large four-year institutions, medium-sized state universities, private colleges, Web-based institutions (e.g., the University of Phoenix, Walden University, and Argosy) offer master's, and in some cases, doctorates in counseling. While students will select the program and delivery method that best match them and their schedules, the money part of the process looms large. Many students are already $10,000 to $20,000 in debt (or owe far more!) after completing their baccalaureate degree. The prospect of spending two to six years for a graduate degree (master's and/or doctorate) can seem daunting when financial issues are considered. After all, many students are married or partnered, have children, hold a job, have a mortgage, and so on. Sadly, due to misplaced priorities, state and federal financial aid are woefully inadequate to cover graduate education.

SOME CONSIDERATIONS

I worked practically all the way through college, and my master's degree and doctorate. Most students I have been around also are working their way through college or graduate school, at least as much as their schedules allow. While most students will have to work at least part-time, some research indicates that working more than 15 hours a week is detrimental to a student's academic performance (Hawkins, Smith, Hawkins, Grant, & Grant, 2005). This very fact makes quite a statement regarding the relationship between affluence and academic success. Regardless of the realities, most readers of this book will need to work part-time to help finance their education. It may also be a good idea for readers contemplating graduate school to work with a financial planner (or a financial counselor) for ideas.

LOOKING FOR SCHOLARSHIPS

Let us examine the first line of financial options for financing graduate school. There are many ways to search for scholarships. One of the most efficient methods is to use search engines. The Sallie Mae Corporation offers some of the most comprehensive information (www.college answers.com), where you can register and open an account. You should also explore the Federal Financial Aid for Student Assistance form. If you are a student at a college, your financial aid office also can provide you information regarding scholarship searches.

Many counseling students become frustrated in their search for financial aid due to the relatively small number of scholarships available for graduate students. But I encourage you to search because many scholarships go unclaimed due to lack of knowledge about their existence. Some tips are as follows:

You will need to put regular time into your search each week, as if it were a job search.

Scholarship deadlines occur throughout the year, not just in the spring.

When you find applications for scholarships, read the application very carefully to ensure you comply with the requirements. Otherwise, your application may be disregarded.

Many scholarships will require an essay. In crafting your essay, make sure you address the theme of the scholarship. For example, if the scholarship is named for a particular person, refer to that individual and her or his legacy in your essay. If the scholarship is sectarian sponsored, mention how you becoming a counselor is a good reflection on the organization that sponsors the scholarship. Also, edit your essay carefully to catch sentence fragments, misspelled words, and redundant sentences.

Keep in mind key words such as social justice, human service, public relations, and violence prevention, to name a few.

Make an appointment with a financial aid worker in your college's financial aid office as these professionals have a lot of ideas and may know of specific scholarships. If you are not in college, I would suggest you speak with a representative in the financial aid office of an institution you are considering.

Remember, there are many privately financed scholarships. Once again, your financial aid office should be able to assist you in identifying such scholarships. Many private scholarships are established as memorial scholarships, while others are supported by various faith-based institutions.

For graduate students, some counseling programs offer select scholarships for their graduate students. These tend to be few in number, but it is still a good idea to ask about them.

ADDITIONAL METHODS OF FINANCING GRADUATE SCHOOL

In addition to scholarships, there are additional methods of financing.

Federal student loans: The U.S. government offers low-interest loans for graduate students seeking to continue their education. The interest rates are significantly lower than what private lenders charge. Ask a professional in a college financial aid office for information. The amount you can borrow will depend upon your financial need.

Work study: Though formerly an option open only to undergraduate students, graduate students have recently become eligible. I have had students work in the library, dean's office, athletics, and so on.

Graduate assistantships: Graduate assistantships tend to be of two types, a GTA or GRA. For the counseling profession, doctoral counselor education programs (PhD, EdD, etc.) tend to offer more GTAs and GRAs than do master's-level counseling programs.

Graduate assistantships usually cover tuition and provide a small monthly stipend in exchange for assisting faculty with ongoing research or teaching master's degree students in classes. Graduate assistantships are highly sought after and provide financial help and valuable experience in the field.

Graduate fellowships: These are similar to graduate assistantships, but the duties may differ from graduate assistantships. Fellowships may be sponsored through cooperative agreements between different institutions or private organizations.

In addition, there are other creative methods to financing graduate study.

- Do you have a 401(K) or Individual Retirement Account you can withdraw from? You may be able to withdraw up to $10,000 for furthering your education without incurring a penalty fee.
- Applying for a home equity line of credit or home equity loan to help finance graduate school. (This may be more difficult in the wake of the recent recession.)
- If you are single and not claimed on your parent's tax forms, you may be eligible for more financial aid.
- Though many students are reluctant to request the maximum in federal student loans due to concerns regarding debt, remember that the interest rate is relatively low. Also, if a loan can help you access the career you desire, it may be well worth it.
- Do you have family members who can help you defray costs? I realize this is a very sensitive issue, as parents, spouses, aunts, or uncles may have helped you finance your undergraduate career. Another method of financing is when parents or other relatives allow graduate students to live with them for little or no cost to assist with costs. Paying for an apartment, utilities, and food is very expensive. If you do not have to pay for these, that would save a lot of money.
- Supervising a collegiate living group, such as a residence hall, Greek letter house, cooperative living group, religiously affiliated house, and so on. In many cases, supervising collegiate residential living communities is part of a graduate assistantship, though not always. I spent almost 10 years as a resident advisor and resident director of college living groups, and though it was a challenging job, it saved me a lot of money and I was able to put my counseling training to good use during those years. In fact, I would suggest that students in a graduate counseling program are ideal professionals to run living communities as they receive training in career and personal counseling, crisis intervention, sexual assault, eating disorders, mediation, and so on.
- Professional organizations such as the American Counseling Association (ACA) and its divisional affiliates (American School Counselor Association, American Mental Health Counselors Association, American College Counseling Association, etc.) offer scholarships. Most of them are for students already enrolled in a counseling program. For example, each spring, ACA sponsors an essay contest for graduate students.

■ Minority and corporate scholarships: Many of these are for under-graduate students, though not all. Check http://www.menominee. edu/newcmm/FinancialAid/Scholarships.htm.

In closing, I strongly encourage all readers of this book to make a diligent search for financial assistance. Check out the resources mentioned in this chapter and also seek the aid and assistance of financial aid experts such as professionals in college financial aid offices and professional financial planners. Solicit professors in counseling programs for scholarship, fellowship, and graduate assistantships. If you are a member of a religious organization (church, synagogue, mosque, temple, etc.), seek out leaders in your spiritual community to see if they can offer any financial aid assistance. Financing graduate school has become a "patch-work" effort for most graduate students I have taught. Good luck!

20 Counselors and the Job Search

A job search involves many facets: preplanning, resume writing, mock interviewing, making an application, actual interviewing (phone and in-person), following up after the interview, dealing with rejection, entertaining an offer, deciding on whether to accept the offer, and negotiating salary to name some specific steps. The remainder of the chapter will focus on the basics (cover letters, resumes, interviewing, etc.). I will recommend a few additional texts to assist students preparing for the job search later in the chapter.

I also must express that because readers may be students in a counseling program, recent graduates, or people considering enrolling in a counseling program, I understand this will make you somewhat a heterogeneous population. What I mean is that some aspects of this chapter will relate better to those already in a counseling program or those who have completed one. But for readers considering counseling as a career, this information will apply to you should you decide to get into the counseling profession. Some of the language in this chapter, because it reads as if you are in the field, may not seem appropriate at the present. Still, I believe the career information herein is very relevant for counselors planning their careers.

THE VISIONING PROCESS: CREATING YOUR DREAM

Career professionals will tell you that the first order of success is the ability to visualize a desired goal. The second, and more important task, is to strategize on how to achieve the goal. One of the most popular methods for strategizing is creative visualization, or "visioning" in short. Visioning is a simple concept arising from the work of seminal figures such as John Holland and Richard Nelson Bolles among others. Successful people in every occupation tend to use some type of visioning process. Notable "visionaries" include Mahatma Gandhi, Martin Luther King, and Mother Teresa. Visioning should likely be the first step in planning and plotting your career path as it provides a sense of direction. Visioning is a simple process requiring just a few basic tenants of information:

- *Personal history.* How did you arrive at where you are? What experiences led you to becoming a professional counselor or counselor educator? Psychologist Milton Rokeach (2000) conducted extensive research in the study of values. Rokeach's work suggests that successful people find work congruent with their personal values. For example, if working in a spiritually affiliated school or agency is important, perhaps you should consider searching for such positions. If working with inner-city youth is where your passion lies, does a job in a wealthy suburban school really seem like a good fit for you?
- *Professional identity.* The issue of professional identity is not always as clear as it might appear. Sure, you know you want to be a professional school/rehabilitation/career/mental health counselor. But, labels such as "counselor" do not tell the entire story. For example, some mental health counselors may decide to become school counselors or vice versa. Also, many experienced counselors may move into administrative roles, such as clinical director and director, and do more administrative work and little counseling. Would your long-term goals include moving into administration? If so, do you understand what changes that would mean for your career (little to no actual counseling, budgeting, staffing concerns, grant writing, lots of meetings, lots of politicking, etc.)? Would those changes be healthy for you?
- *Goals.* What are your short-term and long-term career goals? Are you interested in running a school counseling center? Being director of a college counseling center? Becoming dean of students at a large university? Moving overseas? Becoming president of American Counseling Association (ACA), American School Counselor Association (ASCA), American Rehabilitation Counseling Association (ARCA), American College Counseling Association, etc.? Goals are fluid and subject to personal changes over time, but it is still a good idea to set goals and to review and revise them accordingly.

■ *Action plan.* Everyone with a vision needs an action plan to achieve it. An action plan is a rough roadmap to success and should consist of concrete steps leading up to the vision. The visioning process should also involve estimated time frames in order to get a sense of how you are proceeding toward your goal. If your ultimate goal is to become the president of the ACA, your action plan might look something like this:

- Becoming active in the state affiliate of ACA (one to three years).
- Transitioning into a state leadership role by

   ○ Planning board for the state conference
   ○ Serving on the editorial of the state journal
   ○ Running and being elected as president, vice president, or another office of the state organization

- Submitting manuscripts to the state journal and national ACA-affiliated journals (add 1 to 2 years to the time for the first item above)
- Attending the annual ACA conference for networking opportunities. You apply to make presentations at ACA. Eventually, you are volunteering at ACA, making presentations, and holding receptions for your state affiliate. It could take several years before you are well known at ACA (say, three to six years).
- You are having some success: publishing in academic journals, national newsletters, and in venues such as *Counseling Today.* You even have gotten on a few ACA committees and are meeting well-known members of ACA (estimated three to four years).
- After putting in 7 to 10 years in leadership positions at state and national level, you run for secretary or vice president of ACA. You lose.
- You regroup after losing and run for office the following year. You mount a more effective "campaign" (networking, thoughtful statement in *Counseling Today,* circulating among your state affiliate membership, etc.). This time, you are elected as vice president.
- The following year, you run for ACA president. You lose a close election.
- You run the next time utilizing everything you have learned previously regarding visibility, a coherent platform, networking, and so forth. This time you win.

Total estimated time to reach goal is 8 to 12 years or so. Now, most counselors are not interested in becoming ACA president, but some are. This example illustrates that setting a clear goal helps you strategize on how you might begin to work to reach that goal. You should also be flexible with timelines and remember that you will have some failures along the way, just as in the example. Do not let failures get you too down. Remember, Thomas Edison, a very successful inventor, had far more failures than successes with inventions. So, when creating a visioning plan:

1. *Be conscious of the present.* Think long-term as in the example. But do not let long-term planning trip you up in the present. Doing well in your present is the first step to achieving your long-term goals.

2. *Time frame.* Remember, long-term goals will take time, and you will need to revise them when setbacks and when life circumstances change (e.g., marriage, divorce, children, moves, promotions, and job loss).

3. *Be flexible to change.* You goals will change and that may be good. For example, you may start out with the long-term goal of running a university counseling center but decide over time you are more interested in being training director at a college counseling center. This would be an example of clarification, or simply learning that the original goal was not as congruent with your values and interests as previously thought. Remember, life is dynamic and all about change.

4. *Review your action plan periodically.* You need to regularly check on your progress. If you are not being successful, check why not. Also, what does success actually mean to you? Have your interests and values changed?

5. *Mindfulness.* "Mindfulness" is a very popular term in contemporary Western psychotherapy. Though it has Eastern connotations, mindfulness, defined for our purposes as grounded in the center of our own being while connected to others, has a place in all cultures. Some counselors will create visioning that has little to do with climbing the leadership ladder. (I do believe there are mindful leaders. Gandhi is a notable example and he was very mindful of who he was, the needs of his country, and his vision, action plan, etc.) So, be mindful and search out your values to discern if the goals you have set actually fit with your values. Discerning what goals are and are not congruent with your values may be the most difficult process you encounter in your career journey. There are no easy methods to this discernment process. The old adage of "know thyself" comes to mind, but you may have several years of struggle, professional counseling, and some type of meaningful self-reflecting practice to establish and maintain a "mindful" career.

Some common techniques for career visioning are

- *Asking open-ended questions.* This phase involves simply asking questions such as "What do I want in my career?" and "Now that I know what I want career-wise, how can I create it?"
- *Meditation.* Many people have a meditation practice (or prayer, sitting in silence, a special place, etc.) that calms and centers them. Some people use meditation as part of the creative process. Many ideas may come from meditation, or perhaps the deep relaxation meditation produces assists the practitioner in reducing anxiety and managing stress. Managing anxiety and stress will definitely be good for one's career and health.
- *Visualization.* When you picture yourself 5, 7, or 10 years down the line, what does that picture look like? What does your job involve? Director of a school counseling office, director of an agency, lie counselor, etc.? Where are you residing? State, overseas, large city, small town, region of the country, etc.? Who else is in your picture? Family, friends, colleagues, etc.?
- *Focusing.* This phase assists in clarifying how to plan and prioritize the preceding visualization process. For example, what needs to happen before you can realize your dream of a private practice?
- *Career journaling.* For many people, journaling allows them the opportunity to document how their career is proceeding, what challenges are present, satisfactions, struggles, changes, failures, successes, and so on. Not everyone finds journaling helpful, but for those who enjoy it, journaling can be a type of self-discovery regarding career and personal insights.
- *Collage making.* Do not denigrate this potentially creative, concrete exercise. Collage making can be fun and help you create a picture of your career dreams.
- *Seeking honest feedback.* Choose two or three people whom you respect. These should be people who know you well enough to give you in-depth feedback. Ideally, the people you interview should know you well and be honest enough to provide the type of critical feedback you may not want to hear. But what we do not want to hear may be what we most need to hear. Ask the people you select to answer these five questions either verbally or in writing:

  1. What qualities does this person (you) possess that will help make her/him successful in her/his career?
  2. What steps does this person need to take to realize her/his career goal(s)?
  3. This person's strongest quality is _____.

4. This person's chief weakness appears to be _____
_____.

5. The change this person most needs to make is _____
_____.

Adapted from Hodges & Connelly (2010, p. 14)

THE NEXT STEP: THE CAREER CENTER

Graduate students should make use of a valuable resource on their campus, namely, the career center. One of the most valuable services is the career center's bank of letters of reference. For example, your field supervisor can write a letter of reference on an official career center form and be done with writing reference letters for you. Reference letters in the reference bank can be "open" or "closed" file references. "Open" references mean that the student has the right to inspect the letter. "Closed" letters suggest the student is not able to read what the referral has written. Students have frequently asked me "Should I have an open or closed file?" I always feel somewhat torn because I believe that when we agree to serve as a reference, it should be an open process. (Counseling, of course, has a lot to say about transparency!) But I also know that some hiring committees will view closed files as more authentic. So, graduate students should assess the situation under advisement and make the best decision they can. Students likely may feel less inhibited in closed files if they feel confident in the people who write the reference letters. I have written reference letters for open and closed files, and my reference letter would be the same for both.

Helping students craft quality cover letters and resumes is another important service the campus career service offers. Now, in this high-tech age, most students of all ages have written resumes and cover letters. I would add, however, that many student-written resumes and cover letters are substandard to say the least. Even if you have had experience in writing cover letters and resumes (or curriculum vitae [CVs]), having a pair of "fresh eyes" to review your work is a very good idea. Even the most careful of us will make the occasional typographical error or simply add extraneous detail. So, have the career center staff critique your resume and cover letter. Also, you might run the finished products past your advisor, though be advised that because a professor has numerous students, classes to teach, papers to grade, references to write, and so on, she/he may not have a lot of quality time. For this and other reasons, make use of the campus career professionals. Remember, even professional musicians, actors, and athletes have conductors, coaches, and trainers to assist them in preparing for concerts, dramas, and games.

REQUESTING LETTERS OF REFERENCE

Counselors preparing for the job search should be soliciting letters of recommendation from professors and field supervisors. Because counseling is a professional field, letters of reference ideally should be written by counseling professionals. Counseling professionals would include professors in your counselor education program, field supervisors from your practicum and internship, and possibly supervisors in related fields who may be able to address pertinent areas related to counseling work. Teachers in P-12 schools, student affairs, the ministry, and human services organizations, for example, may be able to provide commentary on your work ethic, attitude, ability to get along with coworkers, initiative, and trustworthiness. When hiring, committees in schools, agencies, college and university counseling centers, and so forth are most concerned about your counseling skill; a strong recommendation from a supervisor in the previously mentioned related areas can be very valuable.

Before you solicit letters of recommendation, make a list of the people you intend to ask to write letters of recommendations. Some definite professionals to seek references from are your faculty advisor/major professor (sometimes these roles are filled by different people), field site supervisors, and professional people who know you well. While most counseling positions you apply for will likely ask for three letters of reference, some potential employers may ask for five. So, be prepared for the possibility of needing additional references. Now, another step you must take prior to sending off your resume or cover letter is to *ask* each person on your list of references if they would be willing to serve as a reference. You might be surprised how many times I have received a phone call from a school principal, agency director, and college counseling center search chair for an applicant who never asked if I would serve as a reference. Such unexpected calls are always embarrassing and usually torpedo the applicant's candidacy. Another factor for the applicant to consider is the strength of their referrals. As a professional who has written innumerable reference letters over the past two decades, my guideline is I must be able to write a strong letter of reference or I will refuse. Graduate students should be aware that weak or nebulous reference letters are worse than none at all. So, while you are busy getting your referrals together, consider the following:

1. Always show the respect of a potential reference by asking if they will serve as a reference for you. This is both basic courtesy and good sense.

2. Regarding the preceding point, find out the relative strength of the reference letter they will write. For example, if you have struggled in the professor's classes, you may wish to ask someone else. Or, if a field supervisor has been overly critical toward you, you may need to solicit another reference. The last thing you want your reference source to do is "damn you with faint praise."

3. Provide your referral sources with a resume or CV. This helps them fill in the gaps they may not know about your vocational life. No matter how well I know a student, I always learn something from their resume or CV. For example, the student may have several years experience as a case manager, served as a director of a residence hall, or won awards I know nothing about.

4. Make sure you do not ask your references to write a letter at the last moment. This shows poor planning on your part and suggests you have not done your homework. Ideally, give your references at least two weeks to write letters of reference.

5. Make sure you keep your references informed as to how your job search is proceeding. As a counselor educator who writes many letters of recommendation for students, I appreciate hearing how my students are progressing on the job search. When you land a job, let your references know about this as they also will be happy to know their supervision and hard work has paid off.

6. Though many of your references may not require it, it is a good idea to provide your references with self-addressed stamped envelopes. Now, as many schools, clinics, and colleges make use of e-mail, reference letters can be e-mailed as attachments, eliminating the need for postage. Still, some schools, agencies, and colleges continue to use the traditional postal service.

7. Keep a folder of the applications you have made for employment. Many students, especially doctoral students, looking for an academic job, may make 20 to 30 applications. You want to keep the positions you apply for from merging together in your mind and a file can assist with organization.

8. Anytime you apply for a counseling position, be sure to examine the Web site of the school, college counseling center, agency, and so on. Probably, everybody knows to do this, but in case you don't, Web sites can provide additional information not listed in the job advertisement. For example, how many staff are employed, how many males or females, is there a dominant theoretical approach (cognitive behavioral therapy [CBT], dialectic behavior therapy [DBT], psychodynamic, etc.), is there a mission statement (if there is, you want to learn it as you may be asked about it at a future interview), and any other relevant information.

DEVELOPING A WINNING RESUME OR CV

"A resume is the equivalent of a passport in the world of business and industry and the curriculum vitae (CV) is its equivalent in most of academia" (Hodges & Connelly, 2010, p. 31). Like passports, resumes or CVs provide a summary description of your educational and occupational life. The resume or CV is what the agency, school, or college knows about you and provides a sketch of you for their perusal. The next step in preparation for your job search is to write a resume or CV. Most readers of this text will be developing a resume. CVs are used almost exclusively by professors and college administrators.

Your campus career center will likely have a number of books on how to write a resume and cover letter and conduct a job search. But to provide some guidance, the below lists a number of books I have used and found helpful in counseling students regarding resume and cover-letter writing, self-exploration, visioning career goals, and the job search process in general:

Bolles, R. N. (2009). *What color is your parachute?* Berkeley, CA: Ten Speed Press. (Updated annually)

Capacchione, L. (2000). *Visioning: Ten steps to designing the life of your dreams.* New York: Tarcher/Putnam.

England, W. S., & Kursmark, L. M. (2007). *Cover letters: Trade secrets of professional resume writers.* Indianapolis, IN: JIST Works.

Hodges, S., & Connelly, A. R. (2010). *A job search manual for counselors and counselor educators: How to navigate and promote your counseling career.* Alexandria, VA: American Counseling Association.

Parker, Y. (2002). *The damn good resume guide: A crash course in resume writing.* Berkeley, CA: Ten Speed Press.

Yates, M. (2007). *Knock' em dead 2007: The ultimate job seekers guide.* Avon, MA: Adams Media.

Because the above list of books covers resumes, cover letters, and job search information in far greater detail than is possible in a practicum and internship book, I will not go into great detail in this chapter. I will offer some tips and cite an example of a cover letter and a resume. I highly recommend you consult one or more of the above books regarding job search.

A Few Points Before You Begin to Construct Your Resume or CV

1. *Your education and transferrable skills are of critical importance.* Your experience, training, education, and skills serve as a bridge to desired employment. Make sure you design your resume or CV in a manner that clearly highlights your training and skills areas.
2. *Claim the highest skills ethically possible.* For example, if you have cofacilitated counseling groups for two years, certainly list

that. Do not, however, list that you "ran and supervised treatment groups" if you only observed them.

3. *Make your resume or CV reader friendly.* Remember, when a search committee member first looks at your resume or CV, she or he will give it a 30- to 45-second speed read (Bolles, 2007). If the search committee does a second reviewing, they will spend considerably more time on it. Make sure your resume or CV makes logical and chronological sense. Check for misspelled words and have a career counselor or someone else you trust read it for content and mechanics.

4. *There is no one "right" resume or CV format.* So, make sure your resume makes sense, flows logically, is factually accurate, and fits with the counseling position for which you have applied.

5. *Cover your most recent 8 to 10 years of work experience in the greatest detail, depending on your age and years in the field.* Faculty counselor education positions are different from positions in schools and agencies and CVs can be voluminous in length, while resumes usually stop at two pages. Do not be discouraged if you are a 25-year-old recent graduate of a counseling program. At your age and experience level, you are not expected to have long years of professional experience. After all, everyone starts somewhere.

6. *Holding multiple jobs is no longer the problem it was in previous generations.* In this era, people are expected to hold three, four, or even more different jobs (Bolles, 2007). In higher education, the general understanding is that you must "move out to move up," and that is likely to be reflected in your resume or CV.

7. *Be factually correct where your resume or CV is concerned.* We emphasize this aspect of the job search throughout this book. You are responsible for anything you list in your resume or CV. Promote your education, skills, training, and experience— just be sure to be honest. If you are caught lying on your resume or CV, on a job application, or in an interview, the least you will lose is a job. In some cases, you may forfeit your career. Be warned!

Adapted from Hodges & Connelly (2010, p. 34)

Action Words

In developing your resume and cover letter, I encourage you to use language that describes your experience, skills, and interest in a concise, descriptive, and eloquent voice. The best way to illustrate your work in the cover letter and resume is with action words that present your case in a lively manner. Below is a sampling of action words:

Accomplished	Directed	Negotiated
Achieved	Drafted	Organized
Advised	Edited	Planned
Assisted	Established	Presented
Chaired	Facilitated	Presided
Collaborated	Implemented	Reorganized
Consulted	Integrated	Researched
Counseled°	Lectured	Revised
Developed	Monitored	Supervised

°Use of this word should be a given!

In writing a cover letter, you want to keep several elements in mind:

1. First, open the letter with a respectful business-like address such as "Dear Director," Dear Search Committee," or another title that conveys respect. Do not use informal titles even if you know the persons to whom you are writing. Remember, the cover letter indicates that you understand professional protocol. Also, tailor the cover letter to the counseling position to which you are applying (school, agency, college/university, etc.).

2. If the ad specifies that you mail in your cover letter and resume, then use "bonded" paper made for resumes. With the advent of the electronic age, much is done through the Internet. Type using a standard 12-point font such as Times New Roman or other more conservative styles.

3. Make sure in the opening paragraph that you express why you are interested in the job and provide brief information demonstrating that you understand the population served. For example, if you are applying for a position as a school counselor in an inner-city school or alternative school, briefly illustrate your knowledge of this student population. I have read numerous cover letters where the applicant seemed to have no idea of the clients we counseled. That suggests to me, the potential employer, that you, the applicant, have not done your homework.

4. Remember that the first time the search committee, personnel officer, or director reads your cover letter they are likely spending around 30 seconds on it (Bolles, 2007). So, keep it brief—one page, or one and a half at most.

5. Hit the highlights of your qualifications for the position. Cite your counseling experience (practicum/internship) and theoretical approach (or if the school/agency uses a particular approach, say CBT, indicate your knowledge and experience with that). Also, if you have special training (DBT, mediation, adventure-based therapy, critical incident stress management/critical incident stress debriefing, etc.), then indicate that as well.

6. If you have experience related to the counseling field, you certainly want to mention that. Related experience, such as working as a case manager, teaching assistant, resident advisor/resident director in a college living community, and bachelor's-level addiction counselor, is important to weave into your cover letter.

7. In the final paragraph, wrap up the letter by stating that you look forward to meeting with them to discuss your interest and fit for the job. Provide a phone number and e-mail address. Then, close with the standard, "Sincerely Yours," or "Respectfully Yours," then sign your name.

In developing a resume, remember several additional tips before you begin writing:

1. This is no time to be overly modest. Your resume is your "calling" card and summary of your professional life. Be your best self. But *be honest!* Overly embellishing on a resume can cost you a job, and maybe even a career.

2. Make your resume reader friendly. Be aware that search committees will give your resume around 30 to 45 seconds on the first read through (Bolles, 2007). Thereafter, of course, they will examine it more closely (Hodges & Connelly, 2010). As with the cover letter, use a common 12-point font, with a traditional style like Times New Roman.

3. Tailor your resume to the particular counseling position to which you are applying. This would be, naturally, one in school counseling (elementary, middle, or high school), university/college counseling, community/technical college, inpatient/outpatient settings, and so forth.

4. Make sure your resume makes chronological sense. Begin with the most recent position and work your way back. Also, I recommend you list your graduate assistantship just as you would list a job, because in essence it is vital.

5. If you are more experienced (perhaps above 40 years of age), focus on the last 8 to 12 years of your professional life. If you have been a bachelor's-level addictions counselor or case worker

for, say, 15 years, definitely list all that experience. Naturally, graduate students who have been working in related fields will have a great advantage during the job search.

6. Remember, no matter how strong your resume is, your attitude can cancel it out. As someone with more than 20 years on search committees in higher education, community mental health, and human services agencies, I have seen highly qualified candidates lose out to lesser experienced ones due to arrogance. Be confident, but tread softly. (Remember that the pronoun "we" has a more pleasing ring to the search committee than "I.")

7. Remember there is no perfect resume. Work with a career counselor in crafting yours. Make certain you know what you have written as you may be asked about it during an interview. Also, have a career counselor, colleague, or classmate read over your cover letter and resume. "Fresh" eyes may catch stylistic errors or fragments that you may miss.

8. An important addition to your resume is that of your membership in relevant professional organizations. Membership in professional organizations demonstrates a stronger commitment to the profession. It also suggests that you are more likely to keep informed of research and emerging trends in the counseling field. Every counselor should be a member of the ACA. In addition, you should join the affiliate division representing your particular counseling specialty: ASCA, American Mental Health Counselors Association (AMHCA), ARCA, and so on. As a former director of two counseling clinics and longtime faculty member, I would be hesitant to hire any counselor or counselor educator who was not a member of ACA or a relevant professional organization.

In the next section, I have provided a sample cover letter and resume to use as a model.

Sample Cover Letter

March 13, 201X

1339 Easy Street
Vista View, AR 72301

Personnel Department
Hickory Ridge School District
5555 Cardinal Lane
Hickory Ridge, AR 72709

Dear Personnel Officer:

Please consider me an applicant for the school counseling position at Hickory Ridge High School. I noticed the advertisement in a recent on-line edition of the *Northwest Arkansas Times*. Currently, I am a graduate student completing my studies and will graduate with my master's degree in school counseling this May from the University of Arkansas. In addition to course work, I have completed 700 hours of practicum and internship at a local high school. I also served as a teacher's aide in a public school for five years and have a good understanding both of academic and of personal issues that impact a student's learning environment.

My practicum and internship was spent at Fayetteville Technical High School, where I assisted the school counseling staff with academic, career, and personal counseling. This past semester, I co-facilitated two counseling groups for students at risk for dropping out of school. I also led an after-school group targeted at gang prevention.

During my counselor education studies at the University of Arkansas, I was selected for the counseling honorary Chi Sigma Iota, and even served as president. During this past year, I also worked part-time at the Beacon Light Center, where I provided personal, career, and academic counseling to at-risk adolescents.

My resume and three letters of reference requested in the advertisement are being forwarded from the Career Center at the University of Arkansas. I would welcome the opportunity to discuss my interest in the school counseling position with you in the near future. If you have additional questions, please feel free to contact me at (870) 474–1998 or through e-mail at aj47@hotmail.com.

Respectfully yours,
Althea Jefferson
Althea Jefferson

Sample Resume

Reggie Martinez, Master's candidate, B.A., A.A.
327 Springdale Ave.
Palouse Hills, WA 96332
(817) 555–0234 (c)
rmartinez@hotmail.com

Profile

Master's degree candidate seeking a challenging counseling position at a community mental health clinic.

Summary of Qualifications

- Five years experience supervising college students in collegiate living groups and providing peer advising, crisis intervention, and educational programming
- Nearing completion of a 700-hour practicum-internship in community counseling agency
- Trained in brief counseling during practicum-internship
- Developed an outreach program for Latino youth
- Selected as the Graduate Student of the Year at Washington State University

Education

Master's degree candidate (will graduate in June, 201X) in clinical mental health counseling, Washington State University, Pullman, WA (CACREP-accredited program).

Bachelors of arts (20XX) in cultural anthropology at Western Washington University, Bellingham, WA (minor: psychology)

Associates in arts (20XX) in psychology at Seattle Area Community College

Related Work Experience

Mental Health Counseling Practicum and Internship (20XX–20XX), the Rainbow Center, Moscow, ID.

- Provided individual and group counseling to clients in Spanish and English
- Cofacilitated support groups for gay and lesbian parents
- Developed a grief support group for parents who have had children die
- Presented psychoeducational workshops to schools, service organizations, and law enforcement officers
- Served as crisis counselor for evening crisis calls
- Assisted in rewriting the *Rainbow Staff Employee's Manual*

Resident Director, Department of Housing and Residence Life, Washington State University, Pullman, WA. (20XX–20XX)

- Director of International Student Residence Hall, with students from 33 countries
- Oversight of 150 undergraduate and graduate students and scholars-in-residence
- Supervisor for five residence advisors
- Responsible for coordinating educational programming in residence hall
- Mediated conflicts between residents in the residence hall
- Provided crisis intervention and referred students to the university counseling center
- Participated in Safe Haven training for gay, lesbian, and transgender students

Resident Advisor, Department of Residential Life, Western Washington University, Bellingham, WA. (20XX–20XX)

- Floor supervisor in coed collegiate residence hall (30 students)
- Responsible for educational programming
- Served as peer counselor for students
- Referred students to the counseling center, health services, and the career center.
- Mediated disputes between students on the floor.

President, Student Government Association, Seattle Area Community College, Seattle, WA (20XX–20XX)

- President of student organization representing 25,000 community college students
- Responsible for oversight of student fee budgeting, programming approval, and selecting committee chairs
- Voting member of Seattle Community College's Board of Trustees.
- Charged with lobbying for student needs, such as a new student union, recreation center, and campus residence halls.

Awards

20XX–20XX, Graduate Student of the Year. Presented by the Association for Gay, Lesbian, and Transgender Student Association, Washington State University, Pullman, WA

20XX–20XX, Seattle Area Community College's Presidential Scholarship

Publications

Martinez, R. (20XX). Barriers to providing counseling services to Latino clients: Some reflections from the trenches. *Journal of the Washington Counseling Association 12*, 22–34.

Martinez, R. (20XX). Experiences as a first generation Latino graduate student. *The Advocate, 10*, 3–5.

Martinez, R. (20XX, October 15). Racism and homophobia: One Latino's struggle for acceptance. *Seattle Post, V.57*, p. A.1, 22.

Additional Trainings

Trained in Dialectical Behavioral Therapy (Rainbow Center, 20XX–20XX)

Washington State Certified Mediator

Solution Focused Counseling, Pullman, WA, June 22–25, 20XX

Professional Memberships

Chi Sigma Iota (Counseling Honorary)

American Counseling Association (ACA)

American Mental Health Counselors Association (AMHCA)

Washington State Mental Health Counselor's Association (WSMHCA)

Hobbies

Running, cycling, traveling, and writing poetry

References

Sam Cogan, PhD, Associate Professor of Counseling, Counselor Education program, College of Education, Washington State University, Pullman, WA; (509) 633–0134, e-mail: scogan@wsu.edu.

Angela Hermes, MS, LMHC, the Rainbow Center, Moscow, ID; (509) 714–1027, hermesa@yahoo.com.

Harriet Wilson, EdD, Assistant Dean of Students/Coordinator of International Students, Washington State University, Pullman, WA; (509) 618–9090, hwilson@wsu.edu.

Regarding the sample resume, this is only *one* acceptable format. In addition, I always encourage people to list hobbies and interests because this illustrates potential methods of self-care. Reggie, for example, is telling the search committee he enjoys aerobic workouts that might keep him fit and healthy. He also engages in creative arts such as writing poetry and this could even be a way to reach difficult clients. You should also remember that people want to work around others they find similar to themselves or people they find interesting. This is where a brief section on hobbies and interests can be very valuable.

WHERE TO SEARCH FOR COUNSELING JOBS

Naturally, in the process of looking for counseling jobs, you will be concerned regarding *where* to look for them. In the beginning of the book, I referenced the Bureau of Labor Statistics figures on counselors in the United States and demand for counselors. Overall, the job market for counselors is good in most areas of the country. Some areas will be more fertile with opportunities than others. Nevertheless, here are some basic guidelines to follow.

1. *The career center:* If you are in a graduate program, meet with your institution's career center for ideas on where to search. Career counselors usually have good ideas and occasionally inside information.
2. *The newspaper ads section:* OK, this is so 20th century, but print and online editions of local newspapers list job ads. Bolles (2007) suggests that most placed ads are already filled, but many counselors do get hired in this manner. So, continue to check out this traditional approach.
3. *Relevant publications and Web sites:* For counselor educators and counselors seeking work in college/university counseling centers (and related student affairs areas), two important places to check are the career section of *The Chronicle of Higher Education* (print and online versions) and higheredjobs.com. *Counseling Today* will also list some faculty jobs.
4. *Inside tips:* If you are completing your last internship and looking to graduate, ask your field site supervisor if she/he knows any job openings in the area. This is one of the most effective job search approaches. Also, some counseling students are offered jobs at their current site. The internship provides a "testing" ground for future employees.

5. *The Internet:* The Internet has become our society's catalyst for information. Use Google and other search engines to locate jobs in your desired region.

6. *Informational interviewing:* I have known a number of counselors who have requested informational interviews from agency directors (or other appropriate agency/college professionals) and later been hired at that agency/school/college. Even if there is no current job opening, there may be one later, and the informational interview is a viable method of making a personal contact.

7. *Use of social networking sites:* LinkedIn may be the most significant networking site. If you are not on LinkedIn, you may wish to join because e-sites are the wave right now. For faculty and student affairs professionals, Academia.edu is a type of "LinkedIn" for college and university faculty and administrators.

8. *Your faculty:* Solicit your faculty to see if they have any contacts. This is especially important for doctoral students in counselor education.

9. *Job fairs:* Be aware of any job fairs in your area that solicit for school counselors, mental health counselors, and so on. Some large agencies even hold job fairs.

10. *Relationships:* Do you know anyone else who might be helpful to your job search? Perhaps a politician, minister, neighbor, family friend, etc. who might have contacts you can tap into? You are not asking them for a job, but seeking information and direction.

INTERVIEW QUESTIONS TO ANTICIPATE

Some questions you will face on an interview will be generic, whereas others are specific to a school, agency, or college counseling center. The sample questions in this section are not comprehensive but are to give you a sense of the types of questions you should be prepared to answer. It may also be helpful to have a career counselor, classmate, spouse, or friend play the role of interviewer. As previously stated, practice is *highly* recommended. Ask the mock interviewer grade you on a scale of 1 to 10, with 1 being poor, 5 average, and 10 outstanding. Also, ask your interviewer whether she or he would be inclined to hire you based on your answers.

Now, there are a couple of important points to consider before interviewing. If you do not know the answer to a question, say "I don't know." This displays both honesty and a lack of pretension. After all, if you have just completed a master's degree, you are not expected to know everything. Furthermore, experienced search committees have heard too many "BS" answers and you want to sound authentic.

Secondly, you do not want to be too lengthy with your answers to questions, as those interviewing you will lose interest. Bolles (2007) suggests the 50/50, two-minute rule. The two-minute maximum suggests that you keep your answers thorough, but brief. The longer you talk, the less interest the interviewer (or search committee) will have in your answers. After all, if you are too wordy at the interview, you may be too talkative as a counselor. Also, the longer you talk during an interview, the greater the likelihood you will disclose something you would rather not disclose (Hodges & Connelly, 2010). As a wily veteran of search committees, I cannot tell you how often a loquacious candidate has said something she or he should have left out. Be brief, thorough, and discrete.

Sample Interview Questions

1. *Why do you want this job?* This is a critical question. You want the search committee to believe this school, agency, or college counseling center is your primary interest and focus. Be able to tie your answer to the job you have applied for.
2. *Tell me about yourself.* This is your opportunity to take initiative in the interview. Now, what interviewers want to hear is how you can tie your brief bio into why you are a good fit for the job. I'd suggest that you weave your personal experience and strengths into a 60-second answer that sums up your "fit" for the position.
3. *What special training or skills do you offer?* This is where additional training or related skills and experience come in handy. For example, if you are a trained/certified mediator, mention that. Or, say, if you have several years supervising collegiate residential living communities, or training in art therapy or adventure-based therapy, mention that and tie the experience into how this enhances your counseling ability. Remember, the search committee is also asking, "What candidate can best *improve* this program?"
4. *What is your experience with this particular clinical population?* (elementary school, college students, nonverbal populations, etc.) This is where your practicum/internship comes in handy, as does any related experience in residential treatment, as a teacher's aide, and so on. Again, craft your professional and related experiences into an answer that addresses the question.
5. *Could you describe your strengths and weaknesses?* Everyone has weaknesses, and you are no exception. A "weary" line I've heard far too many times in job interviews goes something like: "I'm a perfectionist." This is really a non-answer and, to me

anyway, sounds contrived. So, try and relate a weakness that can be "flipped" into strength. For example: "In the past I had little experience with addictions counseling. In the past six months, however, I have completed a certificate in addictions counseling." Another example: "Well, I am young and have just completed my graduate degree. But I'm a quick learner and in a couple of years, I will be older and more experienced."

6. *If offered this position, how long could you see yourself working here?* In most cases, it's best not to give a specific time. Instead, you might answer something like, "I would like to work here as long as I have fresh challenges and opportunities. And, I hope to be challenged and have opportunities here for several years to come."

7. *What theoretical counseling approach do you work from?* This is often a tough question for recent graduates of master's degree counseling programs, as the program may not have provided one single approach. So, cite the approaches (CBT, solution-focused, existential, etc.) and a few examples of techniques you have used and under what situations you used them (e.g., reframing, scaling questions, empty chair technique, and miracle question). Also, let the committee know you are open to learning new techniques and approaches.

8. *What are your professional goals?* (Or, regarding your career, where would you like to be in 10 years?) Naturally, this question is candidate specific. But wise interviewees want to tie in their long-term goals to the job at hand. For example, if you are interviewing for a school counseling position, you might express that you would eventually like to direct a high school counseling office. You might also mention a few marking points along the way (such as attaining licensure, national certification, additional training).

9. *How do you handle conflict?* Given that conflicts in the workplace are the number one reason people change jobs, every search committee or interviewer should ask this question. Be judicious with your answer, but be authentic. A possible answer to this question might go something like: "I work to calm myself and review the main points of the disagreement. Then, I try and seek out the other party from the standpoint of trying to understand their point of view. If we then cannot come to agreement, perhaps asking a colleague or supervisor to mediate might be a good idea."

10. *What if a parent, teacher, or coach demands to know what you and the student/client are working on in counseling?* This is a

question to see how well you remember your professional ethics (and legal issues as well!). You want to demonstrate your knowledge of ethical and legal realities. Some issues to cover are: Does the parent have custody? What is the child's age? (In some states, 16-year-olds may have the right to privacy from parents on issues such as birth control.) Has the client given a written release of information for the coach? Thus, you want to briefly acknowledge such questions before proceeding. In P-12 schools, there is an over-riding issue termed "What's in the educational best interest of the student." In most schools, if it is in the student's best interest to divulge information to a teacher or coach, that is usually done, though in a limited form. It is also worth mentioning that in some cases, especially in college settings, the client will have the right to privacy from coaches, professors, and even parents given their adult status. Naturally, parents, professors, and coaches may not understand the client's right to confidentiality.

11. *Regarding research, what's your specialty area?* (For doctoral-level counselors.) If you are applying for an academic position or a research position, you need to be able to articulate your research interests, experience, and publications. Also, check out the department's Web site to see how your research interests match those of the faculty.

12. *Have you ever been fired from a job?* If you were terminated for cause, explain what that was. Emphasize how you have learned and grown from this experience. Remember, the world is full of successful people who were fired from previous jobs. Also, if you were fired say, 20 years ago but have stable employment history since, make sure you mention that.

13. *What did you like about our school, psychiatric center, college counseling center, counselor education program, and so forth that interested you enough to apply for the job?* This is a critical question. The answer a search committee or interviewer wants to hear involves the candidate's illustrating an in-depth knowledge of programs, missions, goals, population treated, talented staff/ faculty, and so forth of the school, agency, or counseling center. Be brief but thorough. Illustrate that you are knowledgeable about and interested in what they do.

14. *What do you see as the pressing issues in the field for the next decade?* This question is designed to see how well you understand the profession and potential changes. Good answers also illustrate that you have kept up on professional reading in journals (e.g., *Journal of Counseling & Development, Journal of Mental Health Counseling, Counseling Today*). The "pressing issues" are

debatable, so be prepared to support any answers you give. For example, some potential answers might be: "I believe multiculturalism is the most important issue due to growing immigrant and other multicultural populations." Or, "I believe a critical issue in counselor education is the growing number of virtual counseling programs." Or, the global counseling profession as it expands overseas.

15. *How have you or how would you support multiculturalism?* Multiculturalism is the counseling profession's number one issue. Be prepared to address how you support multiculturalism and include specific examples. Concrete examples might be having served on the school district's diversity task force, or college's commission on the status of women, or several years' involvement in the safe-haven training at the college, community college, or having counseled a multicultural population, worked abroad, and so on. Everyone is going to say they support "multiculturalism." The bottom line is you being able to show *how* you have supported multiculturalism. (Can you imagine anyone at an interview for a counseling position actually saying they *don't* support multiculturalism?)

16. *What professional counseling organizations do you hold membership in?* You may or may not be asked this question—though such questions should be asked as they demonstrate a commitment to the field. If you are preparing for a job search, get a membership in a professional counseling organization such as the ACA, ASCA, ARCA, and so forth.

17. *What salary would you expect to receive?* Never quote a specific figure. Answer with something like, "Somewhere in the advertised range," or "Something reflecting my training or experience." *Never state a dollar amount until you receive a job offer!*

18. *What do you know about the mission of this university, school, or agency?* This is a question that is becoming more commonly asked in interviews. I have fielded it myself a couple of times as a job search candidate. Make sure you have read and understood the mission. (Mission statements will be on the Web site.) Also, be prepared to explain why you fit the mission of the college, department, school, treatment facility, and so forth.

19. *Why should we hire you?* All interviews are an attempt to address this overriding question. This question usually comes at the end of the interview and is the candidate's opportunity to express her or his special qualifications and fit for the job. You need to be brief and sound confident, though not cocky. Here is one possible answer: "I believe myself to be the best candidate for the school

counseling position (or rehabilitation counseling position, addictions counseling position, etc.) because I have spent the past two years (or one, five, six years) working in a P-12 setting. I also have experience in vocational and academic counseling and art therapy, and I am passionate about student's well-being and academic achievements. I have already articulated my ideas about educational programming earlier in the interview and would be excited about implementing them here at Salem High School. Hire me as a school counselor, and I'll make you very happy you did."

20. *Do you have any questions for us?* Of course you do! This is your opportunity to take control of the interview and it comes at the tipping point. I cringe when I hear job candidate's state, "No, I have no questions." Such an answer implies the candidate did not do her or his homework. You must always have questions to ask, even if you already know the answers to them. I would suggest you make a list of questions based on your study of the school, agency, treatment center, community college, and so on where you are interviewed. Have a printed handy list of 7 to 10 questions you can ask the committee.

Adapted from Hodges & Connelly (2010, pp. 68–70)

Inappropriate Questions

Unfortunately, some interviewers will ask inappropriate questions during interviews. Occasionally, such questions are asked by an inexperienced interviewer with no ill intent. (Though inexperience is no excuse!) And, of course, some interviewers ask questions they know to be inappropriate.

For college positions, most public and private institutions have a Equal Opportunity Employment Commission (EEOC, a Federal Law regarding employment) statement that pledges they will not discriminate on the basis of race, creed, national origin, disability status, veteran status, gender, and so on. Many schools, agencies, and colleges also include sexual orientation as a status they will not discriminate on the basis of, though some schools, colleges, and agencies do in fact discriminate on the basis of sexual orientation. (Naturally, gay and lesbian counselors and those who support multiculturalism should check out the nondiscrimination statement of the school, agency, college, and so on carefully before applying for the job.) Examples of inappropriate questions might include the following:

- "Are you married?" Or, "Do you have children?"
- "What church do you attend?"
- "Mind if I ask you some personal questions?"

- "What political party do you belong to?"
- "What's your sexual orientation?" "You are normal, right?"
- "How many times a day do you pray?" "You are religious, right?"
- "I don't see a ring on your finger. Are you dating anyone?"
- "Are you related to anyone who could help us politically?"
- "Do you have any kind of disability or illness we don't know about?"

The professional way to respond to illegal or inappropriate questions is to be tactful and ask clarification questions:

Example: Addressing an illegal/inappropriate question: "Are you married?"

Potential answer: "How does that question relate to the job?" Or, "Why is this important information to know?" You might use humor to defuse the situation: "Hmmm...I don't think the interview police allow that question." This type of response is less confrontational that mentioning the EEOC federal employment guidelines. A more low-key, humorous approach does not suggest that illegal or inappropriate questions are any laughing matter, but rather they provide the interviewee an opportunity to send a message in a manner that does inflame the situation.

Given that the interview is the time when both the candidate and the search committee interviewer are on their best behaviors, inappropriate or illegal questions would rightfully lead a candidate to wonder about the day-to-day ethics of the workplace. It should also lead to the candidate wondering about the school, agency, or treatment center's *worst* behavior. Should you be asked illegal or inappropriate question on an interview you may wish to consider whether this is the place you want to work. You do need a job, but you don't need a job where people are routinely disrespected and legal and ethical issues are blithely ignored. Once the interview is over, you may consider contacting the appropriate person (usually in human resources or affirmative action, or in small agencies, the board of directors) and informing them of your experience. Highly paid administrators should be aware of what their subordinates are doing, especially if it runs contrary to federal law and professional ethics. You also have the right to contact your state's Department of Labor and file a complaint. Naturally, as a vulnerable person on a job search, it is wise to consider the ramifications of reporting versus not reporting illegal or unethical behavior to human resources offices and state offices of the Bureau of Labor as word gets around (even if you are told "This is confidential"). So, consider the potential risks versus rewards in reporting illegal or inappropriate interview questioning.

A FINAL CHECKLIST BEFORE THE INTERVIEW

The interview is the most important step in the "getting-hired" process. Here is a checklist for you to consult prior to your interview:

1. Be ready with a 30-second answer to the crucial question of "Why should we hire you?"
2. Review your CV or resume and be ready to expound on it during the interview.
3. Practice a mock interview with a career counselor, classmate, or friend (see the sample questions in this chapter and be prepared to answer them). Also, have the mock interviewer grade you on a 1–10 scale: 1 = poor, 5 = average, and 10 = excellent. Why did they give you this grade?
4. Regarding the practice interview, ask the person interviewing you if they would offer you a job and why or why not.
5. Identify 7 to 10 questions you will ask the interviewer or search committee.
6. Select a clean, presentable, and work-appropriate wardrobe for the interview.
7. Confirm the time and location of the interview and arrive five minutes early. *Under no circumstances will you be late!*
8. Treat everyone you meet (secretary, counseling staff, custodians, etc.) with respect and an attitude that suggests enthusiasm.
9. Be ready to tactfully address inappropriate questions should they be asked.
10. Remember that the first five minutes of the interview are critical. Communicate in a confident manner. (Do this throughout, of course.)
11. Allow the interviewer or search committee to control the flow of the interview. Do not try and take the interview over.
12. Answer questions in 30 seconds or less. If it is a real complex question, answer in 45 seconds or less. (Do not use slang or profanity.)
13. Do not raise the issue of salary until offered the job. If asked about salary at the interview, say, "I would expect something in the advertised range" or, "I'm sure we could come to an agreement."
14. Communicate enthusiasm throughout, without being "overly" enthusiastic. Smile; be genuine; use appropriate body language, active listening, and paraphrasing; and summarize appropriately.
15. Do not argue with the interviewer or search committee. If they state something you disagree with, do not press the point. There

will be a time later to contemplate whether the disagreement(s) is serious and would keep you from accepting the job.

16. Close the interview by briefly summarizing your qualifications for the job. Then say something like, "I am very interested in this position and look forward to further discussions." Unlike many other career professionals I *would not* suggest you ask for the job. My own experience of more than 20 years on search committees is that it often suggests a premature decision on the part of the candidate, or leaves the candidate seeming overly anxious. At this point, the committee already knows how serious you are about the job.

17. When you leave the room after the interview, treat people as when you entered, even if you believe the interview has gone poorly. Remember, you are working on behavioral dispositions and you wish to convey respect regardless of potential outcome.

18. The following day, send the interviewer or chair of the search committee a "thank you" card for the opportunity to interview with them.

DEALING WITH REJECTION

On the path to career success, you will experience some rejection. Although rejection during the application process is as natural as success, it is clearly far less pleasant. This section of the chapter will make concrete suggestions on ways of managing disappointment. It is also important to say that while managing disappointment is certainly possible, it is fair to say that rejection hurts. Fortunately, rejection is not personal (rare cases excepted), will pass, and does not have to keep you from landing another viable job. Rejection is also universally experienced; everyone has been rejected for something they desired, be that a job, promotion, marriage partner, sports team, or club.

SUCCESS AND FAILURE

Thomas Edison held over 1000 patents during his lifetime and was considered the embodiment of success. Yet, Edison himself admitted he had had far more scientific failures than successes. But the failures brought him closer to success. Job seekers should look at their search this way.

So, you have just suffered a setback in your job search. That dream job—the one you seemed perfect for—hired someone else. Perhaps you had a great interview where the search committee seemed to hang on your every word (or so you thought). You left the interview convinced you would soon be getting a call from the school principal, agency director, or dean of the college with a job offer. Perhaps you were even planning the salary negotiations. Then, with a brief, stilted phone call, your dreams burst into flames of disappointment. You hang up the phone stunned and numb from the shock of rejection. You try to make sense of it, but your mind could not seem to accommodate the unexpected setback, especially after your experience during the interview.

The above scenario has been experienced by just about every job seeker in history. On occasion, the anticipated fails to materialize, and the applicant is left empty handed and disappointed. During this phase, it is important to remember, however, that every successful counselor or counselor educator has experienced the above let-down.

The critical factor for job seekers to acknowledge is this: *Expect some failures.* But job rejection means you are actively trying to land a job by networking with friends and colleagues, attending career fairs, or examining the local newspaper, online postings or periodicals such as *Counseling Today, The Chronicle of Higher Education,* or *higheredjobs. com.* For each job advertised, usually only one person will be selected. This means, of course, that if 30 applicants apply for a school counseling opening, 29 will be disappointed. Here are some things to think about the aftermath of job rejection:

STAGES OF JOB REJECTION GRIEF

In the late 1960s, Elisabeth Kübler-Ross published her seminal work, *On Death and Dying* (1969). On the basis of a series of interviews with terminally ill patients, she theorized that dying people progress through a series of five stages she termed the "stages of grief." They are

1. Denial
2. Rage and anger
3. Bargaining
4. Depression
5. Acceptance

(Elisabeth Kübler-Ross, 1960, p. 100)

Mercifully, job rejection is not as painful or serious as anticipating death. But job rejection can precipitate a serious bout of grief or depression. My experience in counseling job seekers is that rejected applicants experience stages similar to the ones Kübler-Ross described. It is also likely that stages of grief should more appropriately be termed "phases of grief" as we tend to vacillate back and forth, rather than proceed through the stages in developmental sequence. It is also likely that many applicants go through these stages very quickly. The stages become more apparent when, like in the above scenario, the applicant is rejected for a job she or he really wanted or when a candidate has experienced multiple job rejections. So, the stages of grief have their limitations regarding applying them to some rejected applicants. Still, the stages of grief can provide some insight into the aftermath of a job rejection. For example:

1. *Denial.* You hung up the phone shocked you were not offered the job. Perhaps you briefly entertain whether or not you imagined the rejection. This is a very common reaction for many people I have counseled.

2. *Rage and anger.* "How could they offer the job to someone else?! Those #@$#% idiots!" Does this sound familiar? If you have not given voice to these sentiments, you may have thought them. This stage is very brief for most (fortunately!). For some, feelings of anger may still emerge months after the rejection.

3. *Bargaining.* "I'll change! I'll do anything!" Reality still has not set in. I have counseled rejected applicants who months later continue to hold out hope that the search committee chair will call to inform them the search committee made a horrible mistake and would they still like the job?

4. *Depression.* Depression in very common in rejected applicants. But depression may also be a sign the applicant is moving through the stages of grief. This stage may actually be a "good" sign, provided it does not last too long.

5. *Acceptance.* This stage represents the end of the long, dark tunnel. Acceptance does not mean absence of disappointment, pain, or bitterness. Rather, acceptance implies the rejection no longer dominates one's waking thoughts. This is the point when unsuccessful applicants began to apply the lessons learned from the rejection.

WHY CANDIDATES ARE REJECTED

There are a number of reasons for job rejection:

1. *A more qualified candidate was selected.* Or the committee thought the successful candidate was more qualified. Remember, hiring is a very rough science at best and a shot in the dark at worst.

2. *The successful candidate seemed a better fit for the position.* This could be different from reason 1 above. A candidate with less experience might be hired because she has a counseling specialty area other candidates lack (e.g., trauma counseling, play therapy experience, and mediation training) or she simply seemed to connect better with the search committee.

3. *Fit has cultural and gender implications.* For example, if all the current school counseling staff are female, a male candidate likely has a better chance at the job. The same statement applies to ethnicity.

4. *You were rejected due to racism, sexism, homophobia, etc.* While the counseling profession is generally a progressive one, not all schools, agencies, and college centers are affirmative in their action. Do not kid yourself; the "isms" are very much alive in this 21st century world.

5. *The successful candidate was simply better prepared than the other finalists.* Bolles (2007) makes the point that the most prepared applicant will likely be hired over a more qualified one. Preparation includes well-crafted resumes or CVs, succinct and error-free cover letters, and good interviews. A more qualified candidate could torpedo their candidacy by lack of preparation in these areas.

6. *Candidate's behavior was inappropriate during the interview.* Inappropriate behavior could be excessive drinking at lunch or dinner, making racist or sexist jokes, rudeness to committee members, or raising inappropriate topics during the interview.

7. *Candidate displayed a lack of confidence at the interview.* You might be the most qualified candidate, but if you do not present yourself as such, someone else will get the job offer. Self-critical comments, such as "It's nothing," or "Anyone could have done it," or, "My colleagues actually did most of the work," send the wrong message. Be confident, not cocky.

8. *Candidate was dishonest.* Were you caught in a lie on your resume or CV? Did you overly embellish your credentials during the interview phase? You might get away with dishonesty. But remember, the counseling world is still rather small and unethical behavior is likely to catch up to you and cost you a job—if not a career. Be positive and show your "best" self, but tell the truth while doing this.

9. *Candidate's appearance was unprofessional.* Granted that interviewing for a counseling position is not like that for, say, banking. But play it conservative: women should wear dress slacks, skirt, or a dress. Men should wear a tie or sport coat. Do not go overboard

with cologne or perfume, as this can have the opposite effect. After you are hired, your dress can be more personally expressive.

10. *The search was a failed one.* Sometimes, a committee will not hire due to a shallow applicant pool or a general dissatisfaction with the finalists.

11. *There was behind-the-scenes politicking.* You can never really know what goes on behind closed doors. Nepotism is still alive in the employment realm despite serious attempts to eradicate it. Politics can play a role, as well as the fact someone on the committee did not like your dress, accent, and so on. Maybe the successful candidate was the one who had the least negatives. You never know.

12. *Candidate posted crude, lewd, or insulting information on Internet sites such as MySpace, YouTube, or Facebook.* Social networking sites have created a medium for sharing information and meeting new people. They also contain and chronicle much outlandish behavior. Google searches to root out embarrassing or crude behavior are becoming routine. Younger counseling students should be aware that something posted during undergraduate years could cost them a job. If you do use social networking sites or write a blog under your own name, do not post anything that might jeopardize your career.

13. *The rejected candidate did nothing wrong, was prepared, was respectful, and was a model of how to meet, greet, and interview with staff. The interviewer, search committee, or some influential people or persons simply did not like the candidate.* This will sometimes happen despite the candidate having done everything correctly. Perhaps she or he simply did not "hit it off" with the personality of the committee, or other influential persons.

Adapted from Hodges & Connelly (2010, p. 88–91)

TRANSFORMING YOUR DISAPPOINTMENT

Fortunately, most applicants are resilient and understand there will be other job opportunities in the counseling field. The important point in managing and transforming job rejection is to learn from disappointment and adapt that knowledge to new opportunities. When you get a disappointing phone call, e-mail, or thin envelope, here are some suggestions for dealing with job rejection:

1. Allow yourself some time to adjust to the situation. Do not push yourself to feel "ok." Talk the situation over with a trusted friend

or colleague. Be honest with yourself about the disappointment and pain.

2. Stay physically active. Activity routines are a staple of health, especially during a job search. Physical activity works off anxiety and promotes relaxation.

3. When you have a little distance from the disappointment, reflect back on the experience. What went wrong? What seemed to go well? How could you improve for the next application or interview? This aspect of self-reflection is a critical task in the job search process.

4. Get feedback from someone in the professional field. If you are seeking a school counseling position, ask a professional school counselor to look over your resume or CV for tips. Practice interviewing with a career counselor or a professional counselor and have them grade you.

5. You may wish to join a Job Club. Many areas have them and they are set up for unemployed people. The Job Club offers personal support from peers and also provides structure to assist you in looking for a job.

Complete self-reflection exercises on a separate sheet of paper (or simply in your mind):

1. How would you describe your current job search? (e.g., What's going well? What's been a struggle? Who has been helpful to you during this time?)

2. Ideally, where would you like to be in your professional life? Describe the job, geographic location, salary, and anything else that seems pertinent.

3. How can you begin to create the professional life you described above? Cite anything that could help you accomplish your professional goals.

4. If you were recently rejected for a job (or jobs) you wanted, what did you learn that can help you in future job searches? If your answer is "nothing," get some feedback from someone you trust or a professional in the field. Learn *something* constructive from every rejection you experience.

5. What supports do you have during this transitional time? Examples of support can be family members, friends, a spiritual community, fellow grad students, a support group, or personal/career counselor.

6. Regarding the Kübler-Ross type of grief process described earlier, if you have recently dealt with job rejection, what stage are

you currently in? Note the date of your answer and then periodically return to assess whether you have transitioned through this stage.

7. What personal strengths do you have that will assist you in coping with this transition time? Examples of personal strengths are a positive outlook, good work ethic, fitness routine, belief that you will eventually be successful (this may be the most important of all attributes), and so on.

8. Think of when you were faced with previous challenges. How have you coped with previous disappointments? How can previous experience with disappointment assist you now?

9. Think of someone who has been successfully transitioned through job rejection and then found success. Ask them for tips on how you can do the same.

10. Ask yourself: "What else can I do to become the strongest candidate possible?" If you can't answer this question, seek out a friend or career professional.

11. When you do land a professional counseling position, how will your life be different?

12. What would potential employers find attractive about you? What criticisms might they have? What is your ratio of strength to criticisms?

13. Networking is an essential component of a successful job search. What can you do to create an effective supportive network? (Use of career center, LinkedIn, support groups, informational interviewing, etc.)

14. When writing cover letters, resumes, or CVs and when being interviewed, what message would you like to convey? How can you create that desired message?

15. If you were looking to hire a counselor or counselor educator, what qualities would you look for? How well do you match up to those qualities? If you do not match up to the desired qualities, what do you need to do to meet them?

16. If a potential employer were to ask, "Tell me five reasons why I should hire you," how would you answer?

17. If it was a job offer you really wanted and are feeling very disappointed, try a focusing technique. With each breath, hold the picture of the job in your mind. Then, exhale and visualize letting go of that job. Do this mindful-type exercise as long as you need.

Adapted from Hodges & Connelly (2010, p. 94–96)

FINAL THOUGHTS ON MANAGING JOB REJECTION

As a counselor, a large part of your job in any setting will be to assist students, clients, inmates, couples, groups, and so forth in moving through their own grief, pain, and disappointment. Naturally, you will have your own experience to fall back upon. Whenever you are tempted to resign or when one of your clients is, stay optimistic. Hope may well be the best single predictor of success in any endeavor (Seligman, 1998). Also, remember:

- Disappointment is transitory. You will also have other opportunities.
- Continually update your skills. Attend professional trainings to build on existing skills (e.g., DBT and mediation training).
- Strategize. Use the self-reflection exercises in this book to assess your capabilities and to enhance your strengths.
- Work on your self-talk. Do not give in to negative self-messages you may be giving yourself. Remember, Ellis (1994) has illustrated that unhealthy behavior follows unhealthy self-talk.
- Practice interviewing through the use of role plays. Get a career counselor or friend to interview and grade your performance. Or perhaps have yourself recorded during a mock interview in order to observe how you come across verbally and nonverbally.
- Remember your strengths. Do not dwell on deficits. Remember that you have come very far in your educational life, so there are likely far more strengths than weaknesses.

ENTERTAINING A JOB OFFER: TO ACCEPT OR NOT TO ACCEPT

Congratulations, you have a job offer! This is a big deal even if you are not interested in the job. When you receive an offer, it may be tempting to accept on the spot, especially during tough economic times. Be aware that if you accept the job unconditionally, you may be losing any leverage you might have in the negotiation process. Certainly you want to express excitement and gratitude on receiving the offer and you may even feel the salary and benefits are very good. Still, as this is a big step and may involve a move, ask for a few days to think it over. Most employers, reasonable ones anyway, will respect this request.

Be thorough in your decision-making process, as you do not want to hastily accept a job only to find there is something you missed in the process (moving expense reimbursement, annual raises, etc.). In the discernment process, there are many issues to consider:

- What life changes would accepting this job entail?
- What expenses would I incur by accepting the job? (e.g., moving expenses, selling or buying a home, uprooting children from school and friends, and moving away from family)
- What would I be gaining by accepting this offer? (Other than a paycheck.)
- What would I be giving up by accepting this job?
- Does the salary range seem equitable or enough to live on? Also, what will my counter offer be?
- How excited am I about this offer? Would I want to work with the staff? Does this position offer good potential for professional growth?

If you are still unsure about accepting the job, a simple and common technique in assessing the benefits and drawbacks to accepting the position is a pro–con exercise. Using a pen, split a sheet of paper down the center. Label the left side *pro* and the right side *con*. Then, list all the pros and cons you can think of. Naturally, you want the pro list to be longer than the con list. If the con list is longer or the lists are of about equal length, this should give you pause before accepting the offer. Let us examine the list below:

Pro	Con
It's a job	Expensive area
Good salary and benefits	Requires expensive move
Desirable area of country	Far from friends and family
Good potential for promotion	I might get other offers
Likable colleagues	
Area has job potential for partner	
I'm excited about the job	

In the above case, the pros outnumber the cons, although there are significant cons in the list. Thus, this candidate has a difficult decision to make. There are some significant pros above, and the most significant one may be the excitement about the job. Some readers may be in the enviable position of entertaining several offers at once, and the pros–cons lists would be longer than a list for one offer. Regardless, the ultimate decision to accept or reject the offer can be a difficult one. Here is another example of a counselor weighing an offer:

Pro	Con
It's a very good job	It's a 500-mile move
We love the location!	I'll be leaving friends
They'll help my partner job search	My partner will need to find a job
Excellent potential for promotion	
I like the staff/faculty	
The salary and benefits are very good	
They will pay $3,000.00 for the move	
We're close to family	
I'm very excited about the job!	

In this example, the pros seem to far outnumber the cons. It is likely that this counselor would have an easier time making a decision of whether to accept the position than the one in the previous scenario.

A SIMPLE EMPLOYMENT DECISION TREE

Another method of assessing whether or not to accept a job involves a decision tree. In the example below, continue down the list until you arrive at a "no" answer. A "no" answer would suggest that you seriously consider whether accepting this job is a wise decision.

Step 1: Do I really want this job? Yes? No?

Step 2: Does this job fit mine or my family's needs regarding professional challenge, financial security, benefits, stability, and lifestyle? Yes? No?

Step 3: If taking this job necessitates a move, would I or my family be willing to relocate? Yes? No?

Step 4: Would the relocation be worth the disruption in our lives? (distance from family, friends, school change, spouse/partner's job change, etc.) Yes? No?

Step 5: Are the administration and staff (or faculty) at this position actually supportive of diversity?* Yes? No?

---

* Regarding the question on diversity above, there are some questions to ask yourself: What does their nondiscrimination statement include? Some aspects of diversity are not included in the federal EEOC guidelines (e.g., sexual orientation). If not, you might want to do a little investigation. For gay and lesbian counselors, search the Web site to see if there are benefits for same-sex couples or if the term "partner" or "significant other" is even used. If not, ask why. Also, during the interview or on the Web site, did you notice any rainbow symbols? Granted, there are no guarantees, but visible signs and verbal acknowledgment provide some window on how supportive and affirming the school, agency, or university might be.

Step 6: Do I feel committed to this job for three to five years? Yes? No?

Step 7: Does the job environment seem healthy? (healthy collegial relations, small annual turnover rate, supportive supervisor, etc.) Yes? No?

Step 8: Can I say, "This is the type of job I'm excited about?" Yes? No?

Step 9: Do the pros of accepting this job outweigh the cons? Yes? No?

Step 10: If you answered "yes" to the question above, do the pros *significantly* outweigh the cons? Yes? No?

(Hodges & Connelly, 2010, p. 81)

IF YOU REJECT THE OFFER

Be professional. Thank the search committee chair or whoever has offered you the position. If the person asks why you are turning down the offer, be as honest as you feel comfortable. For example, if the staff seemed rude, you might want to consider whether you would actually disclose that. If you are rejecting the offer because of money, a "better" job, or because you have found one closer to family, that likely won't be as difficult to mention. Remember, the counseling profession can be very small, so be careful not to impugn reputations over petty misunderstandings.

IF YOU HAVE DECIDED TO ACCEPT THE OFFER

This is the place all job seekers want to be; you have an offer and have decided to accept it. Your work still is not done. Anyone extending a job offer understands that a savvy candidate will attempt to negotiate the best possible terms. Many people, and this may be especially true of counselors fresh out of graduate school, may be uncomfortable with negotiation, especially during tough economic times. Determine what salary you and your family need, then practice negotiating with a career counselor or friend. Now, here are some things to keep in mind regarding negotiation:

- You may have been given a specific salary figure. Your ability to move that figure upward will depend on what you have to offer (special training, related experience, publications, etc.), your apparent skill level, and how much the employer wants you.
- Beyond salary, what are the other negotiable? Is a costly move involved? Are you a dual-income family and losing one income with the move? Can the employer assist your spouse or partner in finding a job?

- How good are the benefits? What and *who* does the health plan include? (domestic partners, step-kids, etc.) What about the retirement package. If you are young, don't discount this issue as it will become increasingly important over time.
- How many vacation days do you receive per year? How many sick days?
- What type of annual salary increase or merit increase is offered? Will you have a probationary period? Does the job involve tenure and if so, what is the length of time before you can apply for tenure?
- What opportunity is there for advancement?
- Will the employer pay for you to receive additional training? (for attending conferences, workshops, etc.)
- Regardless of what transpires, you will be courteous during the negotiation phase. Do not become rigid and make statements such as "This is my final offer!" Be flexible when necessary without giving in on everything. For example, you might be more flexible on salary, but hold the line on moving expenses or in getting the school/college/agency to assist your spouse or partner in finding a job.
- When you agree to a package, get the agreement in writing. There are too many stories of applicants being promised something that did not materialize once they arrived on the job.

SOME FINAL THOUGHTS ON THE NEW JOB

Your new employer will expect you to be enthusiastic when you begin. Be realistic and give yourself time to adjust to a new place, new colleagues, and new challenges. Remember that most people struggle in their jobs not because they lack the skill, but because of conflicts with coworkers (Bolles, 2007). Therefore, extend yourself to your new colleagues by asking for their input, ideas, and critique. Be respectful when you disagree in staff meetings, and learn to listen to people you find difficult.

CONCLUSION: A FEW TIPS TO REMEMBER

Preparing for the job search includes many facets such as meeting with a career counselor; writing cover letters, resumes, and CVs; preparing for interviews; dealing with rejection; accepting a new job; negotiating salary; and often, moving to a new area. The good news is that job placement success rates are promising (Bureau of Labor Statistics, 2010–2011).

Securing the initial, postgraduate professional counseling job can take a few months, so do not get too discouraged if you do not have a job at graduation. Stay focused, make lots of applications, and get support from family, friends, and, if needed, a counselor.

The profession of counseling has entered an exciting time, with licensure in all 50 U.S. states, Washington, DC, and Puerto Rico. Licensed counselors can now bill most insurance companies, work in Veterans Affairs hospitals, bill TRICARE, hold private practices, and much more. The counseling profession has even become a global profession, and many readers of this book will likely have the opportunity to work overseas during their career as a counselor. As new counseling professionals, or as readers entertaining becoming counselors, I will offer some simple tips for you. I call these *My 10 Recommendations:*

1. Achieve licensure. This is the major credential of the field. Or, if you live in Canada or another country, earn the credential your country/province/state/professional association provides.
2. Be a lifelong learner. Update your skills through certification trainings (in trauma counseling, autism spectrum disorders, career coaching, etc.).
3. In addition to licensure, get the particular certification offered through the National Board for Certified Counselors.
4. At minimum, maintain a lifelong membership in the ACA and in your professional specialty division (ACSA, AMHCA, ARCA, etc.).
5. Be active in your state counseling association. Attend state conferences when you can.
6. Make sure you stay current and informed on ethical issues (by reading and referring to your professional ethical code) and on changing state laws related to counselor practice.
7. When you need it, seek professional counseling for your emotional health and to remain professionally fit.
8. When you become a supervisor, be willing to take on counseling interns to help promote the profession. Also, be fair to graduate students in related fields such as social work, psychology, and marriage and family therapy.
9. Be willing to lobby for the counseling profession by calling your local political leaders. These include U.S. Senators and Congressional Representative to Washington, DC, as well as state politicians. The ACA Web site offers simple, easy tips on how to lobby.
10. Know your professional and personal limitations and practice within them.

RECOMMENDED READING

Bolles, R. N. (2011). *What color in your parachute?* (updated annually) Berkeley, CA: Ten Speed Press.

Bureau of Labor Statistics. (2010–2011). *Occupational outlook handbook.* http://www.bls.gov/oco/. Washington, DC: U.S. Bureau of Labor Statistics. Author. (Updated annually)

Hodges, S., & Connelly, A. R. (2010). *A job search manual for counselors and counselor educators: How to navigate and promote your counseling career.* Alexandria, VA: American Counseling Association.

References

American Council on Education. (2008). *Mapping internationalization on U.S. campuses: 2008 edition*. Washington, DC: Author.

American Counseling Association. (2005). *American Counseling Association code of ethics*. Alexandria, VA: Author.

American Counseling Association (2009). *Licensure requirements for professional counselors: A state-by-state report*. Alexandria, VA: Author.

American Counseling Association. (2010). *Licensure requirements for professional counselors*. Alexandria, VA: Author.

American Mental Health Counselors Association (2010, November) AMHCA/NBCC/ACA update: Congress passes NDAA recommended independent TRICARE practice for counselors. *AMHCA update*. www.amhca.org/news/detail.aspx?ArticleId=243. Author.

American Psychiatric Association. (2000). *Diagnostic and statistical manual of mental disorders* (4th ed, text rev.) Washington, DC: Author.

American Psychological Association (2011). *What do I need to in order to become a licensed psychologist in the U.S.?* Retrieved November 11, 2011 from www.apa.org/support/careers/licensure/qualifications.aspx#answer.

American School Counselor Association. (2002). *ASCA's national model: A foundation for school counseling programs*. Alexander, VA: Author.

American School Counselor Association. (2005). *The ASCA national model: A framework for school counseling programs* (2nd ed.). Alexandria, VA: Author.

American School Counselor Association. (2008–2009). *Recommended student/school counselor ratio by state 2008–2009*. Alexandria, VA: Author. Retrieved October 21, 2010, from http://www.schoolcounselor.org/files/Ratios2008-09.pdf

Arthur, N., & Pedersen, P. (2008). *Critical incidents in counseling for international transitions*. Alexandria, VA: American Counseling Association.

Aubrey, R. F. (1977). Historical development of guidance and counseling and implications for the future. *Personnel and Guidance Journal, 55*, 285–295.

Barsky, A. E. (2007). *Conflict resolution for the helping professions* (2nd ed.). Belmont, CA: Thomson-Brooks/Cole.

Bolles, R. N. (2007). *What color is your parachute 2007: A practical manual for job hunters and career-changers*. Berkeley, CA: Ten Speed Press.

Bowen, M. F. (1960). The family concept of schizophrenia. In D. D. Jackson (Ed.), *The etiology of schizophrenia* (pp. 346–372). New York: Basic Books.

Bradley, R. W., & Cox, J. A. (2001). Counseling: Evolution of the profession. In D. C. Locke, J. E. Myers, & E. L. Herr (Eds.), *The handbook of counseling* (pp. 27–41). Thousand Oaks, CA: Sage.

Brewer, J. M. (1942). *History of vocational guidance*. New York: Harper & Row.

Bureau of Labor Statistics. (2010–2011). *Occupational outlook handbook*. Washington, DC: Author. Retrieved September 17, 2010, from www.bols.gov

Cashwell, C. S. (2010, March). In CACREP perspective. *Counseling Today, 52*(11), 58–59.

Corey, G. A., & Corey, M. S. (2003). *Becoming a helper* (4th ed.). Pacific Grove, CA: Brooks/Cole.

Corey, G. R. (2009). *Theories and practice of counseling and psychotherapy* (8th ed.). Belmont, CA: Thomason.

Corsini, R. J. (2008). Introduction. In R. J. Corsini & D. Wedding (Eds.), *Current psychotherapies* (8th ed., pp. 1–14). Belmont, CA: Thomson Brooks/Cole.

Council for the Accreditation for Counseling and Related Educational Professions. (2009). *CACREP accreditation standards*. Alexandria, VA: Author. Retrieved September 2, 2010, from www.cacrep.org/doc/2009standardswithcover.pdf

Curtis, R., & Sherlock, J. (2006). Wearing two hats: Counselors as managerial leaders in agencies and schools. *Journal of Counseling & Development, 84*, 120–126.

D'Andrea, M., & Arredondo, P. (2002, September). Multicultural competence: A national campaign. *Counseling Today, 33*, 36, 41.

Eckholm, E. (2006, September 7). Inmates report mental illness at high levels. *The New York Times*. Retrieved May 11, 2011, from http://www.nytimes.com/2006/09/07/us/prisons.htm.

Ellis, A. E. (1994). *Reason and emotion in psychotherapy revised*. New York: Kensington.

Emener, W. G., & Cottone, R. R. (1989). Professionalization, deprofessionalization, and representation of rehabilitation counseling services according to criteria of professions. *Journal of Counseling & Development, 67*, 576–581.

Etzoni, A. (1969). *The semi-professions and their organization*. New York: The Free Press.

Forest, L. (1989). Guiding, supporting, and advising students: The counselor's role. In U. Delworth, G. R. Hanson, & Associates (Eds.), *Student services: A handbook for the profession* (pp. 265–283). San Francisco, CA: Jossey-Bass.

Freedman, T. L. (2004). *The world is flat: A brief history of the twenty-first century*. New York: Farrar, Straus, & Giroux.

Gladding, S. (2007). *Counseling: A comprehensive profession* (5th ed.). Upper Saddle River, NJ: Merrill/Prentice Hall.

Gladding, S.T. (2009). *Counseling: A Comprehensive profession* (6th ed.). Upper Saddle River, NJ: Pearson.

Granello, D. H., & Granello, P. F. (2007). *Suicide: An essential guide for helping professionals and educators*. Boston, MA: Allyn & Bacon.

Green, M. F., Luu, D., & Burris, B. (2008). *Mapping internationalization on U.S. campuses: 2008 edition*. Washington, DC: American Council on Education.

Grisham, J. (1998). *The street lawyer*. New York: Bantam Books.

Harold, M. (1985). Council's history examined after 50 years. *Guidepost, 27*(1), 4.

Hawkins, C. A., Smith, M. L., Hawkins, R. C., & Grant, D. (2005). The relationship among hours employed, perceived work interference, and grades as reported by undergraduate social work students. *Journal of Social Work Education, 41*(1), 13–27.

Herr, E. L. (2004). ACA fifty years plus and moving forward. In G. W. Waltz & R. Yep (Eds.), *VISTAS–perspectives on counseling 2004* (pp. 15–23). Alexandria, VA: American Counseling Association.

Hodges, S., & Connelly, A. R. (2010). *A job search manual for counselors and counselor educators: How to navigate and promote your counseling career.* Alexandria, VA: American Counseling Association.

Hollis, J. W., & Dodson, T. A. (2001). *Counselor preparation 1991–2001: Programs, faculty, trends.* Greensboro, NC: National Board of Certified Counselors.

Hubble, M. A., Duncan, B. L., & Miller, S. D. (1999). *The heart and soul of change: What works in therapy.* Washington, DC: American Psychological Association.

Kadison, R., & DiGeronimo, T. F. (2004). *College of the overwhelmed: The campus mental health crisis and what to do about it.* San Francisco, CA: Jossey-Bass.

Knell, S. M., & Ruma, C. D. (1996). Play therapy with sexually abused children. In M. Reinecke, F. Dattilio, & A. Freeman (Eds.), *Cognitive therapy with children and adolescents: A casebook for clinical practice* (pp. 338–360). New York: Guilford.

Kottler, J. A. (2003). *On becoming a therapist* (3rd ed.). San Francisco, CA: Jossey-Bass.

Kottman, T. (2003). *Partners in play: An Adlerian approach to play therapy.* Alexandria, VA: American Counseling Association.

Krumboltz, J. D. (1992, December). Challenging troublesome career beliefs. *CAPS Digest,* EDOCG-92-4.

Kübler-Ross, E. (1969). *On death and dying.* New York: Macmillan.

Landreth, G. L. (2002). *Play therapy: The art of the relationship* (2nd ed.). New York: Brunner-Routledge.

Linde, L. (2010). From the president: Counseling is.... *Counseling Today, 52*(11), 5, 37.

Maples, M. F., & Abney, P. C. (2006). Baby boomers mature and gerontological counseling comes of age. *Journal of Counseling & Development, 84,* 3–9.

Marx, K., & Engels, F. (1985). *The Communist manifesto.* New York: Penguin Classics.

Miller, W. R., & Rollnick, S. (2002). *Motivational interviewing: Preparing people for change* (2nd ed.). New York: Guilford.

National Board for Certified Counselors. (2011). *Understanding NBCC's national certifications.* Retrieved November 21, 2011, from www.nbcc.org/OurCertifications

National Center on Family Homelessness. (2010). *What is family homelessness?* (The problem). Retrieved January 28, 2011, from http://www.familyhomelessness.org/families.php?=ts

National Coalition for the Homeless. (2011). *Factsheets.* National Coalition for the Homeless. Retrieved July, 2011, from www.nationalhomeless.org/factsheets/who.html

Nichols, M. (2008, October 15). *A national shame: The mentally ill homeless. Anxiety, panic, & health.* Retrieved May 11, 2011, from http://anxietypanichealth.com/2008/10/15/q-national-shame-the-mentally-ill-homeless

Nugent, F. A., & Jones, K. D. (2009). *Introduction to the profession of counseling* (5th ed.). Upper Saddle River, NJ: Merrill/Prentice Hall.

Remley, T., & Herlihy, B. (2007). *Ethical, legal, and professional issues in counseling* (3rd. ed). Upper Saddle River, NJ: Pearson/Merrill-Prentice Hall.

Remley, T. P., Jr. (1995). A proposed alternative to the licensing of specialties in counseling. *Journal of Counseling & Development, 74,* 126–129.

Rogers, C. R. (1942). *Counseling and psychotherapy: Newer concepts in practice.* Boston: Houghton Mifflin.

Rogers, C. R. (1951). *Client-centered therapy: Its current practice, implications and theory.* Boston: Houghton Mifflin.

Rokeach, M. (2000). *Understanding human values: Individual and societal*. New York: Simon & Schuster.

Romeo, J. L., & Skovolt, T. M. (1998). Henry Borow and counseling psychology: A half-century common journey. *Counseling Psychologist, 26,* 448–465.

Seligman, M. E. P. (1998). *Learned optimism* (2nd ed.). New York: Pocket Books.

Stockton, R., Garbelman, J., Kaladow, J. K., & Terry, L. J. (2008). The international development of counseling as a profession. In W. K. Schweiger, D. A. Henderson, T. W. Clawson, & Associates (Eds.), *Counselor preparation: Programs, faculty, trends* (12th ed.). New York: Taylor & Francis.

Sue, D. W., Arredondo, P., & McDavis, R. J. (1992). Multicultural counseling competencies and standards: A call to the profession. *Journal of Counseling & Development, 70,* 477–486.

Sue, D. W., & Sue, D. (2002). *Counseling the culturally different: Theory and practice* (4th ed.). New York: Wiley.

Sue, D. W., & Sundberg, N. D. (1996). Research and research hypothesis about effectiveness in intercultural counseling. In P. B. Pedersen, J. G. Draguns, W. J. Lonner, & J. E. Trimble (Eds.), *Counseling across cultures* (4th ed., pp. 323–352). Thousand Oaks, CA: Sage.

Tjaden, P., & Thomas, N. (2000). *Full report of the prevalence, incidence, and consequences of intimate partner violence against women: Findings from the National Violence against Women Survey*. Washington, DC: U.S. Department of Justice. Retrieved January 27, 2011, from http://www.ncjrs.gov/txfiles1/nij/183781.txt

U.S. Conference of Mayors. (2007). *A hunger and homelessness survey*. Retrieved November 24, 2010, from http://usmayors.org/uscm/home.asp

Walsh, R. J., & Dasenbrook, N. (2007). *The complete guide to private practice for licensed mental health professionals* (4th ed.). Rockford, IL: Crysand Press.

Wampole, B. (2001). *The great psychotherapy debate: Models, methods, and findings*. Mahwah, NJ: Lawrence Earlbaum Associates.

Wheeler, A. M., & Bertram, B. (2008). *The counselors and the law: A guide to legal and ethical practice* (5th ed.). Alexandria, VA: American Counseling Association.

Whitaker, C. (1977). Process techniques of family therapy. *Interaction, 1,* 4–19.

Appendix

PROFESSIONAL COUNSELING ORGANIZATIONS

American Counseling Association

American Counseling Association (ACA) is the flagship organization for the counseling profession. ACA also has 19 divisional affiliates (as of 2010) and some 50,000 members. Many professional counselors join both ACA and the divisional affiliate of their particular counseling specialty area (e.g., school counselors also join American School Counselor Association and mental health counselors also join American Mental Health Counselors Association). All counselors should hold a membership in ACA and their divisional affiliate (http://www.counseling.org).

ACA's Divisional Affiliate Organizations

Each of the 19 affiliate organizations are themselves separate organizations focusing on different counseling specialty areas.

American College Counseling Association (ACCA)
ACCA is the primary professional organization for counselors working in higher education (http://www.collegecounseling.org/).

American Mental Health Counselors Association (AMHCA)
AMHCA represents the profession of mental health counselors. Mental health counselors work in outpatient and inpatient settings (http://www.amhca.org).

American Rehabilitation Counseling Association (ARCA)
ARCA represents counselor educators, rehabilitation counselors and students in graduate rehabilitation counseling programs (http://www.arcaweb.prg).

American School Counselor Association (ASCA)
ASCA promotes the profession of school counseling (P-12 grades, public and private secondary schools) (http://www.schoolcounselor.org).

Association for Adult Development and Aging (AADA)
AADA serves as a focal organization for professional development and support for counselors working with geriatric populations (http://www.aadaweb.org).

Association for Assessment in Counseling and Education (AACE)
AACE promotes effective and ethical use of assessments (testing) in counseling and education (http://www.theaaceonline.com).

Association for Counselor Education and Supervision (ACES)
ACES is the primary professional organization for professors of counselor education. ACES is also open to counselor supervisors in the field (http://www.acesonline.net).

Association for Counselors and Educators in Government (ACEG)
ACEG is dedicated to counseling issues and concerns in state, federal, and military settings (http://www.dantes.doded.mil/dantes_web/organizations/aceg/index.htm).

Association for Creativity in Counseling (ACC)
ACC provides an organization for creative arts counseling (e.g., art therapy, music therapy, and dance therapy) and for counselors who write songs and poetry, act in the theatre, use humor, and so on (http://www.creativecounselor.org).

Association for Lesbian, Gay, Bisexual, and Transgender Issues in Counseling (ALGBTIC)
ALGBTIC educates counselors and the general public on the issues and needs of lesbian, gay, bisexual, and transgender clients (http://www.algbtic.org).

Association for Multicultural Counseling and Development (AMCD)
AMCD strives to improve the understanding of multicultural issues in counseling (http://www.amcdaca.org/amcd/default.cfm).

Association for Specialists in Group Work (ASGW)
ASGW provides professional leadership in the field of group counseling (in schools, agencies, inpatient and outpatient settings, etc.) (http://www.asgw.org).

Association for Spiritual, Ethical, and Religious Values in Counseling (ASERVIC)

ASERVIC is devoted to exploring spiritual, religious, and ethical values in counseling (http://www.aservic.org).

Counseling Association for Humanistic Education and Development (C-AHEAD)

C-AHEAD is a professional counseling organization to promote and discuss humanistic-oriented counseling approaches (http://www.c-ahead.org).

Counselors for Social Justice (CSJ)

CSJ is committed to equality on a broad array of social issues (http://www.counselorsforsocialjustice.com).

International Association of Addictions and Offender Counselors (IAAOC)

IAAOC advocates for the development of effective practices in substance-abuse counseling, counseling offenders, and correctional populations (http://www.iac.coe.uga.edu/index.html).

International Association of Marriage and Family Counselors (IAMFC)

IAMFC is the counseling organization focusing on couples and families (http://www.iamfc.org).

National Career Development Association (NCDA)

NCDA's mission is to promote career counseling, advising, and development (http://www.associationdatabase.com/aws/NCDA/pt/sp/Home_Page).

National Employment Counseling Association (NECA)

NECA charge is professional leadership for counselors working with the unemployed and charged with job and career development (http://www.employmentcounseling.org).

Additional Related Counseling Organizations

Council for the Accreditation of Counseling and Related Educational Programs (CACREP)

CACREP is the international accrediting organization for graduate counseling programs. CACREP accredits programs such as clinical mental health counseling, marriage and family counseling, school counseling, counseling and student affairs, college counseling, and doctoral programs in counselor education. Counseling programs having earned CACREP accreditation have earned the highest standard in the field. Note that CACREP does not accredit rehabilitation counseling. Rehabilitation counseling is accredited by the Commission on Rehabilitation Education (CORE) (http://cacrep.org).

Commission on Rehabilitation Education (CORE)

CORE accredits graduate programs in rehabilitation counseling (http://. www.core-rehab.org).

International Association for Counselling (IAC)

IAC is an international counseling organization for counselors working across the globe. IAC membership is open to counselors in all countries. IAC also offers Web sites of counseling organizations in numerous countries (http://www.iac.coe.uga.edu/index.html).

National Board for Certified Counselors (NBCC)

NBCC serves as an independent credentialing organization for the counseling profession. Although U.S. states and territories are responsible for licensing counselors, NBCC provides certification for specialty areas in counseling. Examples of NBCC certifications are National Certified Counselor (NCC) and National Certified Clinical Mental Health Counselor (NCCMHC). (http://www.nbcc.org).

Center for Credentialing Education (CCE)

CCE is an affiliate of NBCC and provides a number of services. Most notably, CCE offers credentialing as an approved clinical supervisor (ACS), and certifications in distance counselors and others. CCE's most common credential likely is the ACS that counseling supervisors can earn (http://www.cce-global.org).

Because of the varying nature of training and credentialing, Web sites of expressive arts therapy organizations are provided below.

Creative Arts Therapeutic Organizations

American Art Therapy Association (AATA): http://www.arttherapy.org
American Dance Therapy Association (ADTA): http://www.adta.org
American Music Therapy Association (AMTA): http://www.music therapy.org
American Society of Group Psychotherapy & Psychodrama (ASGPP): http://www.asgpp.org
Center for Journal Therapy (CJT): http://www.journaltherapy.org
International Art Therapy (IAT): http://www.internationalarttherapy.org
International Expressive Arts Therapy Association (IETA). http://www. ieata.org
National Association for Drama Therapy (NADT): http://www.nadt.org

National Association for Poetry Therapy (NAPT): http://www.poetry-therapy.org

Bureau of Labor Statistics

The Bureau of Labor Statistics (BOLS) compiles and publishes occupational demand for all occupations in the United States (www.bls.gov). I have noted statistics for counseling occupations that are tracked by BOLS. BOLS publishes the *Occupational Outlook Handbook* both online and in traditional printed format. The *Occupational Outlook Handbook* can be accessed at http://www.bls.gov/oco.

Index

AA. *See* Alcoholics Anonymous (AA)
AACE. *See* Association for Assessment in Counseling and Education (AACE)
AADA. *See* Association for Adult Development and Aging (AADA)
AAPC. *See* American Association of Pastoral Counselors (AAPC)
AATA. *See* American Art Therapy Association (AATA)
ABC. *See* Adventure-based counseling (ABC)
ACA. *See* American Counseling Association (ACA)
Academic advising counselor, 109–110
Academic dean, counselor as, 113–114
ACC. *See* Association for Creativity in Counseling (ACC)
ACCA. *See* American College Counseling Association (ACCA)
ACEG. *See* Association for Counselors and Educators in Government (ACEG)
ACES. *See* Association for Counselor Education and Supervision (ACES)
ACS. *See* Approved Clinical Supervisor (ACS)
Addiction counseling, 21
Addictions treatment counselor, 130–131

Adopting couples, counselor for, 47–48
ADTA. *See* American Dance Therapy Association (ADTA)
Adventure-based counseling (ABC), 229
case study, 229–232
Adventure-based counselor/therapist, 238–239
After-school programs, counseling in, 82–84
Agency managers. *See* Program manager in nonprofit agencies, counselor as
Alcoholics Anonymous (AA), 129
ALGBTIC. *See* Association for Lesbian, Gay, Bisexual, and Transgender Issues in Counseling (ALGBTIC)
Alternative schools, counselor in, 77–78
AMCD. *See* Association for Multicultural Counseling and Development (AMCD)
American Art Therapy Association (AATA), 208, 314
American Association of Pastoral Counselors (AAPC), 195, 197
American College Counseling Association (ACCA), 311
American Counseling Association (ACA), 8, 85, 222, 240, 268, 311
divisional affiliate organizations, 311

Spotlight: Grief Counselor
Career Counseling Spotlight: Neil Mellor, A/Program Leader, Lecturer in Counseling, Faculty of Arts and Business, University of the Sunshine Coast, Maroochydore DC Qld, Australia

I have worked as a counselor for 30 years and am an accredited Mental Health Social Worker and Level 4 Practitioner with the Australian Counselling Association (ACA). I am in private practice with my wife Kathy at Altogether Psychology Services and I teach Counseling and Social Work at the University of the Sunshine Coast in Maroochydore, Queensland, Australia.

My first professional experience of the importance of grief counseling occurred in 1981 when I was a new graduate social worker responsible for running a men's community housing project. I was coordinating 8 houses with 60 residents located in the inner-city area of Melbourne, Australia's second largest city. The extent of the grief and loss issues experienced by the residents surprised me at the time, as this was not a well-understood problem in the context of welfare practice. My early social work training had provided me with only limited exposure to the "Five Stages of Grief" developed by Elisabeth Kübler-Ross in 1969 in her book *On Death and Dying*. While working in this program, I had an experience that seemed to epitomize the field as it was at that time.

One morning I arrived at one of our houses and found that a long-term resident, whom I shall call Ernie, had suffered a major heart attack and was barely breathing. I immediately called an ambulance, gave him mouth-to-mouth resuscitation, and kept him alive for 25 minutes while waiting for the ambulance. The ambulance came after 30 minutes, but sadly, Ernie had died. When I asked what caused the delay in the arrival of the ambulance, the senior officer reported that the ambulance staff knew this was a house for homeless persons and because the staff had a log of emergency service calls to these premises previously, they did not prioritize the call as urgent! As I spoke to the residents of the house and those who knew Ernie to help them process the shock of his death, I came to understand that residents who suffered from problems associated with psychiatric and physical disabilities were treated as second-class citizens by many health and welfare services, and their issues of bereavement were largely discounted. I found that death and loss were an ever-present reality in the lives of these residents, and although this was not often spoken about directly, grief was present in my daily conversation without being named. Up until this time I had mostly thought of grief as a reaction to death or to an incident resulting in serious injury or disfigurement. I soon learned that grief and sadness took many forms and were caused by a variety of phenomena, including the loss and estrangement of loved ones such as family, friends, and pets, the dissolution of marriages and de facto relationships, lost careers, and lifestyles. When I arranged Ernie's funeral, his former wife, children, and siblings chose not to attend and a Methodist Church organization was the only one who would pay for his funeral. There were virtually no services dealing with death, dying, and grief in those days, except for churches, hospitals, and funeral homes.

As I moved on in my career, I found the themes of grief and loss present in my direct client work in mental health, addiction, problem gambling, relationship, and employee assistance counseling. There were no training programs specifically dealing with issues of grief in those days as there are now, so I developed my competency through a combination of professional training and supervision in transactional analysis psychotherapy and other experiential therapies, and by spending time with those who worked closely with people who had experienced great loss and pain.

Australia now has a robust set of national, state, and locally based centers and services addressing grief, bereavement, and loss. Many of these services are supported by funding from federal and state governments; in some cases, these centers are affiliated with universities, and are generally run by not-for-profit community organizations.

On a national level there is a specialist organization, the Australian Centre for Grief and Bereavement, which was established in 1996 to provide a range of services to those who are suffering from grief and bereavement, or for those caregivers or professionals who want training, supervision, and advice on how to work in this area. There is also the National Association for Loss and Grief (NALAG), which provides accreditation for members working in this area and which has many branches in the major states of Australia. Numerous state-based organizations are also active in this area, including state and local government health and mental health providers. In addition, several other helpful services provide a range of face-to-face, telephone, or web-based assistance.

Grief counseling is addressed in several professional-degree courses in Australia, including Counseling, Social Work, and Psychology, courses that are offered at the university with which I am affiliated (University of the Sunshine Coast). Several prominent professional associations such as the ACA offer support for members specializing in counseling in this area through publishing journals and clearinghouses of resources disseminating research, providing professional development opportunities, and maintaining standards and registers on national members. In addition, organizations such as the ACA provide a register of volunteer members who offer free telephone counseling to victims of natural disasters such as the Queensland floods (2010–2011) and the Victorian bushfires (2009).

Private practitioners in counseling psychotherapy and allied health disciplines such as social work provide grief counseling and other services to community members under several different fee-for-service arrangements and other health insurance and federal government-funded Medicare health plans. For instance, under the Better Access Mental Health Care Initiative, clients may be referred by a medical practitioner to an accredited counselor, at no cost, for problems such as bereavement disorders or posttraumatic stress disorder.

Counselors use a range of psychoanalytic, person-centered, and cognitive behavioral approaches to grief, with cognitive behavioral therapy the most commonly practiced.